HOWARD BRENTON

PLAYS: TWO

The Romans In Britain
Thirteenth Night
The Genius
Bloody Poetry
Greenland

Methuen Drama

WORLD DRAMATISTS SERIES

This edition first published in Great Britain in 1989
by Methuen Drama, Michelin House, 81 Fulham Road, London SW3 6RB
and distributed in the United States of America
by HEB Inc., 70 Court Street, Portsmouth, New Hampshire 03801

The Romans In Britain first published in 1980 by Eyre Methuen, revised in 1981, reissued in 1982 and in this edition in 1989. Copyright © 1980, 1981 by Howard Brenton.

Thirteenth Night first published in 1981 by Eyre Methuen, reprinted in 1983 and re-issued in this edition 1989. Copyright © 1981 by Howard Brenton.

The Genius first published in 1983 by Eyre Methuen, reprinted 1985 and reissued in this edition 1989. Copyright © 1985, Howard Brenton.

Bloody Poetry first published in 1985 by Methuen London, revised in 1988 and again revised for this edition in 1989. Copyright © 1985, 1988, 1989 Howard Brenton.

Greenland first published in 1988 by Methuen Drama and reissued in this edition 1989. Copyright © 1988 Howard Brenton.

Front cover: detail from 'Snowstorm: Hannibal and his army crossing the Alps' by J. M. W. Turner, courtesy of the Tate Gallery, London
Back cover: Howard Brenton by Snoo Wilson

A CIP catalogue record for this volume can be obtained from the British Library.

ISBN 0 413 61490 5

CAUTION

Printed in Great Britain by Cox & Wyman Ltd, Reading

The Romans in Britain, Thirteenth Night,
The Genius, Bloody Poetry, Greenland

Howard Brenton is one of Britain's best-known and most controversial dramatists. Following on from PLAYS: ONE, the plays in this volume represent his writing in the eighties. In them Brenton develops the themes of utopia, political malaise, the ethics of the nuclear age and imperialism.

The Romans in Britain – 'Conjuring up an era that is culturally as well as historically remote is a notoriously difficult task, but Mr Brenton achieves it with great skill and effect . . . a very good play indeed.'

(Bernard Levin, *The Times*)

Thirteenth Night – 'A sharp flinty piece of theatre that had me hooked from start to finish.'

(Michael Billington, *Guardian*)

The Genius – 'This is Brenton at his best, showing how the absurd and awesome often get intertwined.'

(Michael Billington, *Guardian*)

Bloody Poetry – 'Radicalism, artistic defiance, an intellectual rage. These are the virtues celebrated in this extraordinary dream play which begins as it ends, on a foreign shore.'

(Michael Coveney, *Financial Times*)

Greenland – 'Fast, furious and often funny'

(Michael Coveney, *Financial Times*)

HOWARD BRENTON
Howard Brenton was born in Portsmouth in 1942 and educated in Chichester and at St Catherine's College, Cambridge. In 1968 he joined the Brighton Combination as an actor and writer, and in 1969 he joined David Hare and Tony Bicât in Portable Theatre. His first full-length play was *Revenge* (1969) which was performed at the Royal Court Upstairs; this was followed by *Hitler Dances* (1972); *Magnificence* (1973); *Brassneck* (with David Hare, 1973); *The Churchill Play* (1974); *Weapons of Happiness* (winner of the Evening Standard Award, 1976); *Epsom Downs* (1977); *Sore Throats* (1979); *The Life of Galileo* (from Bertolt Brecht, 1980); *The Romans in Britain* (1980); *Thirteenth Night* (1981); *Danton's Death* (from Georg Büchner, 1982); *The Genius* (1983); *Bloody Poetry* (1984); *Desert of Lies* (1984); *Pravda*, (with David Hare, 1985); *Greenland* (1988); *Iranian Nights*, (with Tariq Ali, 1989). His four-part thriller *Dead Head* was broadcast by BBC2 in 1986. A novel, *Diving for Pearls* was published in 1989.

Contents

Howard Brenton

Preface

When I was a boy, I wanted to be an archaeologist. What the Freudian explanation is of this childhood fascination with what is buried, hidden under-foot, leaving upon the surface of the landscape a kind of cloud shadow in reverse from deep below, I don't think I want to know. (Henry Moore was once given a weighty, German psychological analysis of his sculpture. He refused to read it, saying, with Yorkshire phlegm, that if he knew too much about why he sculpted, he might not need to sculpt.)

But the memory of this childhood interest in the buried past did, I must admit, give me the idea for *The Romans In Britain*. Along with dinosaurs, the Roman occupation of Britain is something of an obsession with primary teachers in our schools. I remembered a picture of 'Caesar's legions crossing the Thames' pinned on the classroom wall when I was nine.

So the play takes a rooted, popular myth from the British national consciousness. Everyone knows the Romans came to Britain. This is vaguely felt to be 'a good thing', because they built straight roads and 'brought law'.

It was called an 'anti-imperialist epic'. But the subject of the play is really 'culture shock'. For the Romans, Caesar's second raid on Britain is a minor operation which is not that successful. It is a small war on the edge of the known world that gets bogged down, a wretched summer of little achievement and to Julius Caesar of little interest. The scene in which he appears is titled 'Caesar's tooth'. He has toothache and, irritably, removes the offending tooth and throws it away. That sums up what he thinks of Britain. He notes a few local customs for his memoirs, orders the fields to be salted 'as a reminder', and leaves the stage and these shores for greater things. But for the Celts the appearance of the Roman army is the end of their culture, its touch is death.

I tried to imagine what it must have been like for three young Celts, seeing Roman soldiers for the first time. I titled the scene 'Two Worlds Touch'. The Celts had been swimming on a fine summer's day. On the river bank they fool about, brag and laugh, then stretch out in the sun. From out of the trees come three Roman soldiers. They have had a bad day, losing touch with their platoon in a confused skirmish in the trees, and want a swim. The Celts are between them and the river. To the Romans it's nothing, there are three natives, three 'wogs', between them and a much

vii

needed swim. The Romans kill two of the Celts and grossly abuse the third, who runs off. To the soldiers it is nothing, nothing at all. To the Celts it is worse than death, it is the end of their world.

My scene shocked many, for it is profoundly shocking. What is so hard to take is the flippancy of the soldiers, their jokey indifference, the fact that they 'know not what they do'.

The play took three years to write, through three versions. It was a most difficult undertaking. Ten years on, I think I've forgotten the heartache of writing it. It seems quite simple and straightforward to read.

It does break many of the received theatrical rules of 'the well-made play'. There is no lead character. There are no 'goodies' and 'baddies'. There is no obvious, or usual, 'moral message'. The scenes of the past are haunted by the 1980s with another army, the British, blundering around in another foreign country, Ireland. And the play's dramatic shape is perverse, for it goes from 'dark' to 'light', with a first half that is violent, dynamic and tragic, while the second half is elegaic, still and flooded with an hysterical, light-hearted, comic spirit. You were faced in the theatre with the problem of an audience in the interval saying 'My God! If that was Part One, what the hell is going to happen in Part Two?' For it is a received notion that a funny play should be funniest at its end, and a violent, angry play should end at its highest pitch of mayhem. It is deeply perverse to fly in the face of that expectation. Indeed, the play ends with a perverse joke – one evening, in a time of civil war, a century after the Empire abandoned these islands, two cooks are hiding in a ditch. It is not a good time for cooks. There is famine, and the big houses, with their kitchens, have been burnt down. The cooks realize they need another profession and decide to be storytellers, inventing, there and then, the story of King Arthur . . . which has done rather well since.

The first difficulty was to construct an account of the Celtic society the Romans found. There are some thirteen accounts of the ancient Celts by classical authors, including Caesar's disapproving observation of what he took to be gross sexual immorality. (Was he looking at a quasi-matriarchal society in which women had several husbands? His imperial mentality made him assume he had come across tribes of female sluts.) It was something of a shock to realize how thin the written record is, how rocky the pillars are upon which volumes of scholarship have been built.

So, since in a play people have to say and do *something* while they are on stage, my account of the ancient Celts is highly speculative and academically suspect. Though I did find after a few months of research I could hold my own in an argument with a professor about whether the eaves of Celtic roundhouses were, or were not, painted and decorated with gods . . . the academic world is as full of bullshit as any other, including mine!

When Peter Hall commissioned the play, he said one thing: 'How are they going to talk?' Since, as a rough and ready rule of thumb, the Romans in the play are nearer to us and they are soldiers, I was able, without too much trouble, to develop an anachronistic prose for them. Julius Caesar was a religious man, his family believed they were descended from the Goddess Venus. Historians have puzzled over Caesar's religious reforms, to which he devoted enormous energy when he came to power in Rome. Some see this as power-broking between powerful families, elevating the cults of friends, downgrading the cults of enemies. But one suspects it was from an impulse lost to us. The paganism of the classical world, viewed through Christianized eyes, is dim and difficult to read. Nevertheless, in many respects Caesar in my play thinks like us, that is dialectically, in terms of cause and effect. His mental world is symmetrical, four-squared, logical.

Writing the Celts, I kept staring at the few examples of their decoration we have, which is off-centre, curled, triangular. In the British Museum there is a remarkable relic, a Celtic game. It looks like solitaire but no one is sure how it was played. A simple game, which any British Celt's child would know, that melts our best archeological minds . . . Then there were the Welsh triads (again, thinking in threes), which are the nearest thing we have to their sense of poetry and, therefore, to their mentality. The triads are, to us, infuriating. They mention heroes and battles, but without any sense of what we call history. An 'asymmetrical view of the world'? From puzzling at these cryptic traces in the archeological records and at the triads, and from visiting some sites of Celtic camps – again, triangular, maze-like, once hidden in woods, unlike the square Roman camps dominating ridges and hill tops – I began to find a language for them. A triple-rhythmed speech, fiery, full of a kind of self-display and relish, an unabashedly bodily self-love (nearly every Roman author could not get over what they did to their hair . . .), and a language hopelessly ill-equipped to even describe the Romans. An emissary from another family in the play attempts to do so. He cannot find the words.

But the greatest difficulty I had when I began to try to write the play is a weighty matter. It was what to do about a sense of overwhelming *sorrow*, a grief for the nameless dead, with which the material of the play is drenched. This is, itself, difficult to express. It was what Blake addressed in the terrifying 'proverb from Hell' –

'Drive your cart and plough over the bones of the dead.'

If you do not, you will go mad with grief. But cruelty is hard to dramatize. What you must never do is pretend, by stagecraft sleight of hand, that the cruelty is not as bad as it is. If you are not prepared to show humanity at its worst, why should you be believed when you show it at its best, in a play that attempts to do both in equal measure. You must not sell human suffering short.

That resolution got the play into a good deal of trouble when it was performed at the National Theatre. For a little while it was something of a scandal. Unable to prosecute the play under the laws that govern public performance, since the police and the Attorney General found there was nothing to prosecute, a 'moral campaigner', Mrs Mary Whitehouse, combed the laws of Old England to find a way of attacking the play. She eventually brought a private prosecution against the play's director, Michael Bogdanov, who on my behalf spent a hellish year of threats, abuse, siege by tabloid newspapers and court appearances. He never complained, he was throughout the madness fiercely loyal to the work and quite prepared to go to gaol, knowing all along that it was merely a quirk of the law that stopped Mrs Whitehouse getting the author into the dock, rather than him. It is pleasing to set down here a tribute to his guts, his good humour and his clear-headedness, which never deserted him as the affair took its ugly and, at times, rather frightening course.

And yesterday's scandals evaporate and here is the play, readable and, I think, very much alive. I am immensely proud of it. I'm confident that it will be eventually revived on the British stage and have its day. Future audiences may or may not like the piece, but I'm sure of one thing: they will say – 'What was all that fuss about, years ago?'

While the '*Romans In Britain* scandal' was in train, I was working on *Thirteenth Night*. I remember sitting in Horseferry Road magistrates court, with Bogdanov for one of his three appearances there, the morning after the play's first preview at the

RSC. The theatrical chit-chat of 'How was your preview?' . . .
'Pretty rough, Michael . . .' seemed curiously out of phase with
the massed cameramen on the pavement outside and the bustle of
lawyers and policemen. In the courtroom that day, before Michael
'came on', there was a request from an undercover policeman,
disguised in long hair for which he apologized, for a warrant. The
purpose of the warrant was not revealed in open court. It was
granted in seconds and the policeman was hurried away. It was as
if he had wandered out of my play of the night before. From one
nightmare into another . . .

For *Thirteenth Night* is, literally, a dream play. At the end of its
prologue the lead character, Jack Beaty, is hit over the head. As he
falls to the ground, the play is what streams through his brain. It
is, I suppose, 'a Shakespearean derivative', since, cheekily I know,
for I was having fun with its form, it plays ducks and drakes with
the plot of *Macbeth*. Its title is a code for the play's theme – this
is the play for when the celebrations have to stop.

A critic accused me of 'having my cake and eating it' by writing
a dream play. It is an open licence for improbability. Quite so.
That is what I wanted. You can only do something really good,
perhaps in the end really profound, in the theatre, if you do not
take the theatre too seriously.

Thirteenth Night is addressed 'to the troops', that is, to fellow
socialists. I make no apology for once, just once, writing a play
that dramatizes an internal row, hanging up the left's dirty, indeed
bloodstained, linen in public. I became fed-up with the unreality
of some of us on the left, who would not address the Stalinist
horrors, the repression in what were called 'socialist countries' in
Eastern Europe. The play is an assault on their Orwellian
double-think. Tyranny is tyranny. To quote Mohammed, 'When
oppression exists, even the bird dies in the nest'. That is true
whether a country be nominally socialist or not. The play is, of
course, pre-Glasnost, pre-Gorbachev. The three 'free spirits' in the
play, the three 'witches', were unidentifiable to the author when
he was writing the play. Now, suddenly, there seem to be millions
of them in the Soviet Union, climbing up to the clean air from the
underground bunker where the tyrant's body rots, to quote the
final image of Jack Beaty's dream.

In 1980 I wrote an English version of Brecht's masterpiece, *The
Life of Galileo*, which John Dexter directed at the National
Theatre with Michael Gambon in the lead – a production of great
clarity and force.

I had a somewhat grandiose scheme to write a modern parallel, a Galileo of our time, and to talk the National into performing it in their smaller auditorium, the Cottesloe, while Brecht's mighty play was running on the big Olivier Theatre stage.

The scheme came to nothing, for a number of reasons. I was locked into preparations for the production of *The Romans In Britain*, and was embroiled in another mini-scandal over a little 'knockabout' satire on Margaret Thatcher's first Government, *A Short Sharp Shock!*, which I'd written with the 'rough theatre' specialist Tony Howard. Then the Mary Whitehouse brouhaha began. The 'Galileo' play was shelved. The spirit is always willing but sometimes you just can't get the flesh to the typewriter . . .

I eventually got down to it in 1982, writing the play very slowly, five lines a day, and the Royal Court Theatre put it on in 1983.

Its first title was *Galileo's Goose*. At the end of Brecht's play Galileo's sensuality, an expression of the great scientist's Renaissance 'wholeness' in the play's magnificent first scene, has decayed into gluttony. Having denounced himself and despatched his masterwork, the *Discorsi*, to be smuggled out of Italy, Galileo sits down to eat a goose, cooked with an apple and an onion. The play then ends with a scene, left unfinished when Brecht died, of the book passing surreptitiously across the stage. There is a huge, typically Brechtian irony in this. After three hours of drama spent with a complex, ambiguous leading character, all that he did and said climaxes without him present. A book is smuggled through a checkpoint on a border. That, says Brecht, was what was important about Galileo's life, not his recantation before the Inquisition nor the ambiguity of his personality.

Playing around with the question 'Who would a modern Galileo be?', I thought he'd be an American, glamorous, brilliant and articulate, a man who seems to 'have everything', the good looks of a film star, the brain of an Einstein . . . He should be a 1980s' 'Renaissance man', universally admired and a light in people's lives.

But like Brecht's Galileo, Leo Lehrer cannot deal with the moral dilemmas his work forces him to confront. And, again like Brecht's character, this golden human being falls apart and becomes gross, in a 1980s' manner. He is a dangerous man to know, arrogant, promiscuous, cruel and self-indulgent, a wrecker of the lives around him. I try to dramatize his reformation.

The Genius is, though, about two brilliant people – Leo Lehrer and a student, Gilly Brown. They struggle with a dangerous idea –

that nuclear science is a profoundly malign pursuit and that, for the first time in human history, we must deny ourselves a technological 'advance'. It was a strange play to write, trying to dramatize the intellectual love affair between two characters light years ahead of their author's intelligence.

Through the early 1980s, I wrote three shows for the small touring company, Foco Novo. The first, in 1982, was an adaptation of Brecht's long, discursive dialogue *Conversations In Exile*. Roland Rees, Foco Novo's artistic director, had a one-act play by the Jamaican playwright, Alfred Fagon, *Four Hundred Pounds*. It was a two hander, set around a pool table. Two Jamaican pool hustlers discuss their sense of 'internal exile' over the table, failing actually to play the game they had met to play. Roland Rees had the brilliantly imaginative idea of getting a one-hour version of Brecht's dialogue, which uncut would run for three and a half hours and was never meant for stage production, and setting it around the pool table of the Fagon play, with a game in progress. The two black actors would play the German characters, in exile in Finland from Nazi Germany just before the war. I cut and rearranged it ruthlessly, keeping the 'formless' nature of the piece, the only 'line' through it being the gradual 'trust in distrust' that grows between the middle-class and the working-class refugees. This worked beautifully. Roland Rees is an unsung hero of the contemporary theatre, the most daring producer – that is dreamer up of ideas for plays and shows, with whom I've had the privilege to work in this country.

Roland's second, madcap, scheme was to commission a collaborative play between myself and Tunde Ikoli, *Sleeping Policemen*, which we did in 1983. Roland wanted a play about Peckham in South London, *not* one of the more obvious places to draw poetry and drama from. The three of us met off and on for a year, discussing characters. We invented, from observations made on the Peckham streets, six people, three white and three black. We set a rule – the action would take place on one particular weekend. Tunde and I went away swearing, on Roland's insistence, that we would have no contact and, separately, each wrote his own play, a script of some seventy pages. Then we sat down and did a William Burroughs style, 'cut-up' job, in one long session, slicing the two plays together. Roland's point in setting up this bizarre process, was to keep the sharpness of the voices of two very different playwrights, one white and middle-aged, living a middle-class life, and one young, black and working-class. The result was extraordinary, a kind of cubist *Under Milk Wood*, with a most strange dramaturgy, which had a 'singing' quality about everyday life in a London hinterland where writers do not usually travel with their pens.

The third show, dreamt up by Roland for me to write, was the play printed here, *Bloody Poetry*. I resisted his idea for some time. He wanted a play about the poet Shelley for Foco Novo to tour. My resistance was because I am wary of 'Art about Art' and plays about writers. I had only tried it once before, when I was beginning to write, with a play about Maxim Gorky called *A Sky-Blue Life*, and that was more a dramatization of some of his short stories than a stage biography. I suspect that Roland's impulse was to present Shelley as a revolutionary hero.

But I said 'yes' to the project, when I saw a different way of handling it, writing not just about Shelley, but about the quartet of Shelley, Byron, Mary Shelley and Claire Clairemont, Byron's mistress. Throughout the 1980s I had been wrestling with the notion of writing a Utopian play, a version of William Morris's *News From Nowhere*. Several attempts at doing so had broken down – I was building up a 'bottom drawer' of half-completed Utopias . . . *Bloody Poetry*, which Foco Novo premiered in 1984 and has been widely performed since, with a revival by the Royal Court Theatre in 1988, became a way of broaching the subject, for the quartet are determined to invent a new way of living, free of sexual repression. They make a terrible mess of it. Some found the 'morality' of the play bewildering. I was not concerned with saying whether these people were 'good' or 'bad', I wanted to salute their Utopian aspirations for which, in different ways, they gave their lives. It is a celebration of a magnificent failure.

Greenland, after an extended, bitter prologue, is an outright Utopia. It was greeted, on its first production, with incomprehension. I wanted to stage a world in which Shelley, Byron, Mary and Claire would be happy to live . . . though, thinking of Act Two of *Greenland* in that light, I think George Byron might have kicked over the traces. I know that this play was a reckless undertaking. Gentleness and peace are not meant to make good drama. The mental agony of *The Genius*, the death and defeat of *Bloody Poetry*, the dystopia of *Thirteenth Night* were praised while the sly, quiet contentment and weird utterances of 'The Greenlanders' were derided by the critics.

The first full draft of the play, which ended up on an autumn bonfire, simply went through scenes in the distant future set on one day, without comment.

In the world we have it is difficult enough to understand our different cultures. A common humanity unites us in our basic needs and instincts, food, shelter, love of children, the use of language, curiosity, the pride of being alive, the love or the fear of death, but I have a suspicion that the humanist faith that 'people are the same everywhere and always have been' is too generalised a truth. Cultural *Weltanschauungs*, the 'mind sets' and world views we live in, vary sharply and often cruelly. Witness the confusions between Christianised and Muslim British citizens at the end of the 80's.

Imagine then the folly of a writer trying to describe a new 'world culture', seven hundred years hence, free of conflict and oppression. How do you dramatize *people without fear*? We wouldn't understand a word they said. It was not surprising that the first draft for *Greenland* was not only bizarre, which I didn't mind, but also totally incomprehensible even to its author. Definitely one for the bonfire.

Then I realised there was a model, Shakespearean romantic comedy: *As You Like It* and *A Midsummer Night's Dream*. I took the basic joke – people like us, with all our hates, confusions and contemporary troubles hanging from them like rags, get lost in a 'magic wood', a new, alternative reality. The comedy comes from them loving or hating it, and from watching our assumptions about our 'human nature' challenged and changed. A Shakespearean scholar, Sally Homer, tells me this is now a most dated and discredited view of Shakespearean comedy, originating with Northrop Frye . . .

But no matter. It helped me to write a play. I took a handful of 'travellers' and by a ludicrous device (you can do anything on a stage, and should) threw them into the Utopia I had been trying to imagine for nearly ten years. Act One introduces them, Act Two tries to dramatize how they get on 'in there'. It is a silly idea, but I wanted it to be *wonderfully* silly. The powerful advantage of our theatrical tradition is that it is profoundly comic. Serious matters can be tackled in the theatre by mucking about and having some fun with what is meant to be unstageable. Why shouldn't the exploration of the human spirit be light-hearted?

These five plays were written with a left-wing perspective, in opposition to the dominant political mores of 1980s Britain. It was a nasty decade, a mean time to be a writer at last coming on song. But I'm encouraged, re-reading the plays for this volume, to realize that along with many others, I did manage to get so much on to the stage, in the teeth of fashion, cuts in the Arts and a hostility to the very idea of a subsidized, that is, publicly owned, theatre, putting on plays like these. The theatres and the actors who helped me with this writing held the line, though at some cost. The gallant Foco Novo Theatre Company, which initiated *Bloody Poetry*, went to the wall in 1988, murdered by the grant-cutting knife of the Arts Council.

Also I realize these five scripts are like one long play. The cooks at the end of *The Romans In Britain* could be Greenlanders; Jack Beaty in *Thirteenth Night* is an extension of my version of Julius Caesar, and the lovers in *Greenland* could be the 'witches' in *Thirteenth Night*; *Bloody Poetry* and *Greenland* are twinned by their Utopian themes; Leo Lehrer at the end of *The Genius* is shuffling towards Greenland, and in *The Romans In Britain* a stone is held up, then thrown, in a gesture of liberation by a slave, while at the end of *Greenland* a stone is brought back from the future and held up, shining with light . . .

If these plays were to be given a Shavian title, they could be called *Five Plays For Romantics*. Or maybe: *Five For The Bloody-Minded*.

'Better a long, slow fire than a brief explosion . . .' said Joan Littlewood when I met her in 1980. She claimed this was a quote from Brecht. She may have made it up. But it was a motto I continually recalled, writing in the 1980s.

Howard Brenton, 1989

THE ROMANS
IN BRITAIN

To Jane

The Romans in Britain was first performed on 16 October 1980 in the Olivier auditorium of the National Theatre, London. The play was directed by Michael Bogdanov with settings by Martin Johns, costumes by Stephanie Howard and lighting by Chris Ellis.

On the run — A family and its fields — Two worlds touch — Fugitives and refugees — Caesar's tooth — The gods grow small — Two murders

The action takes place north of the River Thames on 27th August, 54BC and the following dawn.

PART ONE

Caesar's Tooth

Nothing human is alien to me
Terence

I have been dead, I have been alive
Taliesin

Characters

The cast is as for the National Theatre premiere (see page 2).

CELTS

CONLAG	*Criminals*	John Normington
DAUI		James Carter
MARBAN	*A Druid*	Greg Hicks
BRAC	MARBAN's	Michael Fenner
VIRIDIO	*foster brothers*	Roger Gartland
A MOTHER	*A matriarch*	Yvonne Bryceland
TWO ENVOYS		James Hayes
		Peter Dawson
VILLAGE MEN		Gordon Whiting
		Elliott Cooper
		Peter Needham
		Michael Beint
VILLAGE BOY		Malachi Bogdanov
VILLAGE WOMEN		Susan Williamson
		Anna Carteret
		Terry Diab
		Jane Evers
VILLAGE GIRLS		Loraine Sass
		Chloe Needham

ROMANS

FIRST SOLDIER		Robert Ralph
SECOND SOLDIER		Robert Oates
THIRD SOLDIER		Peter Sproule
GUARD		James Carter
JULIUS CAESAR		Michael Bryant
PREFECT		Nigel Bellairs
PRIMUS PILUS	CAESAR's staff	Artro Morris
LEGATE		William Sleigh
BUGLER		Colin Rae
STANDARD BEARER		Glenn Williams
ASINUS	*an historian*	Brian Kent
FOURTH SOLDIER		Peter Harding
FIFTH SOLDIER		Peter Dawson
SIXTH SOLDIER		James Hayes
SEVENTH SOLDIER		Melvyn Bedford
SLAVE		Jill Stanford

Scene One

Darkness. Dogs bark in the distance. Silence.

CONLAG. Where the fuck are we?

By the sea?

Daui?

DAUI. Day in, day out. Lying in a boat with salt round the back of my eyeballs. In a river up to my neck. Marshes with leeches. Moors with birds of prey. Rocks with wild cats. In sun, in rain, in snow — I have heard you ask where the fuck are we.

CONLAG. Well.

Where are we?

DAUI. How the fuck do I know?

All I do know is, three days of forest. Then that. Farms. Stockades. Fields.

A silence.

CONLAG. You can smell their food. Smell how their teeth went into it. The little squirts of fat in the meat. The spit that washed it down.

Yeah, you come out of the trees. You smell the meal, the fire, the family. All that you've lost.

DAUI. All that we've shat upon. And has shat upon us.

CONLAG. The criminal life. It's the boils that get you.

Yeah, when you go on the run, you don't think about getting boils.

He sniffs.

Do you smell fish?

They both sniff.

DAUI. No fish.

CONLAG. Could be near the sea, though. Maybe they don't eat fish for religious reasons.

DAUI. Do you hear the sea?

They listen.

CONLAG. Dogs.

DAUI. Dogs.

CONLAG. Dogfish?

DAUI. Just dogs.

CONLAG. Could be a strange sea, this side of Britain. Sea of dogs! Waves of tails! Rabid surf, all froth and teeth! Dogshit beaches!

DAUI. I'd put nothing past this country.

CONLAG. Better get back in the trees. Come dawn, see where we are.

DAUI. Three nights of trees. I'll not sleep under trees again.

CONLAG. Better, Daui. If men make you live like an animal —

DAUI.   ⎫
CONLAG. ⎬ Be an animal.
       ⎭

CONLAG. True! It's true!

DAUI. Creepy crawlies. Things that are there and not there. Ghosts. Mantraps. Wild animals. Gods. All that rubbish. I'll not take that again.

CONLAG. But maybe these bastards aren't asleep. Maybe they're fucking. Makes your hearing sharp. Makes you see in the dark too. They'll hear us! Run out and see us! With hard-ons! And kill us — or worse!

A silence. They burst out laughing.

DAUI. I never know when your brain's running out your nose or not.

The sound of DAUI *scuttling about.*

Not too wet here.

CONLAG. All right, all right. It's wrong. But I'm not the leader of this robber band.

Robber band of two poor fuckers.

DAUI. Brambles here. Do for the sleeper's wall. You got the bag?

CONLAG. Yes I've got the bag.

DAUI. Let me feel it.

CONLAG. I've got the bag.

DAUI. What have you done with the bag?

CONLAG. There is the bag! Dear oh dear.

DAUI. Is it the bag?

CONLAG. What bag do you think it is?

DAUI. You could have changed it for another.

CONLAG. Look —

DAUI. Back in the trees! Someone you're in league with! Some corpse, ghost, thing! That's following us all the time! That you're winking at, behind my back! When people go as low as you, down in the filth like you, I don't know what you do!

CONLAG. You call me low —

DAUI. I don't know what you do!

CONLAG. Feel the iron in the bag. Feel it.

A silence.

DAUI. The wine —

CONLAG. The wineskin's in the bag. Squishy. Feel it.

DAUI's voice heavy with exhaustion.

DAUI. Iron and wine.

CONLAG. I'm glad we killed that man we met. And took his iron and his wine. Didn't he squeal! Didn't he squeal!

He laughs.

You sleep first. I'll watch.

DAUI. I could sleep.

But don't drink the wine.

CONLAG. Me? Drink our wine?

DAUI. And don't go talking to yourself. And screaming.

CONLAG. Right.

DAUI. And leave my arse alone.

CONLAG. Right.

DAUI. And don't sell me to 'em.

The things in the trees.

While I'm asleep.

CONLAG *sighs*.

CONLAG. Right.

A silence.

Daui?

A silence.

You don't think — that's what we're going to find?

A silence.

After all our sorrows.

A silence.

And heartbreak. And boils. And my pusy ear. And the thing at the bottom of my spine.

A silence.

Find a dogshit beach?

DAUI. A boat. We'll find a boat. Or people are going to die.

CONLAG. Right.

A silence.

Right.

Scene Two

Dawn comes. An early morning light.

A young woman, a SLAVE, is working at the edge of fields, building a dew pond. She hammers clay with a stone bound to a thick shaft. A stave, a bowl and her day's food in a cloth lie a little way off.

Unseen, CONLAG and DAUI are asleep, hidden by brambles and rags.

The SLAVE looks up and stops working.

CONLAG stands stiffly. He stretches and yawns. He rubs the base of his spine. He turns to find himself facing the SLAVE. Both are still, facing each other.

CONLAG. Don't get the dogs. No dogs. Woof woof. No need for that at all.

Throats. Blood all over the place.

No no.

He kicks the sleeping DAUI.

Daui.

He kicks.

Daui. Get up.

DAUI *comes out of sleep and hiding with a rush, kicking and punching.*

DAUI. Where are they, where are they? I'll kick the shit out of 'em, with my own two hands! What?

The three staring, one to the other.

We're not over your boundary.

CONLAG. Just a couple of Irishmen.

DAUI. No disrespect.

CONLAG. But do not take us lightly! Do not take our powers lightly!

DAUI. We are not on your family's fields!

CONLAG. Travellers in trade. Iron? Wine? So we're protected. Right? Right.

DAUI. If we are on your family's fields, tell us. We'll go. No insult. No trouble.

Nothing from the SLAVE. *A silence.* DAUI *squats, turned away.*

CONLAG. What's the name of your family?

The father of your family?

Mother of your family?

Do your fields go to the sea?

DAUI. The thing's a slave.

CONLAG *and the* SLAVE *stare at each other.*

CONLAG. Yeah?

He nods.

Yeah, I see what you mean.

Eh! Maybe it'll get us food. Even a heavy weapon. Food?

He points in his mouth.

Axe? Eh?

He makes a slicing gesture, smiling widely.

I think they've done that —

He indicates punctured eardrums.

to the ears with it.

DAUI. No. It's foreign.

CONLAG. Kill it?

DAUI. I'm tired. So very, very tired. And they almost got me last night. Things like birds. I couldn't move. I couldn't breathe. I could have sworn they were there. To take my balls out at the roots. In their beaks. And all the rest of me, liver, bowels, soul.

CONLAG. I'm smiling at it — it'll run — get its owners — if we don't do something — like kill it —

DAUI. Obviously. Keep smiling and I'll kill it.

DAUI *pulls the bag towards him and puts a hand in it.*

Three young men in their mid teens run on at the back. They are foster brothers, BRAC, MARBAN *and* VIRIDIO. *They are playing ball. The ball is a sheep's stomach, stuffed with rag and clay.* VIRIDIO *has the ball.*

BRAC. Chuck it!

VIRIDIO. Now! Suddenly he feints.

BRAC. What a wanker.

MARBAN. Hedge him.

BRAC *and* MARBAN *feint around* VIRIDIO *to stop him making a run.*

CONLAG. That's fucked it.

DAUI. Get down!

CONLAG (*to the* SLAVE): You. We're not here. Couple o' ghosts, Gods even, out of the woods, just passing through. Bring you good luck, right? So sh.

DAUI. Get down!

CONLAG *and* DAUI *scramble back into their hiding place.*

VIRIDIO *digs his heel into the ground.*

VIRIDIO. My mark!

BRAC. Never!

VIRIDIO. Count of five! Three four five.

BRAC, *a laugh.*

BRAC. Piss off.

MARBAN. Make your play, brother.

VIRIDIO. Want me to make my play, brother?

VIRIDIO *throws the ball high with a feint to wrong foot his brothers. They run after the ball.* BRAC *catches it.* VIRIDIO *and* MARBAN *tear at his clothing.*

BRAC. What's the goal, what's the goal?

VIRIDIO. That hole —

MARBAN. That hole —

BRAC. Oh that hole —

BRAC *makes to go one way then goes another.*

VIRIDIO. Slippery little arse —

MARBAN. Up in the air!

VIRIDIO *and* MARBAN *run after* BRAC, *grab him and throw him up in the air.*

BRAC. Don't throw me up in the air! You know I hate — (*In the air.*) going up in the air.

BRAC *lets go of the ball. They let go of* BRAC. MARBAN *gets the ball, darts away, stops and calmly puts it on the ground.*

VIRIDIO. What's that?

MARBAN. A goal.

VIRIDIO *and* BRAC *stare at him.*

BRAC. What goal?

MARBAN. That goal.

MARBAN *points at the ball and looks at the* SLAVE.

BRAC. I can't see a hole.

VIRIDIO. Hole for the goal, where is it?

MARBAN. It's a small hole.

VIRIDIO. Wormhole.

VIRIDIO *laughs.*

MARBAN. It is a wormhole.

BRAC, *on all fours, scrambles to the ball. He lifts it carefully and looks underneath.*

BRAC. If you want to find a wormhole, send for a priest.

VIRIDIO. Second sight.

BRAC. Second sight, for seeing the turds of worms.

VIRIDIO *grabs the ball and dashes for a few paces.*

MARBAN. Brother!

All still.

(*To the* SLAVE:) What is it?

Nothing from the SLAVE. *The brothers look around, sharply. Then* MARBAN *picks up a stone and tosses it to where* CONLAG *and* DAUI *are hiding.*

DAUI *rises, talking fast.*

DAUI. Travellers in trade. From Ireland. Where the fucking heroes come from. But do not take us lightly, do not take our powers lightly.

CONLAG *stands up slowly. A silence, all still.* DAUI *slowly takes an ingot of iron from the bag. A thin bar, about a metre long, the ends pinched.*

Irish iron. To forge, patting butter. Temper it with blood, the phosphorus will dazzle you. And it is very, very hard. Plough with this iron, gold will grow. And a sword? Go through your enemy's gut, a fish through water. And a man's head?

He swings the ingot, two-handed.

His body will stand there, not believing it's his head, bouncing on his big toes. Eh?

A silence.

So could I see the mother or the father of your family?

A silence.

CONLAG. We'll just go now —

VIRIDIO *walks to* DAUI *and takes the ingot from him. He heaves it into the air, it spins, he catches it.*

DAUI. Got loads back there. Cartloads. And all our friends.

Strong, angry, vicious friends.

We just come on ahead. Out of respect.

VIRIDIO. Traders? Sleeping in the open? Hiding from a slave?

CONLAG. Yes, we'll just go now. Take what we've got. There's wine in the bag. Greek wine.

VIRIDIO. Greek wine from Ireland?

The brothers laugh.

CONLAG. We're on our way —

BRAC. Where's this wine, then?

CONLAG *hesitates, then picks up the bag and takes out a wineskin.* BRAC *walks to him, takes the wineskin and drinks.*

CONLAG. Got a load of wine back there. With our friends.
 Strong —

He falters.

 angry, vicious friends.

BRAC. Greek wine. It's beautiful.

A silence.

Maybe they're Romans.

DAUI. Ha! Ever seen a Roman, farmer boy?

The sun shines out of their navels. Two navels. And big, very big men. In metal. When they walk they clank.

You've never seen a Roman.

MARBAN. Not Romans. (*To* BRAC:) Give me your knife.

BRAC *gives* MARBAN *a knife.*

DAUI. Now don't take that attitude.

MARBAN. They're criminals.

DAUI. Now look, we've not got a disease or anything like that.

MARBAN. Thrown out by their families. Scavenging.

DAUI. Look, we didn't know we were near you, in the dark.

We'll go on our way. Stay in the woods. Move along the hills. Crawl away from your farms. Not steal your animals.

You'll not know we've been past!

A silence.

All right. We're criminals. All right we murdered a man and his wife. All right we were cursed off the land of our families. Our souls taken away by the priests, eh?

But that was in Ireland. A lot of the world away.

You've no cause, boys. To put our blood on your fields.

VIRIDIO. Hard luck, Irishman. (*Indicating* MARBAN.) My brother here, is a priest.

A silence, CONLAG *and* DAUI *taking a step back.*

DAUI. I do have a disease.

The brothers rush at DAUI.

I am a Roman come to fuck your mother —

They up-end DAUI. MARBAN *slits his throat.* CONLAG *runs for it. Blood gushes from* DAUI's *mouth,* VIRIDIO *holding his legs.*

BRAC, *jumping up and down with excitement.*

BRAC. Wonderful! Wonderful!

VIRIDIO. The other one!

BRAC. We'll get the dogs!

MARBAN. Hold him up! Keep him up!

MARBAN *looks around.*

BRAC. Get the dogs and go after him, all day, miles and miles!

MARBAN. A stake. (*To the* SLAVE:) You. Your rope and your bowl.

The SLAVE *stays still.*

Now!

The SLAVE *takes off a rope from round her tunic. She picks up the stave and bowl and holds them out.*

We'll get him right up! Upside down. Let the blood run into his throat.

MARBAN *runs to the* SLAVE *and takes the rope, stave and bowl. He runs back and digs the end of the stave into the ground.*

(*To* BRAC.) Help, then!

BRAC *helps* MARBAN *to drive the stave in securely.* MARBAN *ties the rope round* DAUI's *ankles and knots the rope round the end of the stave. It bends under the dead weight, the corpse's chest on the ground. He puts the bowl under the neck. This, as* BRAC *speaks.*

BRAC. The little one will go into the woods. We'll run with the dogs. All day. A hot day. We'll shout to him. He'll scream back.

Then, in the afternoon, silence. The woods. He and us. Even the dogs won't bark, just breathe. You'll hear their hearts, thumping.

Brilliant light and dark, under the trees.

And we'll kill him in the evening, and come back home with his head, and get pissed.

VIRIDIO. That done right?

MARBAN. It's not 'Right', but it'll do.

BRAC. Let's go, let's go!

MARBAN. Wait.

MARBAN *takes the bowl carefully from beneath the corpse's neck and tips the blood onto the ground.*

A blessing.

SLAVE (*aside*). They are farmers. They want to put some blood into the cream.

MARBAN. (*to the* SLAVE): Don't let the dogs worry him.

BRAC. Come on, come on.

BRAC, MARBAN *and* VIRIDIO *run towards the woods.*

The MOTHER *comes on. Behind her are the* SECOND VILLAGE MAN *leading dogs and, at a distance, two* ENVOYS.

The three brothers stop before the MOTHER.

MARBAN. Mother!

BRAC. Mother!

VIRIDIO. Mother!
The MOTHER *waves them away. They run off.*

MOTHER. Envoys. You say you are envoys.

FIRST ENVOY. We are envoys.

The MOTHER *stares at the dead* DAUI.

MOTHER. Insults! Nothing but insults, all night long!

SECOND ENVOY. There is a Roman Army —

MOTHER. I offer you dogs as a gift. You want the dogs, you don't want the dogs. You take the dogs, you insult me. You don't take the dogs, still you insult me. (*She points at the sacrifice.*)
And now that! That, another insult!

SECOND ENVOY. What?

FIRST ENVOY. We had nothing to do with that.

MOTHER. You kill people on my family's field? You take that right away from members of my family?

FIRST ENVOY. Mother of your families —

SECOND ENVOY. Woman —

FIRST ENVOY. With respect —

MOTHER. You booze the night through in my house. You eat my food. You fight with the men of my family. You eye my women. You won't take my dogs. You kill strangers. Outrage!

FIRST ENVOY. All right, we'll take the dogs —

SECOND ENVOY. We are envoys!

MOTHER (*calls out*). Come in from the fields! Take the children to the house! There has been an outrage!

SECOND ENVOY. Woman! Mother! Cow! Listen!

MOTHER. One of the dogs is a killer. I throw this meat in your face. Five dogs will lick your hands, the sixth will eat your lungs!
The FIRST ENVOY *puts a hand on the* SECOND ENVOY's *arm. The* FOURTH VILLAGE MAN *runs on and sees the sacrifice.*

FOURTH VILLAGE MAN. There is blood on the fields.

Shouts, off, in the distance 'Come in from the fields'.

The VILLAGERS *run on, three children with them.*

FIRST VILLAGE WOMAN. Who did it? Did the guests do it?

SECOND VILLAGE WOMAN. Guests — kill on our fields?

BOY. Is there going to be a fight?

GIRL. Are they the men who got drunk?

FIRST WOMAN. Get in the house and shut up. Or you'll get a thump.

SECOND GIRL. But is there going to be fight?

BOY. Can we watch?

FIRST MAN. You heard!

They go off.

MOTHER. Take the dogs. Kill them. They have been insulted.

SECOND ENVOY. We would be very pleased to accept —

MOTHER. Slit their throats! Bury the blood! Throw their bodies in the cess pit!

She throws the meat high, up the back of the stage. The dogs yelp and strain after it.

The SECOND VILLAGE MAN *takes the dogs and runs off with them as the* FIRST VILLAGE WOMAN *and* FIRST VILLAGE MAN *come running back on.*

A silence.

SECOND ENVOY. There is no insult — we killed no-one.

FIRST ENVOY (*low*). Shut up.

A silence, the VILLAGE MEN *and* WOMEN *around the* ENVOYS.

In all decency. Decency. And with dignity. We came as envoys. Spent the night, with your kind hospitality. Ate well.

A night we could not afford. Full bellies we could not afford.

Over the food I said, over the drink I said, again and again.

There is a Roman Army and it is coming.

It is an army of red leather and brass.

It is a ship.

It is a whole thing. It is a monster. It has machines.

It is Roman.

MOTHER. Year in, year out, stories of Romans to scare the children.

SECOND ENVOY. They — are — there!

MOTHER. Eagles instead of heads to scare the boys. Cocks of brass to scare the girls.

The VILLAGERS *laugh*.

SECOND ENVOY. You won't laugh when you're corpses!

FIRST ENVOY. Meat, sizzling in the debris of your burning homes —

SECOND ENVOY. I beg you, woman! You must send the young men and women of your farms. To fight — today.

FIRST ENVOY. Manhood. Womanhood. War. Fury, battle fury. Raise it now.

The MOTHER *spits at the* ENVOYS.

MOTHER. And who sent you?

A silence. All still.

SECOND ENVOY. We have his rings —

MOTHER. You won't say his name.

All night, drinking, singing, arguing, did you.

Even now, you have not got the balls to say the name.

Of the man who sent you.

Not in my house. Not on my fields. Not to my face.

SECOND ENVOY. Cassivellaunel.

A silence.

Cassivell —

The MOTHER *screams. She rocks, one foot to the other.*

FIRST ENVOY. Let us forget old scores, Mother —

She spits.

SECOND ENVOY. What his Grandfather did to your
   Grandfather?

FIRST VILLAGE WOMAN. The cattle raid —

SECOND ENVOY. Five winters back?

FIRST VILLAGE MAN. But never settled.

SECOND ENVOY. Little squabbles.

FIRST VILLAGE MAN. Cattle in winter are not a little
   squabble.

   Laughter.

THIRD VILLAGE MAN. Your Grandfathers were foreigners.

FOURTH VILLAGE MAN. That's right. We don't even foster
   children with you!

SECOND ENVOY. Cassivellaunel was anxious to foster one
   of his daughters with your Mother —

THIRD VILLAGE MAN. And we booted her out —

SECOND VILLAGE WOMAN. No teeth —

FIRST VILLAGE WOMAN. Boil on the end of her nose —

FIRST VILLAGE MAN. Funny smell —

THIRD VILLAGE MAN. Nipples that scratched —

   The VILLAGERS *laugh.*

SECOND ENVOY. You insult our Father's daughter!
   Sons and daughters of a fucking cow, insult our Father's
   daughter!

SECOND VILLAGE WOMAN. Kill the bastards —

FIRST VILLAGE MAN. Ham string 'em, let 'em drag
   'emselves away on their elbows!

MOTHER. Yes yes yes yes! We've had the meal. We've had
   the formal talk. We've had the insults. Yes yes yes!

   A silence.

   So. You want the fighting men and women of the farms
   under my protection to run off south, over the Thames,
   eh?

And the farms left behind? What will they do? Lie here with their legs in the air, fat, fine slobbery pigs, bellies to be ripped open and gorged, eh? With the harvest nearly come? Eh?

While my children, my brothers and my daughters, splash about on the South Coast, hunting Romans that aren't there, eh?

A trick!

Tell Cassivellaunel I still think fondly of his old cock and — tell him to take it in both hands and piss up his arsehole. One pleasantry one insult. He'll know what I mean.

FIRST ENVOY. The Roman Army is there. I have seen it.

THIRD VILLAGE MAN. See your own fart, floating up your nose.

No laughter. A silence.

FIRST ENVOY. The Roman Army moves through this island. A ship of horror. Smashing the woods and farms. Animals run before it. The ship of horror in the water, pushing before it the animals, men, women and children of the farms. Even in this backwater can't you feel it?

They have come from the other side of the World. And they are one. One whole.

Thirty thousand men. Can you, now, see yourself on a beach, the shingle, the tide coming in, and upon it ships with thirty thousand men, eight hundred ships, all one whole? 'Eh? Eh? Eh?' 'Yes? Yes? Yes?'

A silence.

Understand. The Romans are different. They are — (*He gestures, trying to find the word. He fails. He tries again.*) A nation. Nation. What? A great family? No. A people? No. They are one, huge thing.

FIRST VILLAGE WOMAN. He's shit frightened.

SECOND VILLAGE WOMAN. Get away from our farms. Before your blood's on our fields.

FIRST ENVOY. It's an act of truth. What I tell you.

A silence

I have made an act of truth.

The FIRST VILLAGE WOMAN *stoops, picks up a handful of earth and throws it at the* ENVOYS, *not hard, formally. A silence.*

SECOND ENVOY. You won't defend your fields? You —

The FIRST ENVOY *stops him, a hand on his arm.*

FIRST ENVOY. We crossed your boundary, unharmed. We leave it now, unharmed.

The MOTHER *waves them away. The* ENVOYS *take a few steps back, then turn and walk off quickly.*

THIRD VILLAGE MAN. We ought've — whipped their horses into the woods! Sent 'em off with chicken shit down their necks! Let the wild pigs, ride 'em back to Casivellaunel!

FOURTH VILLAGE MAN. We were the hosts, they were the guests —

MOTHER. We can talk about it all day. Or we can work.

FOURTH VILLAGE MAN. The family must be happy Mother. Happy in its mind.

The MOTHER *squats and spits. The* SECOND VILLAGE MAN *comes back on.*

SECOND VILLAGE MAN. I didn't kill the dogs. Didn't want me to, did you?

Nothing from the MOTHER.

Hunting dogs like that.

He looks around the group.

THIRD VILLAGE MAN. If there was an army, there'd be signs. Animals in the woods, running from it. Birds of prey flying towards it, for the flesh. Stragglers, refugees. Listen!

A silence.

Nothing. Just the animals, just our voices, just a day over the farms.

Mother's right. Let's get back to work.

SECOND VILLAGE WOMAN. Though we could, just about harvest now. Dig pits in the woods, hide the crop. (*A short silence.*) It's the time of year for an army, with the harvest almost on us. (*A short silence.*) If there's an army.

FIRST VILLAGE MAN. If pigs fuck sheep!

THIRD VILLAGE MAN. There's no army. Only the old scores.

FIRST VILLAGE WOMAN. But he was frightened. That made me see what he said. I saw his words. The ships on the beach.

FOURTH VILLAGE MAN. A trick of speech. Probably a poet. Powerful men like Cassivellaunel keep a poet or two for that kind of work.

SECOND VILLAGE MAN. We could move the animals to the fort.

A silence. They all look at him, except the MOTHER.

And the old people and children. That at least we could do.

A silence.

FOURTH VILLAGE MAN. That could take four, five days. To get water up there, fuel, the animals of fifty farms. You've not seen it done in your day. I remember the families, barricaded in up there. Just — I was a child. A religious scare. Some druid went off his head and prophesied the end of the world. It caught on and we all ended up in the fort.

We could all get up there. Arm the walls. Miss the good weather — and watch the harvest rot down below.

SECOND VILLAGE MAN. Well, at least consecrate the ground up there.

FOURTH VILLAGE MAN. Oh, we can consecrate the ground.

FIRST VILLAGE WOMAN. And carry weapons in the fields.

A silence.

FOURTH VILLAGE MAN. Mother? (*Nothing from her.*) Consecrate the fort. Carry weapons in the fields. And no drinking during the day. End up cutting ourselves to pieces.

They all look at the MOTHER.

May we leave you?

The MOTHER *waves them away. The* VILLAGERS *straggle off, the* SECOND VILLAGE MAN *hanging back.*

MOTHER. My husband!

The SECOND VILLAGE MAN *turns back.*

You can get *me* a drink.

The SECOND VILLAGE MAN *runs off. The* MOTHER *and the* SLAVE *alone. The* SLAVE *looking at her. The* MOTHER *still squatting, looking down.*

Work, Thing.

The SLAVE *goes back to work. The* SECOND VILLAGE MAN *comes back on with a wineskin. The* MOTHER *pours wine down her throat. She wipes her mouth handing the wineskin to the* SECOND VILLAGE MAN. *He squats and drinks.*

MOTHER. Listen, husband. There is an army.

A silence.

SECOND VILLAGE MAN. You cunning old bitch. You better tell me what you know.

MOTHER. I better tell you nothing.

She drinks. She wipes her mouth.

Tonight, you and my foster sons, dig pits in the woods. Secretly. I want part of the harvest hidden. And go round the fathers and mothers of the farms, the older ones. Get them to do the same. At night. Fast. Before anyone knows what's happening.

SECOND VILLAGE MAN. You'll not keep that quiet. There'll be a row.

MOTHER. If anyone wants a row. I'll row.

SECOND VILLAGE MAN. What do you know!

A silence.

What!

A silence.

You're my wife. Tell me.

A silence.

MOTHER. Two nights ago. The Trinovan families. Sent me an envoy.

They have made an agreement with the Roman Army.

SECOND VILLAGE MAN. Agreement?

MOTHER. They will not fight.

A silence.

SECOND VILLAGE MAN. What do you expect, from fishermen?

MOTHER. The Romans took five hundred hostages, to keep them to it.

SECOND VILLAGE MAN. Five hundred?

A silence

SECOND VILLAGE MAN. What — did you reply to the Trinovan families?

MOTHER. I said that — we foster children with them, not the Cassivellaun families.

That the children bind us.

That their love for the five hundred taken, is our love.

That we are stupid farmers, thick as pigshit.

And we will farm. Just farm.

SECOND VILLAGE MAN. In peace.

MOTHER. Huh.

SECOND VILLAGE MAN. And we — we! Thanks to the treachery of a load of fishermen, we are in alliance with the Roman Army!

None of us have ever seen a Roman!

He turns a circle then stands still.

The forest. The fields. The boundaries. The stockades. The cattle runs. The kilns. The tall roofs of the houses. The Gods on the eaves.

He stamps his foot three times.

The ground in late summer. The thing I know. The thing that's me. The place. Is it changed? Is it —

Is it —

Is it —

Not what I know?

A silence. He reaches for the wineskin. The MOTHER *pulls it away.*

MOTHER. Ah no.

Keep your eyes sharp. And on the chicken. On the pigs. On what's coming out of the trees.

And it'll go by. Whatever it is. Out there.

She stands, walks to the sacrifice, takes the bowl from beneath the dead DAUI's throat and pours blood onto the ground.

Scene Three

River bank and woods. Sunlight. The clothes of BRAC, MARBAN and VIRIDIO on the stage.

A silence. Then the brothers come out of the river, naked and wet. They lie down.

BRAC. In the winter, I'll grow my hair. In the spring I'll dye it. Three colours. Black at the roots, henna, and at the tips, bright yellow.

It will be fucking terrifying.

VIRIDIO. A short arse like you needs to put on a bit of height.

BRAC and VIRIDIO look at each other. BRAC looks away then does a cat leap onto VIRIDIO.

MARBAN lies back with his hands behind his neck, crosses his legs and yawns. Then he suddenly sits up, listening.

BRAC and VIRIDIO stop fighting and look at MARBAN.

MARBAN. I heard him.

A silence.

And the dogs.

A silence.

In the forest.

BRAC. A long way away —

VIRIDIO. Run with the dogs, the short arse said.

VIRIDIO laughs.

BRAC. The dogs will come back, when they've got him. The

leader of the pack will come to tell us. That dog speaks to me.
Woof woof, a bone from Ireland. Hero beef.

VIRIDIO. We should've taken the horses.

BRAC. We'd never have followed 'em through the trees.

VIRIDIO. The Iceni ride through the trees. The Iceni can ride
into one side of a wood, in chariots, in the shape of an axe-
head, and come out the other side, the axe-head still sharp.
I saw it done once, at a festival. The forest. The screaming
charioteers — disappear.

Silence.

Not even birds rising.

You stare at the wall of trees. Horizon to horizon, a wall of
many dark gates.

Then wham! They're coming at you, from anywhere.

BRAC, *playing with his hair.*

BRAC. Great.

MARBAN. A trick.

VIRIDIO. Magic —

MARBAN. It's a trick. They cut tracks through the trees, only
known to them. They are silent because the companion of
each charioteer muffles the horses' hooves, when they are
under cover.

VIRIDIO. Brilliant.

MARBAN. A brilliant trick.

VIRIDIO. Now what would a priest know about tricks?

A short silence. MARBAN, *quietly.*

MARBAN. I'm not a priest yet. And you know it.

VIRIDIO. Ooh!

BRAC. Ooh!

VIRIDIO. He's angry.

BRAC. I think you touched him on his secret rites.

VIRIDIO *and* BRAC *giggle.*

VIRIDIO. Brother is it true, that for part of the training to get
to be a priest, you stand for ninety days, with a great big

boulder hanging from your testicles?

BRAC *giggles.*

MARBAN. Lie on the ground. A great boulder on your stomach. For ninety days.

A short silence.

VIRIDIO. Well. I s'pose that will come in handy, in later life.

BRAC *giggles.* MARBAN, *quietly.*

MARBAN. Don't be childish, don't be — that. You're my brothers, don't. Eh?

VIRIDIO. Brother, really we are shit scared of you.

(BRAC *giggles.*) I am. Of you.

Because you are going to be a priest. (BRAC *looks embarrassed.*)

MARBAN. Look — no.

If you think — no.

It takes twenty years to be a priest. The thing with the boulder, on your stomach, happens in the ninth year. I've been doing it for three. All right? All right?

Coming home for the harvest.

Though that will stop, in two years' time. And I'll be shut up with them, all the year round.

Huh? Huh?

He looks at BRAC and VIRIDIO. They will not look back.

They're so happy, those old priests. Those frightening old men and women.

Frightening in the way I begin to frighten you.

Do you want to see a ghost?

A silence.

VIRIDIO. Who am I, a mere wanker in the straw —

MARBAN. No no do you? Now? Right.

MARBAN *goes quickly to his clothes.*

BRAC. Look, eh —

VIRIDIO. Let him.

MARBAN. I go everywhere with her.

VIRIDIO. Her?

MARBAN. It's a woman.

VIRIDIO. Oh good.

MARBAN. Though a ghost.

VIRIDIO. Course.

BRAC. Er —

MARBAN (*at* BRAC). Someone dead. Beyond the grave. Not in our world.

MARBAN *takes a flint stone with a hollow ground in it. He puts a powder in the hollow. He takes another flint stone, flaked to a point to fit the hollow in the first stone. He takes a length of cloth and wraps it round his fist as he gives his patter.*

Have you thought why, since we all live beyond the grave, in the sweet fields, the rich woods there — we don't see them more often, the dead?

BRAC. Well —

MARBAN. Because of the pain of dying, brother.

Which is like a wall.

BRAC. Ah.

MARBAN. Solid, thick with pain.

So the cracks in the wall of death are rare. Tiny.

And the life of the dead can only flare through them, for a moment.

As they do, in the lights over a marsh.

Like this.

MARBAN *hits the two flintstones together. A muffled report. A cloud of white smoke drifts up and away.*

VIRIDIO. That was a woman?

BRAC. I saw her —

VIRIDIO. What was it?

BRAC. Lovely thighs —

MARBAN, *unwinding the cloth from his hand.*

VIRIDIO. A trick?

BRAC. Like silver.

MARBAN. A ghost a trick, a trick a ghost.

If the religious shit themselves, what's the difference?

Huh? Huh?

He laughs.

VIRIDIO. They do say 'Never look a priest in the eyes.'

BRAC. Like a dog! Send the dog mad —

VIRIDIO. Which one is the dog though, looker or priest? Eh?

VIRIDIO *and* BRAC *stare at each other.*

BRAC. Yes but —

VIRIDIO *and* MARBAN *staring at each other.*

Look, don't.

A silence.

Don't.

A silence.

Start fucking insulting each other next.

MARBAN (*to* VIRIDIO). I've been taught an insult.

Which, if it's made to you, your eyes melt. Your tongue, tears itself out. Your head — bursts.

It's only a few words.

Want me to say it?

To you?

They stare on. Then VIRIDIO *looks down.* MARBAN *giggles.*

VIRIDIO. Now he's taking the piss.

BRAC. Stories about priests, getting up each other in the woods. My father always hated 'em. Rant and rage, 'bout how the richer families send off their favorite sons to join 'em. How their visions, auguries, judgments of disputes, were always — in your favour if — (*A turning gesture with his hand.*) A fine animal or two, fine iron, fine wine —
Then, round they'd come. And my poor old father — he'd go religious quicker than a billy goat fucks.

VIRIDIO *looks away, then does a cat leap onto* MARBAN. They laugh and fight.

MARBAN. Get off.

VIRIDIO. What, brother —

MARBAN. Get off —

VIRIDIO. Dear oh dear.

VIRIDIO *rolls away. The three brothers lie in the sun.*

Still. It's hot. The water was good and cold.

The dogs are tearing down an enemy, somewhere in the woods.

Along with the wild pigs, and your priests, in there, doing what they do.

Where's the Irishmen's wine?

BRAC *hands* VIRIDIO *the wineskin. He raises it to drink.*

Three ROMAN SOLDIERS *walk out of the woods. The soldiers and the brothers see each other at the same time. There is a considerable distance between them.*

A silence.

FIRST SOLDIER. Three wogs.

A silence.

SECOND SOLDIER. What are they, d'you know?

THIRD SOLDIER. A wog is a wog.

FIRST SOLDIER. Not Trinovante. Not round here.

THIRD SOLDIER. Pretty arses. Give 'em something.

The SOLDIERS *laugh.*

VIRIDIO. They — not got eagles on their shoulders 'stead of heads. We'll see in a moment if they've got brass balls that clang when they walk.

VIRIDIO *laughs.*

MARBAN. Be quiet.

VIRIDIO. They don't know what we're saying. We don't know what they're saying.

BRAC. Kill the leader first. Which one's the leader? Can you tell which one's the leader?

MARBAN. Shut up! (*Low:*) What weapons have we got?

BRAC. My knife —

MARBAN. Where?

BRAC. You had it. To cut the Irishman's throat —

MARBAN. Yes.

A silence.

One knife. Under my clothes — don't look at it!

Stand up.

The brothers stand.

FIRST SOLDIER. A little wander round, and we pick a plum. Not that we don't deserve it. Fine day? Sun? A swim? Three little wogs to play with?

SECOND SOLDIER. There may be others. (*He looks around.*) I mean these are children. Maybe they sent 'em out to play, while they're hiding, waiting to come down on us.

THIRD SOLDIER. No, these wogs are fucked and do they know it. Success is with us, the news of success — right? So — wade right through 'em, into the river, right?

BRAC. Jabber jabber.

MARBAN. They're talking about how to kill us.

VIRIDIO. They're between us and the trees.

MARBAN. We've got one knife.

We don't know who is best to use it.

BRAC. Me —

VIRIDIO. Me —

BRAC. With a knife? Oooh!

BRAC, *a knifing gesture.*

MARBAN. Be still!

A silence.

Get them to circle round. Then we can get into the trees.

The SOLDIERS advance toward the brothers carefully.

SECOND SOLDIER. Don't let 'em get into the trees. I've seen enough of wogs running into the fucking trees.

THIRD SOLDIER. Beads? Pretty beads?

FIRST SOLDIER. For fucksake.

> *The* FIRST SOLDIER *draws his sword.*

> Italian short sword, eh? Want to feel your fist round that? A real hard-on, eh?

> *He spins the sword in the air.* MARBAN *takes a step back. The* SOLDIERS *stand still.*

> *A silence.*

> *The* SECOND *and* THIRD SOLDIERS *draw their swords.*

> *The* SOLDIERS *run at the brothers.* MARBAN *runs to his clothes and gets the knife.* VIRIDIO *and* BRAC *run in different directions.*

> *The* SECOND *and* THIRD SOLDIERS *catch* BRAC *and give him a bad stomach wound.*

> BRAC *rests, pulls himself along the ground, screams, rests — a progress that continues during most of the rest of the scene, gradually slowing.*

> VIRIDIO *stops, turns and stares at his brother's agony.* MARBAN, *with the knife, turns.*

> *All but for the crawling* BRAC *are still.*

VIRIDIO. Foreigners, I will hold your heads in my hands. With my fingers in the sockets of your eyes, I will hold up your skulls, wet with the flesh of your eyes and your blood! I will know you as a killer! As only the killer can know the thing he has killed! To hold you, the guts of you, the kidneys and the hearts of you in my fists! And you will smile, when your heads are dry bone! Over my house! My children and my grandchildren will play with your skulls! And I will tell of the meal we will have tonight! Of you! Of your brain, turned over a fire! With your guts fed to the pigs! Your arseholes gnawed by my dogs! I will hold your bloody hearts, today! Today! Up to the sun as it sets, and squeeze, and your blood will run down my throat, and I will drink you, get pissed on you! And vomit on you and drink more of you! You will be blood in my bones! You will feed me, my meat, my enemy! And your mothers, wherever those stinking sows lie, in your stinking country, will wake with a cry in their own shit, and tear their tits with the pain of how I am going to kill you!

FIRST SOLDIER. Jabber jabber.

SECOND SOLDIER. Keep the one with the knife off.

The FIRST SOLDIER *walks toward* MARBAN *and feints him away from the* SECOND *and* THIRD SOLDIERS, *who, with their shields, calmly crowd in on* VIRIDIO, *slam their shields against him and kill him. They step back.*

VIRIDIO *slides to the ground with a wound in his chest and in his back.*

THIRD SOLDIER. What a waste of pretty arse.

A silence.

The three SOLDIERS *and* MARBAN — *four young men standing still.*

Then, relaxed, the SOLDIERS *walk to surround* MARBAN, *each a good way from him.*

With the knife ready MARBAN *turns from one to the other. Then he relaxes.*

A silence, but for BRAC.

FIRST SOLDIER. I'm just here for a swim.

SECOND SOLDIER. That (*Meaning* BRAC.) may be heard.

THIRD SOLDIER. That (*Meaning* MARBAN.) would've yelled, if there were more.

FIRST SOLDIER. I'm going to get that swim, so let's —

The FIRST SOLDIER *runs at* MARBAN. MARBAN *side steps and slashes the knife at the* FIRST SOLDIER, *catching his arm. Surprised, the* FIRST SOLDIER *falls, turning with a reflex out of his training to cover himself with his shield.*

Fucking little nig nog.

He staggers to his feet.

He cut me!

The SECOND SOLDIER *laughs.*

THIRD SOLDIER. What are we waiting for?

The SOLDIERS *run at* MARBAN, *smashing their shields against him from three sides.* MARBAN's *knife goes flying, he stumbles away and falls. The* FIRST *and* THIRD SOLDIERS *begin to strip.*

Hold him, then.

SECOND SOLDIER. I'll do him in the neck.

THIRD SOLDIER. Don't , he'll shit himself.

FIRST SOLDIER. All this trouble for a bit of a swim.

THIRD SOLDIER. No, I want him to feel this. You can cut him about a bit if you want. Here!

The THIRD SOLDIER *picks up* MARBAN's *knife and tosses it toward the* SECOND SOLDIER.

Use his knife.

SECOND SOLDIER. I wonder about you sometimes.

THIRD SOLDIER. Cut him! Make him look pretty!

SECOND SOLDIER. Dear oh dear.

The SECOND SOLDIER *picks up the knife and makes a cut on* MARBAN's *shoulder blade.*

THIRD SOLDIER. Got no fucking idea at all, have you.

The THIRD SOLDIER, *now half naked, takes the knife from the* SECOND SOLDIER, *kneels and cuts* MARBAN *on the buttocks.*

MARBAN *moans, as if with a question, looking at the* SECOND SOLDIER *who holds him by the shoulders.*

MARBAN. Hunh?

The SECOND SOLDIER, *into* MARBAN's *face.*

SECOND SOLDIER. My friend has been to the Orient. Persia? Funny little ways he's picked up, in his career. But what the fuck do you expect, from a man who's been in Persia?

MARBAN. Hunh?

SECOND SOLDIER. Hunh?

THIRD SOLDIER. Ooh, he's begun to shit himself.

SECOND SOLDIER. Persia? The other side of the world?

MARBAN. Hunh?

SECOND SOLDIER. World?

MARBAN. Hunh?

THIRD SOLDIER. Rub it in. Make it smooth.

SECOND SOLDIER. Empire?

MARBAN. Hunh?

The FIRST SOLDIER *is now naked. He spits on his cut arm and rubs the spit in. The* THIRD SOLDIER *holds* MARBAN's *thighs and attempts to bugger him.*

FIRST SOLDIER. Just a scratch.

SECOND SOLDIER (*to the* FIRST SOLDIER). You pig.

He laughs.

THIRD SOLDIER (*to the* SECOND SOLDIER). Y'can — y'can give us a kiss.

SECOND SOLDIER. Fucking Greek.

THIRD SOLDIER. Yeah.

FIRST SOLDIER (*examining his belly*). I've got little spots. I'm coming out in little spots.

THIRD SOLDIER. Go — and have — a swim — you're taking my mind — off what I'm doing.

FIRST SOLDIER. I will.

The FIRST SOLDIER *cartwheels.*

THIRD SOLDIER. Keep this fucking arse still!

SECOND SOLDIER. Sorry, veteran of Persia.

The SECOND SOLDIER *blows the* THIRD SOLDIER *a kiss.*

FIRST SOLDIER (*cartwheeling*). Days and days — I have wanted a swim.

He cartwheels off, into the river, out of sight.

THIRD SOLDIER. This in't no — in't no — at all —

SECOND SOLDIER. In trouble, comrade?

THIRD SOLDIER. In't no arse at all.

The THIRD SOLDIER *rolls away.* MARBAN *begins to struggle.*

MARBAN. Hunh hunh hunh —

THIRD SOLDIER. Not even got it up anymore!

MARBAN. Hunh hunh —

The SECOND SOLDIER *hits* MARBAN *on the top of the head with the butt of his sword.* MARBAN *is knocked unconscious. His left leg twitches twice then is still.*

A silence.

THIRD SOLDIER. Oh. (*He sits up.*) Oh oh.

SECOND SOLDIER. I said, are you in trouble comrade?

THIRD SOLDIER. Arseful of piles. Like fucking a fistful of marbles. I mean, what do they do in this island, sit with their bums in puddles of mud all year long?

He stands.

Huh.

He looks at himself.

And I'm covered in shit.

The SECOND SHOULDER, *running his hand over* MARBAN's *back.*

SECOND SOLDIER. Good shoulders.

THIRD SOLDIER. I don't want you talking about this.

SECOND SOLDIER. Did I say a word?

THIRD SOLDIER. I don't want to hear a word.

SECOND SOLDIER. If that's your attitude.

THIRD SOLDIER. Marcus Clavius. I do not want to hear, one night out drinking, back home, years from now, on a lovely evening, surrounded by admirers, sons. I do not want to hear — of me not getting it up a British arseful of piles. Right?

SECOND SOLDIER. Right.

THIRD SOLDIER. I know how rumours start.

SECOND SOLDIER. Right.

THIRD SOLDIER. I mean. (*A half laugh.*) Pride. And it's been a fuck of a summer.

SECOND SOLDIER. Go and have a swim. (*They look at each other.*) Wash yourself off.

THIRD SOLDIER. I will. (*He backs away.*) Right.

He runs into a handstand. He jack-knifes out of it. He turns and looks at the SECOND SOLDIER.

Good.

He goes to the riverbank and dives in, out of sight. The
SECOND SOLDIER *runs his hand over* MARBAN's *back
again, under his shoulder, scrutinizing his finger's path, over
the temple and into* MARBAN's *hair.*

BRAC *is now still and silent.*

SECOND SOLDIER. Soft bone, where I hit you.

My uncle, a slave, he was a slave, was hit there.

He spits. He rubs saliva into MARBAN's *hair.*

When he was a man of some years. Thirty. And he couldn't
speak. Couldn't —

A gesture at his mouth. He puts his finger back into
MARBAN's *hair and runs it round to his mouth.*

My uncle was treated kindly, by his master, he began to get
words back. Gave him his freedom, out of kindness. Now he's
with the priests of a cult, oracle, holy oracle. You've got a
lump of phlegm in your mouth.

He turns MARBAN's *head on its side.*

Halfway up your nose, here — bloody too, if you're bleeding
into the back of your nose you'll choke on that — here.

He pulls out the mucus and wipes his hand on the ground.

There. Choke on that. I saved your life, nig nog. A legionary
saved your life, nig nog. Nephew of a slave. Now, a citizen,
upon my discharge.

(*Running his finger round* MARBAN's *mouth.*) If I don't get
gangrene, eh? And get off this fucking island, eh? My discharge,
upon a little bit of bronze — 'Citizen'.

He breathes out and looks up.

Come on come on.

He leans over MARBAN *and kisses him.*

Get you over. Come on.

He turns MARBAN *over with difficulty.* MARBAN *comes to.*

MARBAN. Sacerdos sum. Exsecrationem scio. Te miles romane,
caedet. Foede!

SECOND SOLDIER. A nig nog? Talking Latin?

MARBAN gags. The FIRST *and* THIRD SOLDIERS *come out of the river, wet. The* SECOND SOLDIER *straddles* MARBAN, *knees beside his head.*

This nig nog talks Latin!

THIRD SOLDIER. What do you think you're doing? (*He laughs.*)

SECOND SOLDIER. He talks Latin!

THIRD SOLDIER. Watch it. He may bite off more than you want him to chew. (*He laughs.*)

SECOND SOLDIER. Fucking Latin talking nig nog! Suck me off!

FIRST SOLDIER (*looking at his stomach*). Those spots. They've gone violet.

Scene Four

Deep woodland. Pools of darkness, shafts of sunlight.

CONLAG *is killing a dog, pulling its back legs over its back, rolling, trying to keep the dog from biting him.*

CONLAG. Leader! Leader are you! Leader of the pack are you! 'Ere. (*Winning.*) 'Ere, 'ere. (*Laying over the twitching dog.*) There. There.

He stands, holding the dog by its back legs. He screams at the surrounding forest, turning.

All right dogs! Here's your leader! Fucker of your wives! Eat him now! I'll get out your way now! Up a tree, over a stream!

Eh? Take — (*Whirling around, swinging the dog with two hands.*) him!

He throws the dead dog. It falls on the ground. He runs a few paces then trips and falls.

Oh I've hurt my foot, oh!

He lies still. A silence. He looks behind him.

No dogs?

He jerks himself into a crouch.

I just killed the lead dog of a pack and they're not chewing my balls? Pack of fucking British hunting dogs?

What else they gone off for? What's rawer than me? Juicier?
(*He giggles.*) Something that's died! And I am still alive. I.
Am. Oh my foot.

He sits back from his crouch and looks at his foot.

If your feet go in times like these, you may as well bury
yourself. Right there. Up to the waist. Some warrior band or
another will be along to cut you to peices.

(*He stands.*) It's all right! (*He falls.*) It's not all right. (*He
shouts.*) It's got to be all right!

(*He stands. Low:*) Oh fuck.

He walks a few yards with difficulty.

The SLAVE, *startled in a hiding place, stands up. They stare
at each other. A silence.*

I threw a dead dog away, somewhere round here. Something
to eat, in the days ahead. Eh?

A silence.

Burn the farms, did they? Run off, did you?

He laughs. She steps back.

I'm not after your hole. I've been in and out of it all. That's
nothing to me. Help me to walk. (*She stays still.*)

I'm a murderer. (*She stays still.*)

I've got a bad foot. (*She stays still.*)

Me and Daui. We were going to the sea. Get a boat. Now he's
dead. So you come with me.

She stays still.

There is a land. The stories say it's there so it's got to be. Over
the sea. The forests are thick. The deer are free. The pigs are
there for the taking. Put your hand in a river there, the fish
come to kiss your fingers. And no Gods, no creepy crawlies,
no souls of dead heroes bashing around in the undergrowth,
giving you the shits. And no people! No people! It is there!
The stories say so!

Off we go then.

*They are both suddenly startled. They stare in the same
direction.*

Something —

She gestures 'Be quiet.' A silence. They hear it again.

Your owners, running. Or Romans running after them.

He laughs. The SLAVE *slaps his face. He stares at her. She pulls him down into hiding.*

The two VILLAGE WOMEN *and the* FIRST, THIRD *and* FOURTH VILLAGE MEN *with the three* CHILDREN *come on, quickly, in a bunch. The* THIRD VILLAGE MAN *is wounded.*

FIRST GIRL. Were they Romans?

SECOND GIRL. They didn't have eagles instead of heads.

BOY. Why did they burn us?

SECOND GIRL. Are we going to kill them?

BOY. Why did they burn us?

FIRST GIRL. *Are* we going to kill them?

FIRST VILLAGE WOMAN. Shut up, children!

She gestures to the group. They crouch down, still.

A silence.

A considerable space between the two groups.

FOURTH VILLAGE MAN. Something.

A silence.

SECOND VILLAGE WOMAN. Nothing.

FIRST VILLAGE MAN. I had a sling in my hand. I turned. The house was burning. I ran toward the house. Behind me, the field burst into flames. My daughter ran toward me. Burning. She fell, fire between us. I stood in the smoke. Then I was an animal. Running, to get in the trees. In the dark.

He vomits.

THIRD VILLAGE MAN. Humiliation.

SECOND VILLAGE WOMAN. Catapults. On little machines. Throwing burning —

FOURTH VILLAGE MAN (*to the* THIRD VILLAGE MAN). How bad are you —

SECOND VILLAGE WOMAN. Just like that. From nowhere.

Throwing burning —

FIRST VILLAGE WOMAN. Get to the sanctuary. Leave the children with the priests. Find the families.

THIRD VILLAGE MAN. Hit back. Again and again.

FOURTH VILLAGE MAN. Let me look at you —

The THIRD VILLAGE MAN *pulls himself away.*

FIRST VILLAGE MAN. I didn't even see 'em! Not one of 'em! Just a great ball of fire, rolling over the crops toward me. Then in me.

FOURTH VILLAGE MAN (*to the* FIRST VILLAGE WOMAN, *shaking his head*). Bad.

THIRD VILLAGE MAN. We must get a Roman's head. Carry it alive. In a little bag. On the end of a stick. So it can cry out in terror to its countrymen. And its screams will be clean, clean, clean as a knife, to cut out our humiliation —

FIRST VILLAGE WOMAN. Be quiet!

A silence. They look around. The sound of their breathing.

CONLAG. Crawl away from this lot, girl. They'll be cutting themselves and everything that moves to bits.

The SLAVE *helps him up. They move a few steps. They freeze. The* VILLAGERS *have heard them.*

FIRST VILLAGE MAN. Tracking us. Circle 'em. Stick the pigs.

FIRST VILLAGE WOMAN. Shut up.

A silence.

FOURTH VILLAGE MAN. Only our kind can move as quiet as that.

A silence.

Let them go. Who knows whom we can trust now?

The two groups steal away from each other.

Scene Five

River bank and woods. The bodies of BRAC *and* VIRIDIO *on the ground.*

Upstage a group of ROMAN SOLDIERS *stand very still — a* STANDARD BEARER, *holding a legion standard, two fully armed* SOLDIERS *and a* BUGLER.

A silence.

Two SOLDIERS, *in tunics, run on with a stretcher, on it the bodies of the* MOTHER *and the* SECOND VILLAGE MAN, *her husband. The* SOLDIERS *tip the bodies onto the ground and run off with the stretcher.*

A silence.

A punishment squad of three SOLDIERS, *in tunics, and a* GUARD *come on. They are laden with piles of wooden lavatory seats and spades.*

GUARD. Field lavatory detail!

FIRST SOLDIER. All right all right we're behind you.

SECOND SOLDIER. I am sick of digging lavatories.

GUARD. Then don't end up in a punishment squad.

THIRD SOLDIER. Something to tell your kiddies, when you get back home.

SECOND SOLDIER. Oh yeah. I dug a shit hole on the edge of the world.

They throw the seats down in a heap.

GUARD. A good fathom down, lads.

They begin to dig.

JULIUS CAESAR *wanders forward from the back looking at the ground. He is followed at a distance, though closely observed, by members of his staff —* ASINUS, *a historian in civilian clothes, a legionary* LEGATE, *a legionary* PREFECT, *and a* PRIMUS PILUS — *a centurion of the highest rank, a man in his early sixties.*

CAESAR *stops. His staff stops. The punishment squad stop working and stare.*

A silence, all still.

CAESAR *stoops and picks up* MARBAN's *knife. He walks on. The punishment squad return to work.*

Dangling the knife casually at his side between finger and thumb CAESAR *walks by the* MOTHER's *body, ignoring it.*

CAESAR. Prefect of the Legion.

The PREFECT *runs forward.*

Set the standards.

PREFECT. Yes General.

CAESAR. Don't pitch camp yet. Wait for the order.

PREFECT. Yes General.

CAESAR. Be careful with their bodies. Consecrate the ground.
  Set up an altar.

PREFECT. General.

The PREFECT *goes back to the staff.*

CAESAR. My bugler.

The BUGLER *runs forward.*

Let them know I'm here.

BUGLER. Yes General.

PREFECT (*to the* PRIMUS PILUS). Set the standards. The
  order to pitch camp has *not* been given.

PRIMUS PILUS. Yes Sir. (*He shouts*:) First Standard Bearer!

The STANDARD BEARER *runs forward. The* BUGLER
blows a call.

A runner down the lines. The order is set the standards. Wait
  for the bugle to pitch camp.

STANDARD BEARER. Yes Sir.

The STANDARD BEARER *digs his standard into the ground,
then begins to run off. The* SOLDIERS *take up guard of the
standard.*

CAESAR. Wait.

PRIMUS PILUS. Stop where you are.

The STANDARD BEARER *stops.*

LEGATE. Gaius Julius Caesar. This is my command. It is my
  privelege to receive your orders —

CAESAR (*ignoring the* LEGATE). Primus Pilus. (*The* PRIMUS
  PILUS *runs to* CAESAR. *Privately*:) What did we do here?

PRIMUS PILUS. A couple of cohorts got jumbled up in the
  trees. The runners lost contact. Then they came on this lot —

CAESAR. And had some fun.

PRIMUS PILUS. Without orders, one thing led to another. (*Carefully*:) What with —

CAESAR. What with an invasion that's deteriorated into a squalid little raid, eh Centurion?

Nothing from the PRIMUS PILUS.

I'm not angry with the men. Let that out, down the lines.

PRIMUS PILUS. General.

CAESAR. Stay. (*Calls out*:) Prefect. (*The* PREFECT *runs to* CAESAR.) Any sign of them regrouping?

PREFECT. Nothing. We came on them suddenly and dispersed them.

CAESAR. Prisoners?

PREFECT. Some.

CAESAR. Dead?

PREFECT. No Romans. Of them — (*He shrugs.*)

CAESAR. Think they're getting together in the trees, Centurion?

PRIMUS. What wogs do in the trees, General —

CAESAR. Quite. I want to give the men a rest. What do you think?

The PREFECT *and the* PRIMUS PILUS *uncertain.*

Quite. (*A silence.*)

Divided watch. An hour's recreation for the men stood down. Then change round. No alcohol. For every man swimming a man in battle readiness, watching the trees.

PREFECT. Yes General.

CAESAR *waves them away.*

(*To the* PRIMUS PILUS:) That order down the lines.

PRIMUS PILUS. Sir.

The PRIMUS PILUS *walks quickly to the* STANDARD BEARER. *They talk privately for a few moments, then the* STANDARD BEARER *runs off.*

The LEGATE, *near tears, walks towards* CAESAR.

LEGATE. This is my command. You are humiliating me, before the Legion —

CAESAR *walks away.*

CAESAR. Asinus, my friend.

ASINUS *walks to* CAESAR, *who leads him away from the* LEGATE.

What tribe was it we've just cut to pieces?

ASINUS. As far as I can see, not Trinovante. But a loose grouping, a handful of families —

CAESAR. In the federation of the Trinovantes?

ASINUS. Probably sympathizers.

CAESAR. Sympathizers of sympathizers with us.

ASINUS. Yes.

CAESAR. Wonderful. Is their chieftan killed, or what?

ASINUS. The body of a woman was bitterly fought over. That body.

He points to the body of the MOTHER. CAESAR *doesn't look.*

CAESAR. A woman?

ASINUS. They are not belgaic, they do not originate from the mainland. They are of the ancient stock of Britain. Traces of matriarchy are to be found among them. The Iceni —

CAESAR. All right all right! (*A silence.*) Forgive me. Your scholarship is invaluable. But I've got toothache.

ASINUS. I'll call a surgeon —

CAESAR. No no. (*He calls out:*) The Legate of this legion. (*The* LEGATE *comes forward quickly.*) (*To* ASINUS:) Stand back. But overhear us. Conspicuously.

ASINUS *steps back. A silence.*

LEGATE. Protector of my family —

CAESAR (*angrily*): You what?

A silence. Then CAESAR *holds the knife up by its tip, looking at the handle.*

See, I would like to know how they lay the bronze into the iron. Curling patterns. Like marketry, but with metal. Very fine and on a simple hand weapon. I could have you stoned by your own soldiers for what happened here. (*A silence.*)

Stoned. (*A silence.*) Do these niggers have steel? The Celts of Northern Italy had steel, eh?

> (*Over the* LEGATE's *shoulder*:) Asinus, when we come to a smithy, look to see if there are steel tools.

> *The* LEGATE *looks at* ASINUS *and back to* CAESAR.

> Or did they just trade it from abroad, eh? For a dog, eh?

> CAESAR *tosses the knife and catches it by the handle.*

> I am not the protector of your family, Aurelius Drusius. I just seduced your sister.

LEGATE. I know you are angry with me, I learn from your anger, it is justified, I —

CAESAR. Don't. (*A silence.*) Don't begin to speak like that. Don't go down that path. Ten sentences and you will be promising to kill yourself. Then you will have to kill yourself. And you will never forgive me. Nor will your family.

LEGATE. I speak from the heart.

CAESAR. A disgusting, fashionable habit.

LEGATE. I have no cynicism —

CAESAR. Nor have I! (*He stares at the* LEGATE.) I take rhetoric very, very seriously. In war, what is done is done. In speech, what is meant is meant. You're a young man, learn how a Roman must speak. Of his life, in public, at moments like this. When you are being reprimanded, for having lost control of your command, during a minor mopping up exercise, against a wretched bunch of wog farmers, women and children, in a filthy backwater of humanity, somewhere near the edge of the world.

> *A silence.*

> There. I've spoken of your tiny stupidity — and ended with the world. Textbook rhetoric, little to big? Eh? (*He grimaces, tonguing his bad tooth. He massages his face. He stops.*)

> *A silence.*

> It's an affliction.

> *A silence. He sniggers.*

> I think I am going to make a remark for the Official Biography, Asinus.

ASINUS, *notes at the ready.* CAESAR *sniggers again.*

I was going to say it's an affliction, to see in any one act, its consequence. To see a man — (*He gestures at the* LEGATE.) and see his future. At once. Bang, like that.

In any predicament, its opposite. To build a tower, knowing brick by brick, how it can be destroyed. Even in the victory of an enemy, I see his defeat.

Once I was captured by pirates. Island fishermen really. I told them — when my ransom is paid, I will return and kill you.

My ransom was paid. I raised a fleet. I stormed their islands. I crucified them all, all their communities, twenty thousand of them, men women and children! Wooded islands. The crosses took all the trees. The islands will be rock and turf for ever. A logic. I walked in forests as a captive. Free, the same ground had to be a barren plain. One extreme the mother of the opposite extreme.

After all, my ancestral mother is Venus, Goddess of love, and I am a man of war.

He sniggers. A silence.

LEGATE. What —

CAESAR. What's your future? You — (*He puts his arm round the* LEGATE's *shoulders.*) will die, a little before me, a very old man, very rich, very happy and very senile. You are relieved of your command in all but name and show. The Prefect of your legion will take his orders directly from me. You will stay on my staff. Your humiliation as a military man will be politely obscured. If you protest, you will be stoned by your soldiers, with relish. The political consequences of maltreating so favourite a son would be tiresome, but easily overcome by my party.

LEGATE. I —

CAESAR. No no no. Put it like this, are you my friend, or aren't you, eh? (*Hugging the* LEGATE.) What d'you say?

LEGATE. I'm your friend.

CAESAR. What a fucking island, eh? What a wretched bunch of wogs, eh? Go and have a swim.

LEGATE. Yes, General.

CAESAR. Look, send this knife to your sister, as a present from me. Tell her — (*He toys with the knife.*) to guard with this knife, what I would enter as a knife.

LEGATE. I —

CAESAR gives the knife to the LEGATE.

CAESAR. She reads Terence, she'll understand. (CAESAR *takes the knife back.*) I'll have it cleaned up. A box made. Maybe a human pelt to wrap it in, eh? '

LEGATE. Thank you, Gaius Julius.

The LEGATE *hesitates, then walks away and off the stage.* CAESAR *watches him for a while then turns away.*

CAESAR. The politics of the Roman dinner table are with us, even on the filthy marshes of the edge of the world, eh Asinus?

ASINUS. Yes.

CAESAR. I want him killed. An auxiliary, pissed. A slave with the grievance. Anything — (*An angry gesture.*) trivial. Arrange it.

ASINUS. Yes. Do you want to see something odd?

CAESAR. Odd?

ASINUS makes a sign. Two SOLDIERS *come on with* MARBAN, *still naked, bound.* CAESAR *looks at him.*

Well?

ASINUS. This Celt talks Latin.

CAESAR (*to* MARBAN). Do you? (*Nothing from* MARBAN.) Soldier, go and cut the head off the body of that woman.

The SOLDIER *moves.*

MARBAN. No!

CAESAR stills the SOLDIER *with a sign.*

CAESAR. Why not?

Because then I would own her soul?

MARBAN (*low*). Fitness of things.

CAESAR. What?

SOLDIER. Speak up to the General rubbish!

MARBAN. It would be against the fitness of things!

A silence.

CAESAR. How clumsy your obscene superstitions sound in my language, Druid.

Which is what you are. No?

Nothing from MARBAN.

SOLDIER. Speak up rubbish!

CAESAR (*to the SOLDIER*). No no. (*To* ASINUS:) We know Druids on the mainland speak Greek. Even write it. It's no surprise to find a little Druid in Britain, talking Latin.

ASINUS. All the tools of civilisation. And they keep their people in ignorance.

CAESAR. Hunh. Let him go.

The SOLDIERS push MARBAN forward. He stands, still bound, shivering. CAESAR, with disgust.

Look at the way they live.

A silence.

I'm going to let you run back into the woods, little Druid.

CAESAR takes a pendant from his neck.

Tie that round his neck. Tight.

The SOLDIER does so, MARBAN writhing.

Let him go in the woods. Still bound. His fellow priests will find Venus around his neck. (*Suddenly fierce.*) Listen listen to me! On the mainland I burn your temples. Your priests that will not serve the Roman Gods — I kill. I desecrate their bodies. Desecration according to your beliefs. The head off and burnt, etcetera. Because there are new Gods now. Do you understand? The old Gods are dead.

Nothing from MARBAN.

Yes, you understand. We are both religious men. (*To the SOLDIERS:*) Give him fifty lashes before you let him go. To make the point.

SOLDIER. Yes General.

CAESAR waves them away. The SOLDIERS take MARBAN off.

CAESAR. What did we come to this island for, Asinus?

ASINUS. Fresh water pearls —

CAESAR. So we did. Leave me.

ASINUS. Gaius Julius.

    ASINUS walks away then, at a discreet distance, turns and watches CAESAR.

CAESAR. Primus Pilus. You and two men.

PRIMUS PILUS (*to the* SOLDIERS *guarding the standard*). You and you.

    They go to CAESAR.

CAESAR. Stand with your backs to me.

PRIMUS PILUS. General.

    The PRIMUS PILUS nods to the SOLDIERS. They stand with their backs to CAESAR. CAESAR stoops forward, feeling his tooth with his fingers. Then he holds his lips back and loosens the tooth with the point of the knife. The punishment squad stop work and look.

FIRST SOLDIER. What is our General doing?

SECOND SOLDIER. The moody sod wants to be alone.

THIRD SOLDIER. Sometimes a man has got to be alone. (*They laugh.*)

GUARD. Get on get on.

    With a grunt CAESAR pulls his tooth out. Blood on his fingers. He looks at the tooth.

ASINUS (*aside*). He is a man waiting on the edge of the world. For what? In a sense, he does nothing. He only reacts. And finds himself master of continents. It is not surprising that he pays historians to find omens of great things at the time of his birth.

    CAESAR throws his tooth away.

CAESAR. Vinegar.

    The PRIMUS PILUS gives CAESAR a flat bottle. He sluices his mouth out and spits.

    Stones begin to fly over the stage, landing amongst the Romans.

FIRST SOLDIER (*this is, of the* SOLDIERS *guarding* CAESAR).
Wogs. Throwing stones.

SECOND SOLDIER. Slings.

PRIMUS. General —

CAESAR. Yes. Quickly.

SOLDIERS *running, shields over their heads. The* SOLDIERS
guarding CAESAR *hold their shields* above him.

PRIMUS PILUS. Bugler! Standard Bearer!

CAESAR. Prefect of the legion.

The STANDARD BEARER *and* BUGLER *run to the*
PRIMUS PILUS. *The* PREFECT *runs to* CAESAR.

PRIMUS PILUS. Men out of the water. First and second
centuries of the fourth cohort, up to the trees with missiles —
they are not, *not* to enter the forest. Bugler, defensive
formations.

The BUGLER *blows a call. The* STANDARD BEARER *runs
off.*

CAESAR. Yes?

PREFECT. Can only be a handful. With slings. Even children.
Dying down now.

CAESAR. We will not pitch camp. We go south, now.

PREFECT. General. Primus Pilus!

PRIMUS PILUS. Sir.

PREFECT. Strike the standards.

PRIMUS. Sir. Bugler! Marching order!

The BUGLER *makes another call.*

CAESAR. Asinus, record this order.

ASINUS. Yes General.

CAESAR (*to the* PREFECT). Take their animals. Salt the fields.
Kill the prisoners. Do what you can in the time.

PREFECT. Yes General. Primus Pilus, with me.

They hurry away.

CAESAR (*to* ASINUS). Even a little massacre must look like
policy. They'll take it as a warning. Or that we knew these

people were traitors. Probably leave a little local war behind us — no bad thing.

(*To the* SOLDIERS *shielding him*:) Join your squads.

The SOLDIERS *run off.* CAESAR *walks away upstage, followed by* ASINUS.

The SOLDIERS *of the punishment squad.*

FIRST SOLDIER. Not making camp? What about our lavatories?

GUARD. Leave 'em for the Britons. Teach 'em an healthy habit.

SECOND SOLDIER. I am always digging lavatories on this campaign which are never used.

GUARD. That's the speed of modern warfare.

Scene Six

Moonlight. The fields.

MARBAN *is sitting on the ground, legs skewed beneath him, still naked and bound, the Venus pendant round his neck.*

A silence.

The FIRST *and* SECOND VILLAGE WOMEN *and* FIRST, THIRD *and* FOURTH VILLAGE MEN *come on. They have weapons at the ready, and dart about searching, stopping, listening, looking.*

Then they are all still.

A silence.

FIRST VILLAGE MAN. They've gone. (*A silence.*) Into the ground?

SECOND VILLAGE WOMAN. There.

She points to MARBAN. *The* FIRST VILLAGE MAN *approaches him cautiously.*

FIRST VILLAGE MAN. Where are your brothers?

FOURTH VILLAGE MAN. Salt! Salt on the fields! (*He weeps.*) They'll put salt on the fields.

FIRST VILLAGE MAN. Where is our Mother?

FOURTH VILLAGE MAN. They've poisoned us.

FIRST VILLAGE MAN. Your brothers and your mother —

THIRD VILLAGE MAN (*nursing his wound*). Maybe they're defeated. Maybe —it's peace.

FOURTH VILLAGE MAN. Maybe they tortured him, put him here as a decoy, ambush, while we weep with him for our fields —

THIRD VILLAGE MAN. No. It's peace.

FOURTH VILLAGE MAN. And poison.

FIRST VILLAGE MAN. Boy —

SECOND VILLAGE WOMAN. He's tied up. Cut him free.

The FIRST VILLAGE MAN *hesitates.*

Go on!

The FIRST VILLAGE MAN *cuts* MARBAN *free and steps away quickly.*

At once MARBAN *tugs at the Venus round his neck, gets it off and throws it away.*

MARBAN. Give me a knife.

A silence.

When they let me go I stayed in the trees, near them.

I knew I was — filthy! Filthy! Defiled! With one of their Gods round my neck! Give me a knife!

FIRST VILLAGE WOMAN (*quietly, to the* FIRST VILLAGE MAN). Don't.

A silence.

MARBAN. They're marching to the coast. To cross to the mainland. Give me a knife.

A silence.

FOURTH VILLAGE MAN. Gone.

MARBAN. No.

THIRD VILLAGE MAN. Defeated?

MARBAN. No.

THIRD VILLAGE MAN. But —

They look at each other. A silence.

FIRST VILLAGE WOMAN. Make clearings in the forest, before the cold weather. New fields, hidden —

SECOND VILLAGE WOMAN. Get through the winter, to plant them —

FIRST VILLAGE WOMAN. We'll see in the morning, how much they've burnt —

MARBAN. Give me a knife! (*He laughs.*) I am a priest. A seer. I see. (*He laughs.*)

Three years, the salt will drain out of the fields. And in the fourth year? Will you dare creep out of the hidden fields in the forests, to plant another harvest? To watch the nightmare of another raid, ripening through the year?

Oh the life of the farms will go on.

But you'll never dig out the fear they've struck in you. With their strange, foreign weapons.

Generation after generation, cataracts of terror in the eyes of your children. And in the eyes of husband for wife and wife for husband, hatred of the suffering that is bound to come again.

They've struck a spring in the ground beneath your feet, it will never stop, it will flood everything. The filthy water of Roman ways.

He laughs.

They'll even take away death as you know it. No sweet fields, rich woods beyond the grave. You'll go to a Roman under-world of torture, a black river, rocks of fire.

We must have nothing to do with them. Nothing.

Abandon the life we know.

Change ourselves into animals. The cat. No, an animal not yet heard of. Deadly, watching, ready in the forest. Something not human.

FIRST VILLAGE MAN. And live off what, priest?

MARBAN. Visions. Visions. Stones. Visions. (*A silence. Then, dead voiced:*) The ghosts of our ancestors, slink away. The fabulous beasts, their claws crumble. The Gods grow small as flies.

He weeps quietly.

FIRST VILLAGE WOMAN. Give him a knife.

The THIRD VILLAGE MAN *puts a knife before* MARBAN.
*He looks up from weeping, at the knife. He holds it upwards
in his fist, on the ground, his arm extended. He raises himself
up and is falling on the knife —*

Scene Seven

Dawn. The north bank of the River Thames.

CONLAG *and the* SLAVE *are wandering downstage, she helping
him to hop along. He is feverish.*

CONLAG. The sea!

SLAVE *(aside)*. It's not.

CONLAG. The beach!

SLAVE *(aside)*. It's the River Thames.

CONLAG. The shingle's slippery.

SLAVE *(aside)*. It's mud.

CONLAG. Don't get the dogshit on my bad foot! In a day, in a
    night, how can a foot puff up, right up to your groin? It's not
    fair! It's not right! After all I've been through! There's a
    boat.

SLAVE *(aside)*. It's a log.

CONLAG. Sh. Fishermen.

SLAVE *(aside)*. Branches on the log.

CONLAG. Down down down down.

   They fall in a heap. He crawls over her, toward the 'log'.

   I'll kill them.

SLAVE *(aside)*. He did rape me in the forest.

   CONLAG *and the* SLAVE *pick up stones at the same moment.*

CONLAG. Pick up a stone. Sharp edge. Cut off their heads. Blood
    on the sea. A holy road, over the waves.

   The SLAVE *walks to the crawling* CONLAG *and hits him on
   the back of the neck with her stone. He grunts, then turns
   over on his back and looks up at her. She stands there
   relaxed, the stone in her hand.*

You can be my wife, in the forests, in that land. The animals are so tame, you just kill them for food. They'll not learn fear of men and women. For generations.

She raises the stone high above her head and brings it down hard on CONLAG's *forehead. He dies at once.*

SLAVE (*aside*). On the island where I was born. Over the sea. Where he wanted to go. Only stone. Nets for the fish. The tomb, where my mother was buried, along with all the others. The children saw the ship first, with a sail with an animal on it. We were clever with stones. All the children. Wherever I am it's not left me. When they kept me in a pit. When they fucked me in the forest. When they made me work in a field. I always knew what stones were near me. How many steps to them. Count one, two — and what stone would be in my hand. The men from the ship burnt my home. Now home is where I have a stone in my hand.

In the distance, the sound of an approaching helicopter.

From the back the Roman Army advances in British Army uniforms and with the equipment of the late 1970's.

First a patrol of five soldiers, four privates and a CORPORAL. *The* SLAVE *looks at them.*

FIRST SOLDIER. There's one of 'em.

SECOND SOLDIER. Drop that, or I will have to open fire!

The SLAVE, *still.*

SECOND SOLDIER. Drop that, or I will have to open fire!

THIRD SOLDIER (*into a two way radio*). Charlie Bravo, we have a contact.

The SLAVE *throws the stone at the* SECOND SOLDIER. *and hits him in the face. The* FOURTH SOLDIER *opens fire with his automatic weapon, the* SLAVE *is blown back by the impact, dead.*

CORPORAL. } What the fuck do you think you're doing!
FOURTH SOLDIER. ∫ Chucked it right in his throat!

FIRST SOLDIER. Jack!

THIRD SOLDIER ⟩(*into the radio*). Charlie Bravo we have a
                  ⟩casualty.
CORPORAL. ⟨ Look! Look for more of 'em!

All but the FOURTH SOLDIER *crouching, covering the area. He runs at the* SLAVE's *body and kicks it.*

FOURTH SOLDIER. Fucking bogshitting mick!

CORPORAL. All right all right!

FOURTH SOLDIER. In his throat!

CAESAR and his staff, in the dress of British Army Officers have driven on in a jeep and are getting out.

CORPORAL. All right!

The FOURTH SOLDIER *kicks the* SLAVE's *body again.*

FOURTH SOLDIER. Kick the shit out of your fucking country!

CORPORAL. Shut up lad!

CAESAR. What's that?

PREFECT. A contact, Sir.

FOURTH SOLDIER. Sending little girls out against us now.

CORPORAL. All right.

The noise of the helicopter is louder now.

FOURTH SOLDIER. Sorry.

CORPORAL. Yeah yeah. Just walk away lad and have a good spit. (*To the other* SOLDIERS:) Come on! See if that's wired. Then roll it into the water.

The SOLDIERS *inspect the* SLAVE's *body.*

PRIMUS PILUS. The 'copter will have to hover Sir, too risky to land —

CAESAR. Yes thank you. (*Aside.*) That everyday life will begin again. That violence will be reduced to an acceptable level. That Civilisation may not sink, its great battle lost.

CAESAR and the staff turn away.

CORPORAL. Anything on her?

FIRST SOLDIER. Just stones.

The helicopter roaring.

A blunder — An old man and his fields — A soliloquy — The dead Saxon — The contact — The last Roman Lady — An execution — The making of Arthur.

The action takes place in Britain in 515 AD and in Ireland in 1980 AD.

PART TWO

Arthur's Grave

The world's enigma: Arthur's grave.
The stanzas of the graves

Characters

The cast is as for the National Theatre premiere (see page 2).

MODERN TIMES

THOMAS CHICHESTER	Stephen Moore
CORPORAL	Michael Beint
BRITISH SOLDIERS	Robert Ralph
	Robert Oates
	Peter Sproule
	Peter Harding
	Peter Dawson
	Melvyn Bedford
BOB MAITLAND	William Sleigh
IRISH WOMAN	Yvonne Bryceland
O'ROURKE	James Hayes
IRISH MEN	Greg Hicks
	Michael Fenner
	Roger Gartland

515AD

PRIEST		Brian Kent
CAI		Gordon Whiting
VILLAGERS		Elliott Cooper
		Glen Williams
		Nigel Bellairs
SAXON SOLDIER		Melvyn Bedford
MORGANA	CAI's	Terry Diab
CORDA	daughters	Anna Carteret
ADONA	A Roman Matron	Susan Williamson
FIRST COOK		John Normington
SECOND COOK	ADONA's	James Carter
STEWARD	servants	Peter Needham

Scene One

A field, harvested, the corn in sheaves. Dawn light. THOMAS CHICHESTER, *in farm worker's clothes, walks about the field. He smokes.*

CHICHESTER. Dawn. Waiting. Near the Irish border.

Who are you talking to? You Tom. Right Tom? Dawn near the Irish border.

He turns a full circle on his heel, scanning the countryside.

Who are you waiting for, Tom?

A man called O'Rourke.

Come on, Sheamus Naill O'Rourke.

He is startled. He crouches down. He looks about him nervously. He takes out a drinking flask.

Got the hoojahs, Tom. Because of the field. Four pine trees. The dead likeness of the Old Acre. A field back home, on the family farm.

Could see my mother — coming out of the trees now. Telling me to get my hair cut — that I'm drinking too much.

And where is home, Tom?

England, Tom.

Four pine trees. Traces of banks.

Hard men can weep for home, Tom.

Shut up.

Yes shut up you bloody idiot.

He is about to take another swig of the flask when a whistle blows. British Army SOLDIERS *come into the field at the back through the trees.*

No! No!

CHICHESTER *scrambles into a hollow, trying to hide.*

You bastards.

CORPORAL. We go from this field. Right down through the woods, to the track.

CHICHESTER (*to himself*). No. No, no, no, no.

CORPORAL. And anything. Anything. A fucking blade of grass pointing the wrong way — you call an NCO.

FIRST SOLDIER. Our Corporal is jumpy this morning.

The two SOLDIERS *near him laugh.*

SECOND SOLDIER. Your first time on the border, in't it lad?

THIRD SOLDIER. You don't know yet.

FIRST SOLDIER. Know what?

THIRD SOLDIER. Look at it. Little fields, little hedges. Hills in the pale blue yonder. Pretty, in't it?

FIRST SOLDIER (*shrugs*). Yeah.

THIRD SOLDIER. Could be anywhere. Well it's not. 'Cos you are a Brit and a Squadie and to you what you are walking on is the surface of the moon — and very, very dangerous.

FIRST SOLDIER. Still. Nice day for it.

SECOND SOLDIER. Oh dear oh dear, a little hero.

THIRD SOLDIER. We're moon men. We should have space suits, oxygen, the lot.

FIRST SOLDIER. I joined the Army 'cos I liked canoeing.

SECOND SOLDIER. Oh we all joined the Army 'cos we liked something.

CORPORAL (*walking past them into the trees*). Stop talking over there!

Two SOLDIERS, *downstage, see* CHICHESTER.

FOURTH SOLDIER. Corporal!

All the SOLDIERS *in the field stop. The* FOURTH *and* FIFTH SOLDIERS *cover* CHICHESTER *with their guns. The other* SOLDIERS *are dead still.*

FIFTH SOLDIER. Do not move or I will have to open fire!

CHICHESTER. Piss off.

The FIRST SOLDIER *raises a whistle and blows it. The* CORPORAL *comes running out of the trees.*

CORPORAL. Oh my God.

As he runs he takes out a pistol. He reaches the FOURTH *and* FIFTH SOLDIERS.

(*To* CHICHESTER:) Get up on your feet, slowly.

CHICHESTER. Why does the British Army have to be so bloody British? Brains like boots. Balls like King Edward potatoes. Thick as pigshit.

FIFTH SOLDIER. Shut up!

CORPORAL. Stand up slowly. Put your hands behind your head. If you do not we will have to open fire.

CHICHESTER (*does so, speaking in Bertie Wooster*). Don't twist your knickers, Corporal. I'm touring Ireland for my hols. To have a look at the Celtic crosses and the Guinness.

FOURTH SOLDIER. He does — ah — sound British, Corporal.

CORPORAL. Are you? British?

CHICHESTER (*in immaculate Belfast*). I take that badly, coming from a British Soldier. Who's walking all over my country, like he did God Almighty's job and made it.

FIFTH SOLDIER. Sounds fucking West Belfast to me —

CORPORAL. Shut up. (*To* CHICHESTER:) Right. Who are you, where do you live and what is your business here?

CHICHESTER (*in immaculate Dublin*). I am the Bishop of Dublin. Smuggling the sacred relic of St Patrick's foreskin, over the border for Ian Paisley to suck on.

FOURTH SOLDIER. He's a joker. (*He laughs.*)

CORPORAL. I'm sick of fucking jokers in this country. Search him —

CHICHESTER. Stay where you are!

They hesitate at CHICHESTER's *tone.*

Get me an officer. Now.

CORPORAL. Search the bugger!

FIFTH SOLDIER. Down! On your face! Hands behind your back!

CHICHESTER *makes a kiss to the* FIRST SOLDIER, *who hits him in his stomach.* CHICHESTER *doubles up and goes down.*

CHICHESTER. Not — clever — get an officer —

FOURTH SOLDIER. Shut up!

The SECOND SOLDIER *kicks* CHICHESTER *who rolls to protect himself.*

CHICHESTER. You silly buggers — (*He laughs.*)

FIFTH SOLDIER. Want more do you, Bishop —

CORPORAL. Just search him. (*To the other* SOLDIERS:) And you lot. I want every little Irish worm in this field shitting up his little worm hole.

CHICHESTER (*weeping*). Mummy! Mummy! Mummy! Can I have a British Army Soldier to play with at Christmas?

He laughs. Beyond himself, the FIFTH SOLDIER *pulls* CHICHESTER's *head up by the hair.*

FIFTH SOLDIER. Shut up! Shut up!

CORPORAL. Stop that!

FIFTH SOLDIER. He is annoying me!

CHICHESTER (*calmly*). Just tell an officer to pop along old chap.

CORPORAL. I said let go his hair!

The FIFTH SOLDIER *does so.*

Go over him, carefully. (*To the other* SOLDIERS:) All of you! Be careful! Keep your eyes open! (*Into a two-way radio:*) Red Bravo. Red Bravo. We have a suspect.

The FOURTH SOLDIER *finds a pistol in* CHICHESTER's *clothes.*

FOURTH SOLDIER. A pistol, Corporal.

CORPORAL. Oh yes? (*The* CORPORAL *takes it.*) Czechoslovakiaı

CHICHESTER. Funny little souvenirs a tourist picks up in Ireland.

FIFTH SOLDIER. Be quiet!

FOURTH SOLDIER. Drink on his breath. And not breakfast time yet —

The FOURTH SOLDIER *hands the* CORPORAL *the hip flask.*

CORPORAL. This kind of thing makes me nervous. Why isn't anything straight in this fucking country?

LIEUTENANT BOB MAITLAND, *walks down from the back of the field quickly.*

MAITLAND. What is it, Corporal?

CORPORAL. A suspect, Sir. Armed.

He gives MAITLAND *the pistol.*

MAITLAND. Czechoslovakian.

CHICHESTER. Is that an officer?

FIFTH SOLDIER. Keep your face on the ground.

The CORPORAL *hands* MAITLAND *the flask.*

CORPORAL. And this Sir. He's half-cut Sir.

CHICHESTER. Nothing but the real thing. Irish booze and iron curtain gun.

MAITLAND. Stand him up.

CHICHESTER *is hauled to his feet. He and* MAITLAND *stare at each other.*

Oh no.

CHICHESTER. Keep your mouth shut.

MAITLAND. What the hell are you doing here —

CHICHESTER. Shut up!

A silence.

MAITLAND. All right, Corporal. I'll talk to this johnny.

CORPORAL. Yes Sir. You two!

The CORPORAL *leads the* FOURTH *and* FIFTH SOLDIERS *away.*

CHICHESTER. Don't let them chuck the sheaves about. I harvested this field with my own bare hands.

MAITLAND *stares at* CHICHESTER, *then turns to the* CORPORAL.

MAITLAND. Corporal. Do it neatly.

CORPORAL. Neatly. Yes Sir.

FOURTH SOLDIER. What's all that about?

CORPORAL. We don't see, we don't hear.

FIFTH SOLDIER. Sometimes I think we're just in Ireland to dig toilets.

CORPORAL. Enough. (*To all the* SOLDIERS:) Come on lads! The Pope is hiding somewhere in this field. Give his holiness a big surprise.

MAITLAND. Sorry if they pushed you about.

CHICHESTER. Don't worry old man. I have had special training to deal with pain. Pain is not the problem.

MAITLAND. You do owe me an explanation. Am I going to get it?

CHICHESTER. Bobby, Bobby Maitland. What a prick you are, Bobby.

How are all the other chums in my old Regiment?

MAITLAND. Oh the Regiment's in good fettle.

CHICHESTER. 'Good fettle.' Ha! With their tanks on the Rhine. Short of brains and spare parts —

MAITLAND. I am trying to keep my temper!

CHICHESTER. I am trying to keep my life!

Three months I've been setting up an operation here. Building respect. There's an old woman up in the farmhouse — don't bother her.

MAITLAND. All right all right —

CHICHESTER. I work the farm for her. Her sons are in the Kilburn High Road — or the Costa del Sol.

MAITLAND. How do you, of all people, pass yourself off as Irish?

CHICHESTER. Oh I sing a few rebel songs in the local pub.

MAITLAND. Tom, are you following orders? Or are you off on some madcap scheme of your own?

A silence.

Tom —

CHICHESTER. I am doing my bit to win the war in Ireland. Now you and the Queen's baboons in Army boots are putting my operation here in jeopardy, so piss off.

MAITLAND. I have to ask you again. Are you following orders?

CHICHESTER. A kind of order.

MAITLAND. What does that mean?

CHICHESTER. A sense — of the order — of things.

MAITLAND. What are you talking about?

CHICHESTER. It's a Celtic idea. Pagan.

MAITLAND. Not gone native, have you?

CHICHESTER. Ha!

It's Celts we're fighting in Ireland. We won't get anywhere 'til we know what that means.

Look at this field. It's like one on my mother's farm, not far from Colchester. The Roman city of Camulodunum.

One Spring, ploughing, we found a God. That big. Celtic, pagan. And Camulodunum could be the site for Arthur's last battle. AD515.

King Arthur! Celtic warlord. Who fought twelve great battles against the Saxons. That is, us.

MAITLAND. What are you talking about?

CHICHESTER. The Celts! Ha! Very fashionable, the Celts, with the arty-crafty. Ley-lines. Druids. But show them the real thing — an Irishman with a gun, or under a blanket in an H-block and they run a mile.

If King Arthur walked out of those trees, now — know what he'd look like to us? One more fucking mick.

MAITLAND. You're a maverick, Tom Chichester. And a romantic and a bloody menace. God! I joined the Army for tanks. Where are my tanks? On the banks of the River Rhine. Where am I? Poking about on foot, in an Irish field.

This may be some kind of crusade for you. But for me — Irish, Celt, they're all murdering bastards.

CHICHESTER. Look, old regimental chum. I out-rank you.

MAITLAND. I thought that was coming. Sir. (*Offering the pistol and the whisky flask.*) You want these back?

CHICHESTER. Not in full view!

MAITLAND. There's no sign —

CHICHESTER. They're here. They're always here. This is
   their bloody country. If they saw you take them off me —
   you've done for me, old chum. Give me the whisky and drop
   the gun in the straw.

MAITLAND *does so.*

Now get me that Corporal.

MAITLAND. Corporal!

CORPORAL. Sir! (*He approaches.*)

CHICHESTER. Corporal. Why are Catholic tarts the best?

CORPORAL. Er —

MAITLAND. Answer Corporal. This is an officer.

CHICHESTER. Because they've got rhythm. Sir.

   Corporal!

CORPORAL. Sir?

CHICHESTER. Who was the hardest man who worked on the
   M1 Motorway?

CORPORAL. An Irishman who got his cock stuck in the cement,
   Sir!

CHICHESTER. And Corporal —

CORPORAL. Sir?

   A short silence.

CHICHESTER. What does careless talk cost?

CORPORAL. Lives, Sir!

CHICHESTER. Your balls for sure. Tell every man in this
   field that.

CORPORAL. Sir.

CHICHESTER. Now hit me again.

CORPORAL. Sir?

CHICHESTER. I am an Irish labourer in a field, who gave
   you some lip.

   So hit me hard.

MAITLAND. Do it.

The CORPORAL *hits* CHICHESTER *in the stomach.*
CHICHESTER *doubles up.*

CHICHESTER. (*shouts in Northern Irish*): Hey, Soldier. You
know what your Queen is? A cunt wrapped up in a Union
Jack.

The CORPORAL *kicks* CHICHESTER, *angrily.*

MAITLAND. All right thank you Corporal!

CORPORAL. Sir!

MAITLAND. Pack up here.

CORPORAL. Sir. (*To the* SOLDIERS:) All right. That's it.
Back to the transport. (*He moves away.*)

MAITLAND. You're probably a brave man. But I think you're
off your head.

CHICHESTER. That may get me the first Victoria Cross in
Ireland.

MAITLAND. Only if we declare war.

CHICHESTER. Quite. Now stop endangering my life and limb
and get out of here. Right away.

MAITLAND. Right —

CHICHESTER. Bob, if I get bumped off ask my mother to
throw my ashes on the Old Acre field.

MAITLAND. I —

CHICHESTER. My mother is a stern old cow. Insist.

MAITLAND. Are you serious?

CHICHESTER. Fuck off.

MAITLAND. Yes. Goodbye.

CHICHESTER. Toodle-oo.

MAITLAND *walks away quickly. The* SOLDIERS *go off at
the back.*

CHICHESTER, *alone. He sits. He covers his face with his
hands. Then he drinks from the flask and lies down, curled
up.*

He stays on the stage as —

Scene Two

515AD. A long silence. CAI, *an old man, walks into the field. He is followed at a good distance by a* PRIEST *and three* VILLAGE MEN: *The* VILLAGE MEN *carry the bundles of refugees. The* PRIEST *carrys a staff with a cross at its top.* CAI *squats.*

PRIEST. Saxon soldiers, Cai. Coming North, over the Thames.

FIRST VILLAGER. They've been seen!

SECOND VILLAGER. A mile from the village!

PRIEST. At least think of your daughters.

CAI. Bah. (CAI *spits.*)

THIRD VILLAGER. They may be here, in your field — in the heart of Britain. Today!

PRIEST. We leave under Christ's cross. Carrying what we can of the harvest. And belongings and weapons.

Come with us Cai. There is nothing to fear.

CAI. Fear is it! (CAI *spits again.*)

PRIEST. We will go to Camulodunum, for the protection of the Government.

FIRST VILLAGER. Can't stand here arguing with you, Cai!

SECOND VILLAGER. Let the old fool stew.

THIRD VILLAGER. You want to see your daughters raped? And have the Saxons eat your brains, over a fire?

SECOND VILLAGER. Leave him behind. Gaga old bugger.

PRIEST. No no.

A silence.

Saxon raiders, Cai. After all these years of peace.

But you're an old fighter.

You know what an English raid means.

CAI. I am!
I am an old fighter of the Saxons. I don't need you — come and stand on my field to tell me that. Priest.

FIRST VILLAGER. We're wasting time. Let the old heathen be cut to bits. (*He turns to go.*)

SECOND VILLAGER (*going*). Can't wait any longer, old man! All the village, the women and children, out on the tracks in the woods already.

We don't go now we'll lose 'em —

PRIEST. In the name of pity, Cai!

CAI. Get off! Get off my field!

And you, Priest. With your cross of Jesus.

SECOND VILLAGER. That's it then.

He turns away. The other VILLAGERS *follow. They shout back as they go. The* PRIEST *stands still.*

FIRST VILLAGER. Ought to stone the bugger.

THIRD VILLAGER. We did right by you and yours, Cai. As neighbours.

PRIEST. Christ go with you.

CAI. Good riddance.

The PRIEST *hesitates, then goes off quickly after the* VILLAGERS. *Then* CAI *laughs.*

You're running the wrong way!

The Saxons will burn Camulodunum!

First thing to burn!

He laughs. Then is silent.

(*Aside:*) An old fighter of the Saxons. Here I sit, by the ruin of my field.

Me, veteran of Badon Hill.

When we cut the Saxons to bits. Once and for all. Smashed them back into their Kent marshes. Once and for all.

Huh.

As a soldier, how many commanders have I heard say, as a villager, how many times have I heard priests say — 'Once and for all.' Fight! Repent! Go on, on and on, once and for all!

After a life-time of it, I forgive myself.

I'll stay where I was born. And watch.

It all —

come —

again —

He lifts a wooden idol from the ground. He wipes the earth from it. He kisses it.

N.B. *During* CHICHESTER's *speech he stays on stage and carefully reburies the idol in the ground. At the end of* CHICHESTER's *speech he goes off.*

Scene Three

CHICHESTER *sits up suddenly.*

CHICHESTER. I'm soaking!

He stands up, brushing his clothes.

How is the intellectual at war?

Soaked with dew and pissed by eight in the morning.

He looks up.

Hot day. The banners will be bright. The horses, the shields and the swords.

He starts, looking at the trees.

God. Losing your marbles, old son.

With a parade ground manner.

Captain Thomas Chichester!

Yes Sir?

What are you doing?

Waiting to kill a man called O'Rourke, Sir!

Get on with it then!

Yes Sir!

Men have died with the training you've had, lad! So what is your problem?

No problem Sir!

He is out of breath. He waits.

Just one question Sir!

(He breathes, then shouts again:) When will peace come?

(Then, low:) When will peace come, Sir?

England out of Ireland? Swords into plough-shares, machine-guns to rakes, ammunition to fertilizer?

The dead in any war would vote for peace, Sir.

He breathes. Parade ground again.

You're a British Army Officer! Stop wanking! Put myself on a charge, Sir! Do that Captain! Thank you Sir!

He covers his face with his hands, he takes them away quickly.

He turns on his heel, eyeing the countryside.

He takes off his coat, puts it on the ground and lies on it. He lights a cigarette. He blows a cloud of smoke up.

(He shouts:) O'Rourke! Come on brother, le me blow your head off!

He sends another cloud of smoke up, as —

Scene Four

CORDA *and* MORGANA *run on on opposite sides of the stage. A* SAXON SOLDIER *crashes through the trees into the field. He is mortally wounded.*

SAXON. Feta gehwone. Ic eom gewundod: welc hearm maeg ic to the gedon?

He falls. The sisters watch him. He crawls a little way then stops.

MORGANA. What was he shouting?

CORDA. What do you think? At women.

MORGANA. His arm was jerking in a funny way.

Oh Corda, is he dead?

CORDA. Where's father?

MORGANA. Messing about.

CORDA. Get him.

MORGANA. But —

CORDA. Go and get our father! Go on!

MORGANA (*as she runs off along the edge of the field*). Oh he's got to be dead, oh Mary Mother of Jesus let him be dead.

MORGANA is off. A silence. Then the SAXON stands.

He and CORDA stare.

CORDA picks up a stone.

SAXON. Waelhreowan men! Is eower hete swa to anum eltheoditan geriht?

CORDA throws the stone. It misses him widely.

Wielisce wyrgen! Ic the on twa gescieran wille.

He stumbles a few paces towards her then falls. He drags himself a short distance.

Ic eom anhaga, iserne wund.

He grabs a sheaf, it falls about him.

A silence.

Then MORGANA comes on, pulling CAI by the hand.

CAI. Saxon in my field —

MORGANA. Come on, father — please —

CAI. The old stories, the old lies.

Plagues. Dragons. One-eyed giants eating girls.

CORDA. Look!

Just look at what's wandered into your field!

Turning away.

My poor old, stumbling, brutal father.

CAI. Damage to crops? Wild boar, chasing field mice.

Bah! When wild animals come out and fool in your fields, what is that? When there's nothing to keep 'em down, what is that?

The ruin of Britain.

The SAXON groans and shifts in the sheaf. They all see the movement. They are still.

Then CAI strides to the SAXON, takes his sword and kills him.

MORGANA *prays, weeping.*

MORGANA. Oh love of Christ our Lord. Oh love of the Mother of Christ our Lord, gentle Mary.

CORDA. Now we know there is a war.

Now we know there is a war.

Now we've got to run away.

CAI. Shut your mouth, girl.

CORDA. Don't you even see what you've just killed? Are you that far gone? Gaga old fool.

CAI. Give you a beating girl!

MORGANA (*to* CORDA). Please, don't —

CORDA. A Saxon Soldier.

Look.

That dead thing. Pagan thing.

MORGANA. The Priest said the Saxons believe God is a giant. Who smashes children's heads with a hammer.

CORDA. Don't be stupid, Morgana.

MORGANA. Oh and you're so clever, just 'cos you want to go to a townhouse. And a steward gave you a town dress which father made you burn —

CORDA. Shut up!

CAI. Peace!

CAI *clenches the sword.*

CORDA. We must go!

CAI. Peace!

CORDA. There'll be more of them!

A silence.

Father!

CAI. Twenty-one years of peace. And the killing when I was a boy, forgotten. The Saxons from the South, the Irish from the West, only stories and lies, told by monks on the road out for alms. Poets in winter, out for a good meal. And powerful men, only rumours. Bandits calling themselves 'Emperors', 'New Romans'.

Twenty-one years. A kind of peace, on the same fields, under the same skies.

He gestures at the SAXON.

We'll bury that. Harvest our fields.

CORDA. We'll die.

CAI. That one was alone. Legs torn to bits. Been stumbling about in the forest. Lost his troop.

Dunno. What's it to me?

He begins to dig with the sword at the edge of the field.

CORDA. I'll go with Morgana.

CAI. Do that and my curse goes with you.

CORDA. Better cursed than dead.

CAI. You'll be a leper, girl.

He digs again.

Like all the others. On the roads, in the ditches.

He stops digging.

I remember it. Families on the roads. Following my mother's skirt. Her feet clay and blood.

He digs again, angrily.

Running from the Saxons. Huh!

MORGANA. We'll be all right, Corda! I'll put up a little shrine by the field. To the cross of our Mother of Christ —

CORDA *kneels.*

CORDA. I kneel in front of you like a daughter asking for your blessing, to be married.

CAI. Out of my way.

MORGANA. What are you digging?

CAI. She sleeps here.

CORDA. But I don't want to be married. Just to stay alive.

CAI. Get back!

He lifts a blackened wooden idol from the earth.

MORGANA. What —

CAI. Goddess of this place, girl.

MORGANA. A saint? It's not a saint.

CAI. Huh! Why didn't you die when you were born?

Both of you, eh?
Why didn't all of us die of your mother's sickness?

Touching the idol, gently.

Because of the blood put on the ground where I buried her.
Twenty-one years ago.

MORGANA. Filthy! A filthy pagan thing —

CAI. Right girl. She's not like your skinny rabbit Jesus, nailed
up, soaking up prayers. This one don't soak up prayers.

He laughs, then stops.

(*Low:*) Get a little bowl. For blood from the Saxon's
throat.

MORGANA. No —

CAI. She'll see none of his kind come to this place again.

CORDA *and* MORGANA *hear something.* CAI *does not,
absorbed by the idol.*

CORDA. What did you hear?

MORGANA. Don't know. A woman cried.

CAI (*to* CORDA). You girl! Get a rope and a knife.

CORDA *picks up a stone. She and* CAI *stare at each other.*

CAI. Ah. Ah.

Kind against kind.
The cow gives birth to wolves who tear her belly to bits.
Ah.

CORDA *brings the stone down on* CAI's *head. He goes on
all fours, staring at her.*

Then he stands and staggers away.

MORGANA. Corda.

Don't.

She tries to hold CORDA *back.* CORDA *pushes her away.
She holds* CORDA *about her knees.*

CORDA *kicks her away. She turns and runs after* CAI.
They disappear into the trees.

Saint Pelagius said we're not born into the world evil. We
make our own sin.

Corda! Please! We've not murdered our own father, on our own field!

(*To herself:*) Yes, we make our own sin. The Priest said they call that a heresy and they sent a Bishop from Rome, with soldiers to make us learn —

CORDA *comes out of the trees, the stone still in her hand and bloody.*

She stops a distance from MORGANA.

Learn — that we're born in sin. Even in the cradle, bad. Filthy.

Please, we're not murderers —

CORDA, *moving quickly to where the idol lies on the ground.*

CORDA. He's got some old coins, buried. Maybe by this thing —

MORGANA. He must have a mass, with a priest. Or he'll not go to Heaven —

CORDA *throws the idol to one side. She starts to dig with the sword.*

CORDA. Come on. Help me!

MORGANA. If we drag him into the field, they'll think he was killed by the Saxon —

CORDA. What an evil thought, sister.

MORGANA. I loved him.

CORDA. I hated him. Ever since he lifted my skirt when I was only just a woman.

He did the same to you.

MORGANA. No.

CORDA. Don't lie.

MORGANA. I've only seen the village. All my life, never out of sight.

What's out there? Dragons? Giants?

Is there a war out there?

CORDA *lifts a handful of coins.*

CORDA. I've found them. They're shiny. They're gold. Hurry up, take yours.

MORGANA. No.

A silence.

CORDA. You're right. We don't know anything.

Has there been a battle with the Saxons? We don't know. Are the towns burning? We don't know.

Sickness travels in the air. Whatever it is out there, the war — travels in the air. We're breathing it. It makes a daughter kill her father and rob him. Just like that.

If you won't come I'll kill you too.

In the far distance a woman's voice screams.

MORGANA. I heard it again.

CORDA. Get up to the little wood. Along the ditches.

CORDA, *holding the money in her skirt, scampers away.* MORGANA *hesitates and crosses herself, looking at the idol.*

Come on little sister.

They run off.

Scene Five

CHICHESTER *asleep. The light changes to a sunlit, late afternoon.*
An IRISH WOMAN *comes on.*

WOMAN. You.

CHICHESTER *wakes with a start. A silence. Then he stands, hurriedly. He speaks in upper-class English.*

CHICHESTER. Where's O'Rourke?

WOMAN. The British Army was here.

CHICHESTER. I didn't see them. What did the bastards want?

A silence.

WOMAN. What's your name?

CHICHESTER. O'Rourke knows my name.

A silence.

My name is Henwick. Lliam Henwick.

WOMAN. You've been putting it about you're an Irishman,
Mr Henwick.

CHICHESTER. Of Anglo-Irish parentage. My family's house was
burnt down in 1918 because my grandfather, something of
a romantic drunk, went over to the Republican cause.

But you will have telephoned the backwater in County-
Limerick that gave my father breath.

Don't piss me about love.

WOMAN. You have a token of your good faith.

CHICHESTER. For O'Rourke.

The WOMAN, *impassive.*

All right!

He takes out the pistol. He hands it to her. She examines it.

I'm a friend of the Republican cause.

And a businessman.

The WOMAN *turns and walks away, taking the pistol.*

Tell O'Rourke to come today!

The Republican cause is just!

Trust me! It's in my blood! The great wrong of England in
Ireland!

The WOMAN *has gone.*

(*To himself:*) Believe it, don't you Tom. In a way, Tom.

I am the great wrong in Ireland.

He retches.

The fear worse than you thought, Tom?

He wipes his mouth.

But then a trained assassin is bound to be a dangerous man
with dangerous thoughts.

He laughs.

In the distance, a woman's voice screams.

*He goes to the edge of the field. He takes out another pistol
from a hiding place. He puts it in his clothing.*

A woman's voice screams again.

CHICHESTER *lies down and closes his eyes. He flicks at a
fly.*

Bugger off. Bugger off, Celtic fly.

He falls asleep.

Scene Six

CHICHESTER *turns over on his side, fast asleep, stretching an
arm up.*

CHICHESTER. Ah!

His arm falls. He settles in his sleep.

The WOMAN's *voice screaming, nearer.*

Again, the voice even nearer.

Then two COOKS, *both young, the* FIRST *fat and the*
SECOND *thin, carry* ADONA *on an improvised stretcher. Her
face is hidden by veils of silk, her body covered by richly
embroidered and coloured cloths. A* STEWARD, *a fit, capable
man, walks by the side of the stretcher.*

When ADONA *speaks, the silks of her veils flutter.*

ADONA. Don't bump me!

FIRST COOK. My back's gone!

STEWARD. Watch the crops! I won't have crops kicked about!
Even in this godforsaken —

FIRST COOK. But it's my back, it's gone.

SECOND COOK. His back's gone.

FIRST COOK. Oh!

The FIRST COOK *falls to his knees. The stretcher lurches.*

ADONA. What are you doing!

STEWARD. Put her down.

ADONA. Don't you care? Don't you have any respect?

FIRST COOK. Sorry.

STEWARD. Gently!

The STEWARD *helps them put the stretcher down.*

Shit.

The three men squat, exhausted. They look at the sheaves then at each other. They each stand and rush to a sheaf. They rub ears of wheat between their hands blowing the chaff away. They eat desperately, throughout the scene.

SECOND COOK. First field for miles, not harvested or burnt. We could bake bread! Stone bread — last us for days —

ADONA. Steward! Up again!

STEWARD. My Lady —

ADONA. Where I am — the household is! The house may be burnt! But the household is here!

The man who fell down! Whip him!

FIRST COOK. I'm just a cook Madam, who worked in your kitchens!

ADONA. Whip him. Where I can see.

STEWARD (*to himself*). Shit.

SECOND COOK. That's right Ma'am. We know about feeding you, not carrying you about.

STEWARD. We have to rest my lady, if we're going to stay alive.

ADONA. You're going to abandon me.

The STEWARD *shouts.*

STEWARD. No!

ADONA. You'll all be punished. Do you hear? When things are put to rights. When the Legions come from Rome.

SECOND COOK. She goes on and on about Romans coming to save her.

I don't believe there ever were Romans.

Or the children's story is right. The Romans were giant, stone snails. The roads are the slime they left behind.

FIRST COOK. I've seen the recipes of Ancient Rome. They were real enough. Bastards with bellies lined with iron.

The FIRST COOK *winces and holds his back.*

SECOND COOK. Your back bad?

FIRST COOK. Nothing wrong with it. I'm going to talk to this bastard.

The FIRST COOK *winks. The* SECOND COOK *touches his nose. The* SECOND COOK *begins to wander away, eating ears of wheat. The* STEWARD *is hunched.*

(*To the* STEWARD:) A powerful lady, our Mistress.

STEWARD. Indeed.

FIRST COOK. Three days lugging her about. What she got under there?

SECOND COOK. Must be wine. She's pissed.

STEWARD. Huh.

SECOND COOK. Smells like she's shat herself.

STEWARD. That's enough.

A silence.

The SECOND COOK *moves further away.*

FIRST COOK. I say run. Leave the old bag.

STEWARD. I didn't hear that.

The STEWARD *grabs the* FIRST COOK *by the throat.*

FIRST COOK. I just want to get on with my trade.

STEWARD. Cooking?

The STEWARD *scoffs and pushes him away.*

FIRST COOK. My family goes back a long way. To the kitchens of the Emperors of Rome.
There's a story in my family. One of us, a long time ago, served up an ox to an Emperor. Whole. 'What?' cried the Emperor. 'Cook an ox with the entrails and all the shit entire?' And my ancestor is dragged in on his knees. He begs a sword. But not for his throat. He slashes the ox's basted belly — and out tumble, why chicken hearts, stewed larks, the tasty livers of little lambs. The kidneys of the ox drained of the blood and folded in the delicate flesh of marinated,

white fish. All of it bound with butter, garlic, parsley and dry white wine.

The Imperial Ox! I've always wanted to cook it.

The trick is that with all that offal you don't need salt in the stuffing.

STEWARD. Huh. Things being what they are you're going to be out of a job.

FIRST COOK. Yeah, I wonder what they're all eating out there, these days.

S'pose I can go and cook for the Saxons. Human brains. Tricky, brain dishes.

STEWARD. Where did you hear the Saxons are cannibals?

FIRST COOK. Aren't they?

STEWARD. They're dirt farmers. Just like us.

FIRST COOK. Be better to kill her. Kinder.

You know we're going to have to.

STEWARD. I am her lover.

FIRST COOK. Oh?

A silence.

Nice work?

STEWARD. Lords, ladies, masters, workers in the fields — cooks — what do you all want of me?

I breathe my first breath. Look up. I am the son of a tin miner. A godforsaken trade on this good, sweet earth.

But as the priests say — 'The world, cold thing, is a sermon.'

I get education from the priests. I get out of the Cornish mines by selling myself as a bondsman.

I please a master by doing a murder. I am released from my bondsmanship.

I learn. Gain dignity. I become, in early middle-life, a steward to a great estate.

I carry the estate in my head, in my dreams. Seed-times. Debts. Tallies. Who's sick, who's stupid, who can be relied on.

Like a huge riddle that only I can answer.

And when the mistress of the estate, of the riddle, wants me in her bed, do I go?

Do I. Like a rat down a hole.

Cook, you run off, I will find you. When the raids have stopped. And I am back in my lady's bed. I will manacle you to a wall and, with great pleasure, drive a nail through your tongue.

FIRST COOK. Yeah. Well. We'll see.

STEWARD. You will.

The SECOND COOK *finds the dead* SAXON.

SECOND COOK. Oh no. I'm standing here looking at a corpse. And I think it's Saxon.

The STEWARD *and the* FIRST COOK *look at each other.*

And I'm going to be sick.

FIRST COOK. He's going to be sick.

STEWARD. You two are the lowest of the low.

FIRST COOK. Dunno. When you come down to it, I'm meat and he's vegetables.

The SECOND COOK *is sick.*

STEWARD. Oh dear oh dear.

The STEWARD *walks over to the* SAXON.

ADONA. Steward, what are you doing? Steward!

John!

SECOND COOK. Bad habit for a cook, throwing up all the time. And I think I'm going to see one or two corpses in the days ahead.

ADONA. John. I'm hurting.

STEWARD. They've gone further North than we thought.

He kicks the SAXON *and turns away.*

We'll leave, now.

SECOND COOK. How about threshing this lot —

STEWARD. Too dangerous.

ADONA. You're going to kill me and leave me in a ditch. I'm getting up!

STEWARD. No, My Lady —

He runs to her.

ADONA. You won't whip them? I will!

FIRST COOK. Run for it.

SECOND COOK. He'll kill us —

FIRST COOK. Come on!

SECOND COOK. We won't work in better kitchens than hers —

FIRST COOK. By now our lovely kitchens are gone up in flames — her great house with it —

ADONA. Where is the whip?

STEWARD. I beg you my love —

ADONA *stands. She throws her veils back. She is disfigured by plague.*

A silence.

SECOND COOK. Help me. What's she got?

Someone, what's she got? Oh help me, please.

The SECOND COOK *vomits.*

ADONA. Yellow plague.

What do you expect when civilisation dies? Good health?

STEWARD. Stay in her service.

That's your best chance.
Carry around someone with that, no one will dare come near you.

And come the winter — the fields empty — no crops for the English to scavenge for their troops — it'll all stop.

Powerful men will drink themselves back into some kind of Government, through the winter.

The great houses will be rebuilt. Kitchens with big ovens.

I beg you, don't leave us! It's only a disease! It can only kill you!

FIRST COOK (*low*). On the whole, is the world falling apart?

SECOND COOK (*low*). On the whole, yes.

FIRST COOK (*low*). Run up to that little wood.

SECOND COOK (*low*). Right.

STEWARD. If you won't help us out of fear, how about pity?

ADONA. Whip them! Chain them!

(*To the* COOKS:) You're staring at a Roman matron.

Restore the Empire! Rebuild the towns. Appoint magistrates. Drive the raiders back. Set up gibbets in the fields to punish deserters.

FIRST COOK. Lady, the Romans left Britain a hundred years ago.

ADONA. Whip him! I am a Roman.

SECOND COOK. There weren't any Romans. And if there were, they're all dead.

A silence.

ADONA. The slave's right.

We are ghosts. Roman standards lie rotting on the ground. We stoop to pick them up. Our hands pass through them, like smoke.

FIRST COOK (*to the* SECOND COOK). Run.

The COOKS *run off.*

ADONA. Now you have no one to carry me.

STEWARD. No.

They stare at each other.

ADONA. Rob me then.

STEWARD. I have to, my Lady.

He goes to the stretcher. He takes three small sacks from beneath the covers.

ADONA. Like a dog.

No, not a dog. A dog would sniff around my grave. Whine for me.

The STEWARD *takes out a knife.*

ADONA. I was a great lady. I took you into my bed. You were my pleasure, my fields were my pleasure, my gardens, my harvests, the roofs of my house in the sun, my place in a civilised world.

STEWARD. Now you're a refugee too. With runny bowels and a dangerous disease.

She tries to run, falls and crawls. He takes her by the shoulder and puts the knife into the back of her neck.

She screams, then is silent.

What kind of animal am I?

A survivor.

I was a bondsman. I was a servant. I was a prostitute.

Goodbye my dead Lady, goodbye my dead masters. Now I'm free of you.

Thank God war has come.

He walks away quickly into the trees, the three bags on his shoulders.

Scene Seven

The light changes. A sunset. Golden yellow light, O'ROURKE *walks out of the trees.* CHICHESTER *opens his eyes, sees him and sits up.*

O'ROURKE. Good evening to you.

Two MEN *with automatic weapons come out of the trees. The* WOMAN *walks quickly across.*

So you're a friend of the Republican cause, Mr Henwick.

CHICHESTER *stands. A silence.*

You're a strange and puzzling man to us, Mr Henwick. Here you are on an Irish farm, out of the goodness of your heart helping a bedridden old woman, her sons being scattered by British economic imperialism. You are heard singing in the pubs. Spreading it about that you are no friend of the British Government. Then sending us messages that you are a gun-runner, with communist weapons for sale.

Now as I see it, you're either a madman, or an intelligence officer with the Special Air Services Regiment.

One way or the other.

So you'd better convince me quick that you're stone crazy.

See if he's armed.

The two armed MEN *advance on* CHICHESTER.

CHICHESTER. I am —

I am a British Officer.

The two MEN *stop dead still.*

A long silence.

My name is Thomas Edward Chichester.

Henwick was my cover.

I come from an old English Army family. My father was killed by a landmine in Cyprus, when I was a baby.

My mission was to assassinate you, O'Rourke.

A silence, then:

O'ROURKE (*slowly*). Now why, in God's name, do you tell me that?

A silence.

FIRST MAN. Kill the bastard.

O'ROURKE. Be quiet.

SECOND MAN. This could be a set-up —

O'ROURKE. I don't think so. What is your rank?

CHICHESTER. Captain.

O'ROURKE. You have just spoken your death warrant, Captain Chichester.

Why?

CHICHESTER. I keep on seeing the dead. A field in Ireland, a field in England. And faces like wood. Charred wood, set in the ground. Staring at me.

The faces of our forefathers.

Their eyes are sockets of rain-water, flickering with gnats. They stare at me in terror.

Because in my hand there's a Roman spear. A Saxon axe. A British Army machine-gun.

The weapons of Rome, invaders, Empire.

O'ROURKE. This is one hell of a way to deny your Imperial heritage. That what you're trying to do, Captain?

CHICHESTER, *gripping the wrist of his right hand, shaking it.*

CHICHESTER. The weapons. I want to throw them down.

And reach down. To the faces. Hold the burnt heads in my hands and pull them up. The bodies out of the earth. Hold them against me.

Their bones of peat and water and mud. And work them back to life.

Like King Arthur —

FIRST MAN. Christ Almighty! He's raving mad.

He laughs.

SECOND MAN. Let's have done with him.

O'ROURKE. I think he may just be an honourable man, having a hard time of it. The assassin, humanised by his trade.

O'ROURKE *laughs.*

Is that it Captain? The horrors of war?

WOMAN. What right does he have to stand in a field in Ireland and talk of the horrors of war? What nation ever learnt from the sufferings it inflicted on others? What did the Roman Empire give to the people it enslaved? Concrete. What did the British Empire give to its colonies? Tribal wars. I don't want to hear of this British soldier's humanity. And how he comes to be howling in the middle of my country. And how he thinks Ireland is a tragedy. Ireland's troubles are not a tragedy. They are the crimes his country has done mine. That he does to me, by standing there.

O'ROURKE (*to the two* MEN). When you've disarmed him, shoot him.

A silence. CHICHESTER *begins to tremble.*

CHICHESTER. You murdering bastards —

The SECOND MAN *shoots him.*

CHICHESTER *fumbles for his gun.*

When will peace come? When will peace come? When will peace come?

The SECOND MAN *shoots him again.*

O'ROURKE. Ah Moraed. What will we do when we have peace?

WOMAN. Peace will take care of itself. War will not.

The THREE MEN, O'ROURKE *and the* WOMAN *walk away.*

A moon shines, the light goes as —

Scene Eight

Brilliant moonlight. CORDA *and* MORGANA *creep into the trees.*
CORDA *still carries the* ENGLISHMAN's *sword.*

MORGANA. Father's not here! He's still alive!

CORDA. No. Here he is. Touch him.

MORGANA. No.

CORDA. We came back so you could. Touch him.

   MORGANA *touches* CAI's *hand.*

MORGANA. Oh.

CORDA. We'll get his clothes off.

MORGANA. Why do that?

CORDA. Men's clothes. We can sell them.

MORGANA. I can't.

CORDA. Sister, we're beggars now. This is how we'll live.

MORGANA. Oh why aren't there fires in the village? Why
   aren't the cattle mooing and coughing? Why aren't husbands
   and wives laughing or rowing at their evening meal?

CORDA. Help me.

   Then we'll rob the dead Saxon. Come on.

   The two COOKS *come on.* MORGANA *sees them.*

MORGANA. Corda —

CORDA. What?

   Sh.

   CORDA *and* MORGANA *hide.*

SECOND COOK. Why do we have to come back down here —

FIRST COOK. We saw him kill the old bag. Maybe he left something.

SECOND. So quiet. Could be a trap!

FIRST COOK. Why are Saxon Soldiers going to set a trap for a Second Cook?

SECOND COOK. This field. Standing among corpses. Their ghosts will be out.

FIRST COOK. There she is!

The FIRST COOK *goes to the dead* ADONA. *He throws the coverings from the stretcher about.*

Nothing but cushions.

SECOND COOK. That smell.

Oh, it's her. I can't be sick anymore. I have given my all.

He sees CORDA *and* MORGANA.

Now I'm seeing the ghosts.

FIRST COOK. For fucksake.

The FIRST COOK *sees* CORDA *and* MORGANA.

CORDA. We're women with Saxon Soldiers. You touch us, they'll cut your bollocks off.

SECOND COOK. Yeah, well actually we're cooks.

MORGANA. Cooks?

CORDA. Have you got food?

SECOND COOK. You give us food and we'll cook it.

MORGANA. We've not got any food.

SECOND COOK. Goodbye then.

FIRST COOK. No wait, wait.

Where are the soldiers you're with then?

MORGANA. Don't you try and touch us. We're sisters — we killed our father —

FIRST COOK. Oh really?

CORDA. Oh really. We've got a Saxon sword.

She raises the sword.

MORGANA. And we don't care! We've killed once so we're going to hell anyway.

FIRST COOK. So he's dead. Your father.

A silence.

Our Mistress is dead too.

SECOND COOK. He's right! That was her! Don't you think her smell's like a little cloud — over everything?

FIRST COOK. Shut up.

(*To* CORDA *and* MORGANA:) So what you going to do?

MORGANA. What's that to you?

CORDA. Go on the road. Get away. Kill the Saxons.

SECOND COOK. Oh aye —

FIRST COOK. Look — now don't wave that about. And don't run off. But maybe we'd better stay together for a bit — be a bit of an Army.

CORDA *laughs.*

CORDA. An army of cooks? What use are cooks now?

SECOND COOK. That had crossed our minds.

MORGANA. They're dangerous men —

SECOND COOK. We're not dangerous. Utterly fucked, actually.

CORDA. So what can you be?

FIRST COOK. What can you be?

CORDA. A mother of killers, Cook. Children brought up right. Like stoats, like weasels, like otters.

A cook's not going to be much good for that.

FIRST COOK. I'm changing my trade.

CORDA. To what?

FIRST COOK. Poet.

SECOND COOK. What are you talking about? You can't even read —

FIRST COOK. Shut up. We're on here —

MORGANA. What do we want with them, Corda?

CORDA. We're going to have to travel a long way. We need all the men and women we can find.

What poem you got then? In your new trade.

FIRST COOK. 'Bout a King!

A silence.

CORDA. Yes?

FIRST COOK. King.

Not any King.

CORDA. No?

FIRST COOK. No.

CORDA. Did he have a Queen, this King?

SECOND COOK. Yes.

He hesitates.

Yes, oh very sexy —

FIRST COOK. Look let me do the meat, right?

SECOND COOK. Oh yeah, I do the vegetables even when it comes to fucking poetry.

FIRST COOK. Actually, he was a King who never was.

His Government was the people of Britain. His peace was as common as rain or sun. His law was as natural as grass, growing in a meadow.

And there never was a Government, or a peace, or a law like that.

His sister murdered his father. His wife was unfaithful. He died by the treachery of his best friend.

And when he was dead, the King who never was and the Government that never was — were mourned. And remembered. Bitterly.

And thought of as a golden age, lost and yet to come.

CORDA. Very pretty.

MORGANA. What was his name?

FIRST COOK. Any old name dear. (*To the* SECOND COOK:) What was his name?

SECOND COOK. Right. Er — any old name.

Arthur?

Arthur?

THIRTEENTH NIGHT

A dream play

To Marion and George

Thirteenth Night was first presented by the Royal Shakespeare Company at the Warehouse, London on 2 July 1981, with the following cast:

JACK BEATY	Michael Pennington
JENNY GAZE	Domini Blythe
BERNARD FEAST	John Bowe
BILL DUNN	David Waller
HENRY MURGATROYD	Derek Godfrey
ROSS	Paul Webster
ROSE	Avril Clark
CYGNA	Shelagh Stephenson
JOAN	Sara Mason

FEAST doubles an an AMBASSADOR, DUNN and MURGATROYD as MURDERERS, ROSE, CYGNA and JOAN as CIA AGENTS.

Directed by Barry Kyle
Designed by Bob Crowley
Music by Nick Bicât
Lighting by Leo Leibovici

Induction

Night. A South London street.
A PUBLICAN'S VOICE, *off-stage.*

VOICE. Time, time, come on everyone.

    JACK BEATY *and* JENNY GAZE *come on.*

BEATY. Good meeting.

GAZE. Think so?

BEATY. The issues were very sharp.

GAZE. Oh, in the pub afterwards. Very sharp. The sound of
    Labour Party democracy – breaking glass and men's voices
    raised at closing time.

BEATY. Still. All shall be well and all manner of things shall be
    well. Can we go to your place tonight, Jenny?

    They stare at each other.

GAZE. Why?

BEATY. She's – going to ring tonight.

GAZE. 'She' meaning your wife.

BEATY. I can't face another of those calls. Three-hour calls. Not
    after a Labour Party Ward Meeting. Human flesh is human
    flesh.

GAZE. 'Human flesh' meaning 'Male flesh'?

BEATY. We can't be there – with her on the phone –

GAZE. Take it off the hook –

BEATY. She'd ring all night, just to listen to the engaged tone –
    come the dawn, get the GPO to make that buzzing noise –
    please.

    BERNARD FEAST *comes on.*

FEAST. Better get a taxi. Bill's well away.

BEATY. All right, Bernard.

FEAST. We going to talk later tonight?

BEATY. Yes – yes –

FEAST. I'll give a hand with Bill.

    FEAST *goes off.*

BEATY. God –

GAZE. Why does every Ward Meeting end up with our Chairperson drunk?

BEATY. Water the grass-roots. Can I? Come back?

GAZE. You're going to talk to Bernard.

BEATY. Do that at your place. Or –

GAZE. Doesn't it strike you as sickening, a little bit sickening – working for a Socialist Britain when we can't even run a little love affair? I mean – have we the right to call for a New Social Order when we can't even keep our own bodies under control?

BEATY. Dark thoughts, Jen! (*Low.*) I want love.

GAZE (*low*). Oh, we all want love.

BILL DUNN, *supported by* HENRY MURGATROYD *and* FEAST, *comes on.* ROSS *follows and walks a distance away.*

DUNN. In 1937 my old Dad – said he were going out for a walk. Tea-time it were. Three year he were gone and not a word! Bugger had enlisted for 'International Brigade' in Spanish Civil War! My old Dad –

MURGATROYD. Yes, Bill, we know the story –

FEAST. Not a postcard –

MURGATROYD. } Or an 'and-grenade –
DUNN.   }

FEAST. Someone getting a taxi?

FEAST *wanders off,* MURGATROYD *keeping* DUNN *upright.*

ROSS. Are you and Bernard meeting tonight?

BEATY (*looking at* JENNY). Don't know. Yes.

ROSS. We need two more Wards to get the Selection Committee our way. That means a lot of telephone calls, tonight.

BEATY. We're only a piddling little caucus in a Ward Party – can't we sleep?

ROSS (*low*). It matters!

BEATY (*low*). I know it matters!

GAZE. You can come to my place.

BEATY. Thanks, love.

GAZE. We must get rid of our resident right-wing Labour pig of an MP, must we not? (*She looks away.*)

DUNN. Fixing it up are you? Between you? Carving it up?

FEAST. Jack, over the street.

FEAST, BEATY, GAZE *and* ROSS *staring across the street.*

DUNN. You're a bloody menace, all of you. Tell you what your trouble is – anal fixation. That were Clem Attlee's trouble. And Robespierre's.

MURGATROYD. Don't quite get the connection there, Bill.

DUNN. Too precise. Turd counters, the lot of you.

FEAST. Those thugs who were in the other bar.

ROSS. I know them.

FEAST. Get that taxi –

DUNN. Bloody paperback Marxists. Ah, no no, the young. Dialectically engaged. I love to see 'em scrum.

MURGATROYD. He's going to throw up.

DUNN. Just hold me while I breathe!

MURGATROYD. Help me hold him –

ROSS. Here they come.

MURGATROYD. Tell you what, Jack, Jenny –

ROSS, *taking out a length of piping.*

FEAST. Taxi, there's got to be a taxi –

ROSS. Fascists.

DUNN. If a socialist party really came t'power in Britain, not Labour Party, real Socialist Party – what would it face? Eh? Jack? Jenny? You come to power tomorrow, prison notebooks o' Antonio Gramsci and all – what do you do, eh?

They all stare. They take a step back. DUNN *lurches forward.*

Nazis? Blackshirts? Get 'em all –

As if the attackers are a few feet away, running toward them. Then GAZE *is hit, she goes down.*

BEATY. Jenny –

He moves towards GAZE *and goes down.*

FEAST. Scum!

DUNN. Get 'em –

MURGATROYD. Bill, don't –

DUNN. Get 'em all!

ROSS, *his piping coming down on a head.*
Blackout.
The sound of a fight, then cut off.

Silence.

Scene One

BEATY, *alone on the ground.*
From a dreamscape to the Central Hall, Westminster.

BEATY. Get 'em all, get 'em all.

I'll put on my gloves, not to make the piano dirty, Mum.

Ha!

He sits up.

I still get a nightmare. I am a concert pianist, in black tails, white bow-tie, shiny black dress shoes. Hands manicured and flexed I walk from my dressing-room alone, along the corridor. I listen to my breath. Then I'm on the platform. Wham! The audience a mountainside of humanity, raging for music. The orchestra a band of brilliant men and women, disciplined and honed, all their eyes blue. And on the conductor's podium, his baton one mile long – why, Karl Marx. I flip the tails of my dress suit. Sit upon the stool. Caress my knuckles over the keys. It's the big one! The great concerto! Karl's baton moves, the tip a star dancing among the constellations! The orchestra crashes in, the great chords ascend – intolerable excitement – my ribcage burns – Karl nods to me – my entrance – I raise my hands like hawks to bring them down, and –

I remember I can't play the piano.

It's a ghastly mistake, why am I here – I can't play, I –

And it's frozen, the moment, I – wake up.

He scrambles away wiping his face with a handkerchief. The buzz of a three-thousand-strong crowd. A batch of microphones rises from the stage. He turns towards them.

So, how long can I go on grinding out the notes of a music I can't believe in? Who is playing for whom? Who is dancing?

Comrades. After decades of dereliction. Of the working class on right-wing adventures at the ballot-box. Of the Labour Movement mis-led, split, done down by petit-bourgeois politicians, messing their pants with fear at what real socialist policies would mean to them. Personally. To their cosy little world, the cat's cradle of how Government right or centre or left has always worked in this country. The secret deal. In the leather armchairs of London clubs, over bone china in the House of Commons tea-room, everyone with their tongue in the right ear and everyone with a seat on the board of a City bank being kept warm. No messy, grass-roots democracy. Just leaders in *The Times* and *Daily Mail*, telling them what the country thinks.

Well, we've struck a blow at that. Go to Heathrow Airport these days. See what fabulous refugees are on the wing to the swamps of Florida.

I am proud to serve in a Government which is driving so many of our so-called 'powerful people' abroad.

But. The rub. But.

We have been in power twelve months. And I do not yet know whether we really do mean what we say. Let alone if we are going to do – what we say.

A 'Great Agitation' has put us in power. At last a majority of the electorate is against Death. Which is a wonderful thing. More, they are against Nuclear Death. Which is a very wonderful thing. It's taken a long time, but wonderful. We are to disarm our nuclear forces, unilaterally. The electorate says we are, the Cabinet says we are, even the Prime Minister says we are.

But are we? Abandon nuclear weapons and we leave the Western world. And the Western world leave us. I mean, of course, American money. But since half our country is owned by America we would be left a bleeding corpse on the shore of Northern Europe. Right! The only course, nationalise American assets. And get poorer. For the cost of international sanity will be poverty. Which can only be made tolerable by a new equity. A new social justice – the policies we have all striven for. With new friends abroad. For socialism in this country will, like it or not, drive us to our only moral place in the world. Britain must join with the Third World. New friends. And a new enemy. America.

A roar from the crowd. Then BEATY, *low.*

I have a kind of fear. That – we don't have the politics to do it. That it is going to be so troublesome, the strain, the subversion against us, the terrible strain cannot be borne by Government as we know it. That we need a new democracy, new forms, a politics to end politics.

For if we do not take a stand from which there is no going back – once and for all –

We –

He freezes.

Will –

Be –

Lost –

A silence. Then the crowd very loud and a blackout.

Scene Two

A bunker beneath Whitehall.
BILL DUNN *and* HENRY MURGATROYD. MURGATROYD
holds a red telephone.

DUNN. How bad is it?

> MURGATROYD *listens to the telephone then replaces the
> receiver. He is silent.*

> Come on. How many shop windows smashed? Cars turned
> over? Slogans daubed?

> (*To himself.*) Daubed.

MURGATROYD. The Commissioner says it's only a matter of
time before someone gets killed.

DUNN. Hunh.

MURGATROYD. Ninety minutes since the meeting broke up.
Flowed out of Central Hall, over Parliament Square. Whitehall,
red paint on the lions in Trafalgar Square –

DUNN. Par for the course –

MURGATROYD. Eighty-four policemen have been injured. One
hundred and twelve arrests, so far. Grosvenor Square is
jammed. The crowd wants to burn the American Embassy.

DUNN. Ha! Someone's dream come true, eh?

MURGATROYD. What are you going to do about him, Bill?

> *A silence.*

DUNN. Give us a fag.

MURGATROYD. Given up.

DUNN. Since when?

MURGATROYD. Two days.

DUNN. Hunh! We're two of a kind, Henry. Big, shambolic men who yearn to have tidy minds. S'our destiny to smoke. Ash burning knees of our suits —

MURGATROYD. For Godsake, Bill! On his feet in Westminster Central Hall. TV lights blazing in his hair. Tearing into your leadership —

DUNN. Jack Beaty is hero of the night, all right.

MURGATROYD. Save us from heroes of the night.

DUNN. Hunh!

DUNN, *patting his suit for cigarettes.*

MURGATROYD. Dismiss him.

DUNN *sighs and sags.*

From the Cabinet. It's dissension! It's disloyalty! It's wild, it's adventurism, it's — mess. You know what Lenin called it — infantile disorders.

DUNN. Lenin called many things many things, according to temperature o' water.

MURGATROYD. 'Politics is about power.'

DUNN. Aye aye —

MURGATROYD. } 'Who does what and to whom.'
DUNN.

DUNN. Don't let's end up quoting Lenin at each other, not at this hour o' night. That would really be 'bloody end. I can handle Jack Beaty. An idealist is Jack.

MURGATROYD. And like all idealists, a menace. They get too many people singing loony tunes.

DUNN. Party loves it, though. Pressure from below. That not what we want, what we slobber for?

MURGATROYD. The mob up there tonight, baying at the American Embassy, that's not pressure, working-class pressure for social justice. That's just — steam. Come the dawn, a bit of damp on the pavement.

DUNN. Aye aye.

The telephone rings.

I could do with a drink.

MURGATROYD. And a havana cigar?

He lifts the telephone.

You know what this place is, down here?

He puts the telephone to his ear.

DUNN. I know I know. Churchill's War Room. Ha! Look at me. Prime Minister o' first elected Marxist Government in England's green and pleasant, hiding underground.

Someone's got to look at me, I don't dare. A political heavy, jerking about – pulled by the strings of his dilemma. What is leadership? What is a vanguard?

Ha! Thank you, great public, you great electoral roll. Years you elect governments of right-wing yobbos, or Social Democratic ditherers. Then at the eleventh hour, twenty-third hour, you turn round to me and my brothers and sisters and say – 'Right. You're on. The road to Socialism.'

Well it's too bloody late, it may just be too bloody late. The country's all but stripped bare.

MURGATROYD *replaces the telephone.*

MURGATROYD. Twelve have been killed. There may be more.

The first floor of the American Embassy is blazing.

DUNN. Blazing –

MURGATROYD. On fire.

A silence. Then DUNN *shouts.*

DUNN. Ross! Get in here!

How many of the twelve are policemen?

MURGATROYD. Three. Two uniformed, one Special Branch in the crowd.

ROSS *comes on, unobserved.*

DUNN. Well!

He claps his hands.

Tasty.

(*He shouts.*) Ross! Get in here! Oh, you are in here. Got a drink on you, Ross? No, you are a teetotal vegetarian. Gentlemen, you stink of carrot juice and menthol chewing-gum.

Right.

Public statement. No distancing of my Government from tonight's hoo-ha. 'We're all Red Indians now' – summat like that.

MURGATROYD. We can't —

DUNN (*angrily*). Shut up!

> We're old comrades, Henry. But don't try to teach your Grandma to suck eggs.

> *A silence.*

> Jack Beaty.

ROSS. The man of the hour.

DUNN. I love the bastard. I want all your best men on him, Ross. Surveillance, everything.

ROSS. Yes.

DUNN. Not that you've not got your electronic eye on all of us already, eh, Ross?

Nothing from ROSS.

> But I want reports on him, round the clock. First thing every morning, last thing every night. Who he phones, who he meets, where he scratches himself. Then — we'll get tonight's little holiday back to earth. Back into 'politics we know, eh, gentlemen?

> *He laughs.*

> Prime Minister's bunker under the Admiralty? Churchill's War Room? Break open a good rich London sewer. Flood the place.

> (*Angrily.*) I'm sick of being a leader who believes in no more leadership.

Scene Three

An underground car-park. ROSE *and* CYGNA.

ROSE. Where have you been?

CYGNA. One more room, one more meeting. You?

ROSE. Watching pigs get stuck.

CYGNA. Too many agendas. Too many points of order glittering like razor blades.

ROSE. How can we keep the richness of dreams, yet be fully awake?

ROSE *laughs.*

CYGNA. Not, I begin to think, in endless meetings. Resolutions, referrals back. And nothing changed.

ROSE. You're right of course. Everything is changed and nothing is changed. 'A People's Government' elected but where are the people? Power still flows along the wires of late-night telephones.

CYGNA. And in men's voices.

ROSE. Oh –

ROSE *holds her face.*

CYGNA. Are you all right?

ROSE. I think there's glass in my eye.

CYGNA. Get to a hospital.

ROSE. There'll be a policeman on every ward tonight. Let it melt, into the blood-stream.

JOAN *runs on.*

JOAN. Beaty's coming.

ROSE. The bloody man.

CYGNA. Wind him up. Set him going.

JOAN. We must do it right. We must remember –

ROSE. Sh!

JACK BEATY *and* BERNARD FEAST *come on.*

FEAST. Where are the security guards?

BEATY. Securing a good night out. Will the police police themselves? No.

BEATY *stops.*

FEAST. Let's get to the car.

BEATY. Bernard. Twelve dead. And the Embassy on fire –

FEAST. We'll get hard news on the phone, in the car –

BEATY. But think.

He holds FEAST *back.*

If the American Ambassador is one of the twelve.

FEAST. We don't know that.

BEATY. But that will be my doing, tonight. Ha! Every public
speaker dreams of making a riot, just once in his life. Of the
audience – getting up – and actually doing what has been said.
Eh?

It's coming over me. A rosy glow. I feel sick.

FEAST. Beaty, pull yourself together.

BEATY *retches.* FEAST *looks about them, nervously.*

For Godsake –

BEATY. I see his body. In front of me. On a little trolley. On little
rubber wheels, soundless. I'll push it about in front of me.

FEAST. We don't know it's happened. It's just rumour, in the
crowds.

BEATY. But don't you understand – I want it to have happened?
Part of me does.

He laughs.

The rhetorician, dreaming of reality.

And haven't you always said – America will no more allow
Britain to be independent and socialist than Russia allowed
Czechoslovakia to be independent – and socialist?

FEAST. You're whirling. You're – we'll talk in the car.

He pulls BEATY's *arms.* BEATY *looks around him.*

ROSE, CYGNA *and* JOAN *in the shadows.*

ROSE. Comrade Minister. Why do you park your car
underground?

A silence.

For crying out loud –

FEAST, *pulling out a gun.*

BEATY (*to* FEAST). No!

(*Into the dark.*) Who are you?

ROSE. Women with a question.

BEATY. What?

CYGNA. Is the revolution won or lost, Jack Beaty?

FEAST. I know what this is. Don't stand and listen to this.

BEATY. Sh!

JOAN. Go everywhere with your dog, Beaty?

BEATY. We all need dogs these days, comrade. If you value your life, guard it like an off-licence.

FEAST (*low*). Thank you. Thank you very much.

BEATY (*low*). Bernard, no.

(*A silence. Then* BEATY, *aloud.*) Well? Are you going to show yourselves?

FEAST. They're loonies, Jack, I know the tone.

BEATY. Who is a loony and who is not, when it comes to politics?

FEAST. Have nothing to do with them.

ROSE. What is that man afraid of?

CYGNA. People in the streets.

JOAN. They'll come into the streets for you, Jack Beaty.

CYGNA. They did tonight.

JOAN. And burned down a big eagle.

FEAST. Nothing Beaty said tonight sanctions the fire at the American Embassy. Or has anything to do with that.

You Anarchos! Ultras, dreamers. After years we have an elected Socialist Government in this country. But will you work for it? Keep it to its policies, its duty to the working class? Oh no. You are too pure in mind. When you can't bend the real world into Paradise, you want to smash it. For you it's all or nothing. The Garden of Eden or a planet of dust.

ROSE. What, in Paris, made De Gaulle leave for Germany by helicopter? What, in Prague, made Stalin piss in his grave? What, in Teheran, broke the Shah? A new politics.

JOAN. The politics to end politics.

BEATY (*to* FEAST). God! I said that.

CYGNA. Then live it.

ROSE. The road from Evil to Good is worse than Evil.

JOAN. But what decent man or woman dare not go down the road to good?

FEAST (*to* BEATY). Another quote from your collected works?

ROSE. You're the man, Beaty.

BEATY. A saint? Don't we know by now all saints are killers?

ROSE. You raised a ghost tonight.

  JOAN *laughs.*

JOAN. Spooky, spooky.

CYGNA. Give it flesh, Mr Politician. Give it flesh.

  ROSE, CYGNA *and* JOAN *disappear into the shadows.*

CYGNA. Call on us, when they betray you.

JOAN. We will on you.

BEATY. What are you –

ROSE. Delegates. Delegates, Comrade Minister.

  They have gone. FEAST, *shouting after them.*

FEAST. You represent nothing!

BEATY (*low*). Or do they?

FEAST. Activists crawl away from us, into holes.

BEATY (*low*). Holes, under walls.

FEAST. My daughter's got it. Terminal Maoism. Or 'Small is beautiful' anarchy – of some bloom. The boils look the same.

  BEATY *tries a laugh.*

BEATY. Maybe they know something we don't.

FEAST. Come on, Beaty. That mumbo-jumbo can't get to you. That's nothing to do with the grind of actually being a Socialist Government trying to run this bloody country. The scene on the far left is one big hospital for ideological disorders. Get to the car.

BEATY (*aside*). The Government car. Little curtains in the back window. Careering through the streets. Inside, a Minister, 'careering'. Frightened to look out. Did the streets speak to me with these women? What are people really thinking, what do they feel, what do they want? Is the Revolution won or lost, Jack Beaty?

FEAST. Jack!

BEATY (*aside*). Stop the car. Get out. Show my face?

Scene Four

A bathroom in 10 Downing Street. DUNN *and* MURGATROYD. DUNN *is in the bath.*

DUNN. Have we got the American Ambassador's body?

MURGATROYD. The head. The Special Branch are looking for the other bits.

DUNN. God, I need a holiday. Or a good back rub. I phoned the President, half-an-hour ago.

MURGATROYD. To say what?

DUNN. Woops, sorry.

MURGATROYD. Was he pleased?

DUNN. Oh m'bones, m'dreaming bones. Have m'shoulder blades – slide out under the skin – and scraped. If I laid on 'floor, would you walk up my spine? – no, forget that.

MURGATROYD. No going back.

DUNN. What?

MURGATROYD. Going back. After –

DUNN. Oh. In life, maybe not. But in politics – y'can always go back.
(*Low.*) Promised the President the body. Sneak it out of Heathrow. Old tea chest or something.

MURGATROYD. The far left will go potty.

DUNN. I know I know! But I live in 'real world. Real life, y'know. Backache. National debt. Wear and tear. Inflation. Wondering why y'pee comes out bloody in the john, late some nights.

MURGATROYD. You want an international loan.

DUNN. If we were 'old-style bourgeois government – one phone call and I'd have had a Swedish masseuse in here, giving me a special.

MURGATROYD. A loan. From the IMF. From the Americans –

DUNN. Still. Party's anti-sexist stand kissed goodbye to all that.

MURGATROYD. We wink at the sacking of their Embassy, damn well nearly condone the assassination of their Ambassador –

DUNN. Negotiating position. If y'not got a position of strength – DUNN *shrugs.*

MURGATROYD. Get one of terror —

DUNN (*angrily*). Two real worlds, actually. Soviets or them. (*Wagging two fingers.*) Two! Sup wi' one or the other!

MURGATROYD. The KGB or Coca-Cola?

DUNN. Weakening, Henry?

DUNN *lifts a little cup of water and pours it over his upturned face.*

MURGATROYD. We can't —

DUNN. You know I'd go for a treaty o' friendship with 'Soviet Union. But oh no. British democratic tradition. All right. She's got two tits, sweet Mother Earth — one East one West. We all find ourselves in one or —

He sighs.

The other. Ha! And I still get heckled as 'Paternalist', 'Stalinist pig'.

He splashes the water, angry again.

Thirty-seven years hard I've done. Street corner. More meetings than hot dinners. Union and Party, Branch, District, National Executive. And now I lead a Socialist Government. And do I, under the pressure, in between sandwiches, the phone calls, betray its very name?

DUNN *sags.*

MURGATROYD. Bill —

DUNN. I am so tired. So successful and so tired.

DUNN, *splashing again.*

The great sea of a Socialist Party! But am I riding 'waves or being smashed on 'beach? Cut me.

MURGATROYD. What?

DUNN *lifts a pumice stone out of the water.*

DUNN. From the shoulder blades down to the small of me back.

MURGATROYD. Oh, all right.

MURGATROYD *takes the pumice stone. He stares at it.*

DUNN. Go on.

MURGATROYD. Right.

He runs the pumice stone from DUNN's shoulder blades down to the small of his back.

DUNN. They used to argue, where does 'soul live? Heart? Head? Testicles, vagina? No. In 'muscular wall of your back.

He grabs MURGATROYD's *hand.*

Late night colley-wobbles all this, in me bath. Not a word of it. Soviet Union, smashed on a beach. I go down, you go down.

MURGATROYD. And down goes sanity.

DUNN. What? Oh. Yes.

Ever since I got here, to Number Ten, I've had a bath at midnight. Bad habit. Know why?

MURGATROYD. No, Bill.

He hands DUNN *the pumice stone.*

DUNN. Before I became Prime Minister, every midnight, for three and a half decades, I'd go for a walk. Wherever I was. To look at the streets, listen. Now I do not dare.

He looks at the pumice stone then tosses it into the water.

Instead I wash myself.

BEATY, FEAST *and* ROSS *come on. They hesitate.*

DUNN. N' n' n' no, come in! To m' bathroom!

FEAST (*low*). We have.

BEATY (*low*). Sh.

DUNN. Well?

An embarrassed silence.

MURGATROYD. Bill, you asked for an inner Cabinet, at midnight –

DUNN. I know that. Well, Jack?

BEATY. Well, Bill?

DUNN. I hear on the News you're an English hero. Bring me my bow of burning gold, eh?

He looks at them in turn.

Eh?

He smiles. They begin to smile.

After tonight, the Yanks go home at last, eh?

FEAST. A socialist Britain, free of the spheres of influence, Russia and America.

DUNN. Yes, thank you, Sonny. Henry! Towel. Ross! Clothes. Suit for 8 a.m. briefing. Be up from now 'til then.

MURGATROYD *with a towel,* ROSS *goes off and comes back on with clothes and a suit on a hanger.* DUNN *gets out of the bath and wraps the towel around him like a toga as he talks.*

Comrades! How many years hard? All our life-times. Years hard, for the Party to be built. Years hard to come to power. And now, years facing us to get any socialism into daily life at all.

He stumbles. The others glance at each other.

BEATY. All right, Bill?

DUNN *points at the suit.*

DUNN. Why isn't there a check handkerchief in that breast pocket? I said I wanted a check handkerchief in that breast pocket.

ROSS. There is, Bill.

Delicately ROSS *pulls a check handkerchief up out of the top pocket.*

DUNN. Right.

He hitches his towel.

There'll be a lot of hoo-ha. I want a show of solidarity. Jack here's invited us all up to his neck of the woods for 'weekend.

BEATY. Have I?

FEAST. You have now.

DUNN. Brass Band Gala. In your constituency. Asked me to speak and all, haven't you, lad?

BEATY. Why not –

DUNN. Don't mind me pulling your balls on this one do you, Jack?

BEATY. My balls are in your gift.

DUNN. Hunky dory.

MURGATROYD (*to* ROSS). Ah – a. He's wearing the accent extra thick. This means murder.

ROSS. What?

DUNN. So. Weekend off.

He ruffles BEATY's *hair.*

How d'you think this son of the bourgeoisie got his hand on 'working-class constituency – Brass Band Gala and all? Pass y'self off as some kind of red, did you, Jack?

Eh?

False laughter.

MURGATROYD (*low*). Blood, blood.

Scene Five

JENNY GAZE, *reading a letter.*

GAZE. 'They talked of politics to end politics. The power of the streets. I felt a terrible, secret joy. My love, I heard your voice in what they said.'

She screws the letter up and throws it away.

Why must the good always be weak?

JACK BEATY *comes on.*

BEATY. Bill Dunn's coming up by train. In the morning. For the Gala.

A silence.

I drove up, to get here before the circus. You've been reading my letter.

Jenny?

He tries to embrace her. She turns away.

I haven't slept for two nights. I'm – wildly happy. But it's dangerous. Dangerous days! I think they're losing their grip, Jenny. They can't govern. I think it's even beginning to get to Bill Dunn. The old way, Cabinet deals, pushing back-benchers about, a favour in the Party there, a threat there – it's coming apart! There'll have to be a massive extension of democracy, right through the movement –

GAZE. Oh, shut up!

A silence.

BEATY. What's the matter?

GAZE. You babble, you –

She turns away again.

Get back to your wife if it's pillow talk you want. About what a big boy you are taking on the government.

BEATY. What-is-the-matter?

There is always something the matter when you bring up my wife.

GAZE. Come up to your Northern love nest. To step out of your clothes and be admired.

Go on, get back to her. Let her breathe warm air on your neck to puff you up.

BEATY. My love, I –

She hits him.

All right! All right!

All right.

GAZE. The matter, what's the matter? Everything we believe in. 'The matter' you talk of endlessly, smoking in bed. Weep for, lying on my tit. Night after night in adultery. 'The matter' of a socialist Britain.

BEATY. You don't realise. Unless I am very sharp, they'll lay the corpse of the American Ambassador at my feet. I'm pushing a corpse around –

GAZE. Then chop it up. Feed it to your kids.

BEATY. God. If this century's going to flower it had better get one green leaf up above the mud, quick.

GAZE. Ha!

BEATY. 'Ha' meaning?

GAZE. A political argument with you is like trying to have a conversation under water. What is the special relationship of Britain to America? Rape, I think. Unreported out of shame. My country is a woman in a dark park. America whispers 'Scream and it'll be worse'. And down she lays. And he stuffs the lot up her – from intercontinental missiles in East Anglian lanes to 'The A Team' up her TV tubes. 'Thank you' whimpers Britannia, through clenched teeth.

The politics we have betray us. To America. To the greed of a vicious few at home. Betrays me, an Englishwoman. So don't ask me, Mr Politician, to step out of my clothes and love you. I am a victim of rape. Right now I'd rather masturbate with broken glass than have you.

BEATY. What – do you want me to do?

GAZE. Get – the – politics.

BEATY. Get the politics. Yes. Right. I'll nip out to a take-away.

A silence.

I can't find the politics.

GAZE. I can. Our so-called Marxist Prime Minister, who comes here by train tomorrow to hear the workers play brass bands – was on the phone to the President of the United States of America – while the smoke was still in the eagle's feathers.

He wants an American loan.

BEATY. Bill Dunn.

GAZE. Bill Dunn.

BEATY. No.

GAZE. Think it.

BEATY. No.

GAZE. Think it then do it.

BEATY. How do you know that?

GAZE. I know.

A silence.

BEATY. If that were true – and I can't believe it's true – we'll vote him down.

GAZE. Ha.

BEATY. In the Party, in the Commons.

GAZE. And force a General Election? Would a Socialist Party win again, right now, in Britain?

BEATY. If we can't, we have no right to be the government.

GAZE. Socialists have every right to be the government.

BEATY. Majority vote or no?

GAZE. You believe in a vanguard in power or you don't. Political power is political power. Got by the farce of a General Election or other means.

BEATY. I see corpses when you talk like that. Strung on the wire of camps, stretching for miles. We can't betray an elected Socialist Government.

GAZE. It's betrayed itself. Its leader has lifted a telephone and sold us to America.

BEATY. So what do you suggest? Tomorrow in my home I take the Prime Minister into the toilet and knife him?

GAZE *(calls out)*. Ross!

ROSS *comes on.*

BEATY. Ross.

ROSS. Jack.

BEATY. You've got a habit of walking out of dark corners.

ROSS. Good. Then let me give you a thought from a dark corner.

A silence.

Do you know how vast the security system of this country is? How deep it lies, in the landscape, in the streets, waiting? Telephone lines, TV and radio masts, the Cornish cliffs to the Norfolk Broads, to the Clyde to the Northern Isles – linking secret operations rooms in odd buildings in the suburbs, in market towns, on the top floors of office blocks in city centres? And do you know how many men and women, in the police, the Special Branch, the Army, the intelligence services, the Civil Defence, drill, week in week out, to work those rooms?

All this trouble is gone to in case one of two things happen. A nuclear war with the Soviet Union or civil disorder at home. 'Civil disorder at home' meaning 'A Revolution'.

The system is very professional. It aches, it drools, for orders to obey. It's a giant, sleeping just beneath our daily lives. Ready to take over courts, TV, press, Parliament, even the Cabinet.

Here is the dark thought.

What if a bunch of determined men and women – ?

A silence.

How many years have we known each other, Jack? Since we were kids, sitting on the roads to nuclear power stations. On the phone 'til three a.m. trying to screw up the right wing in the local Labour Party. We were very young. Yet here we are. Tonight in this room. And with an opportunity. You, for the moment, able to jam the streets. I, no doubt for the moment, with responsibility for internal security. It couldn't be done without you. I am a policeman, but you're a leader. Look. It's there. Now. In front our faces.

He makes a grasping gesture before his face.

The means for the Dictatorship of the Proletariat.

He makes a little laugh.

Funny. Trotsky, Lenin, on the night of the 11th October, 1917, were just men in a room. And younger than us.

I'm next door.

He hesitates, then goes off.

GAZE. Yes, he and I are lovers. Yes, we talk about you. Yes, I slept with him long before I dragged you away from your long-suffering, and loving wife.

What do you expect? Sexual fidelity? I am a political animal and a woman in a man's world. I despise women who say 'I am a woman' and don't say, in the same breath, 'I am a revolutionary socialist.'

BEATY. An armed coup.

A silence. Then he shouts.

Ross!

Scene Six

DUNN, MURGATROYD, ROSS, FEAST *and* BEATY *come on. They carry pint mugs of beer, except for* ROSS *who carries a pint mug of orange juice. They wear plastic mackintoshes over their suits and are wet.*

DUNN. Umpa umpa, stick it up your jumper. Brass band music. Sound like the movement of healthy bowels. I love it. Pity about rain. Still!

(*He raises his glass.*) To Lads and Lassies with the puff!

The others mumble and sip.

MURGATROYD. Good speech, Bill.

DUNN. Meant every word. Backwards.

Laughter.

(*To* ROSS.) Can't you just have a half? Bloody carrot juice.

ROSS. Orange. Orange juice.

DUNN. Don't look right, Cabinet Minister walking off platform of Brass Band Gala with a pint of carrot juice in his hand. What do you lace it with, blood?

Laughter and glances.

Someone get him a pint!

MURGATROYD *slips away.*

Day's a day for getting tipsy on 'grass, muddy though it be. Good for us, a beano like this. Eh, Bernard?

FEAST. It's a shock. Just to see people in their thousands, out of doors. A minister never goes on the tube, on a bus, in a pub. Your world is committee rooms, TV studios, the back seats of government cars. You end up never hearing how people talk.

DUNN. Aye. It's nice to be reminded 'working class is really there.

MURGATROYD *comes on with a pint of beer.*

Eh up! Here we go.

DUNN *takes the pint from* MURGATROYD.

There you are, Ross.

MURGATROYD *and* FEAST *on the side.*

MURGATROYD. Funny how we never use Ross's first name.

FEAST. Maybe he sees himself as an idea, more than a man.

MURGATROYD. Indeed.

DUNN *and* ROSS *stare at each other. Then* ROSS *takes the pint of beer and* DUNN *takes the pint of orange juice from him.* DUNN *sloshes the orange juice off-stage and throws the pint pot after it. He raises his glass.*

DUNN. Gentlemen. Prosperity, health and peace of every working man and woman on these islands. You'll drink to that, Ross.

DUNN *chinks his glass against* ROSS'*s. They all look at* ROSS. *Then he sips.* DUNN *roars and slaps* ROSS *on the back. Beer splashes.*

Give me men who're half cut. Decision making may be a bit unpredictable but it'll be human.

He puts his arm round BEATY. *They keep their public smiles speaking privately.*

Your feelings comradely to me, Jack?

BEATY. I'd never – split the Party.

DUNN. Personally. Personally. I've been a father to you. No, don't pull away, y'pull away. Don't like people much, do you?

BEATY. I –

DUNN. They'll never live what you want, y'see Jack. People. Bits fall off 'em, they wander away – can't live it all the time, y'see. Human perfection. That being what you're after, eh?

BEATY (*hesitates*). Yes._____

DUNN (*very low*). You're riding high, Jack. But I'm going to screw you.

I want you to know.

He squeezes BEATY *and goes public again.*

And now with our hero to the Grand Hotel. Then to a little party of my own. To which you will all bloody well come. Drink yourselves silly. Forget politics for a night. Talk about gardening, love, football. Y'know – real life!

Scene Seven

A bedroom in the Grand Hotel. BEATY *alone.*

BEATY. 'Once and for all.' 'A decisive blow.' 'The dash for Socialism.' All the slogans coming home to roost. Black crows on the chimneys of the Grand Hotel, in a northern English town.

Do it now. After all the agendas, party conferences – it comes down to this. Boot in a hotel door at night. Kill a drunken man. Simple. Brutal. The politics is in the consequences.

And consequences of consequences. I can't think. There's a little theatre in my head. Right and wrong shout at each other like actors.

GAZE *comes on.*

What's happening?

GAZE. They're still drinking. Why aren't you in there?

BEATY. Did he ask for me?

GAZE. Of course.

BEATY. We can't do this.

GAZE. You mean it won't work.

BEATY. Morally.

GAZE. Why does it slip away from you again and again? One moment you're a grown man with experience, the next you're a child. Or idiot – vacant eyes, amnesia. Why do you always go back to nothing? Why do you have to convince yourself, over and over from scratch, every second?

BEATY. Endorse political murder, for crying out aloud – in England.

GAZE. Oh, I'll cry out loud. Why do the English call themselves 'moral'? The rest of the world knows we're a race of ruthless bastards who stamped all over a quarter of the planet. Tore nations apart. Distorted continents.

And now our Empire's gone, we're not left standing in the pure air of a high moral plateau. We're one more nasty little European country, trying to get our politics up out of the slime.

BEATY. Just – be quiet.

Let me think. Let me feel.

GAZE. I tell you, my love, if tonight all you want to do is 'think' and 'feel' – you had better slink away from this hotel. Go and dig your garden.

BEATY. All right!

All right.

But, you see, I have a thought in my head. It grows. It pushes against my skull. It pressures every other thought. It has got to the nerves of my eyes. So I see, even in the world outside, the strands of the thought, looping every movement of my fellow human beings, tangling, pulling everything, by a terrible logic into one hard knot.

He laughs.

The presumption. I fear the English Revolution is a tumour in my brain.

My mind.

GAZE. I've had the thought for years.

She laughs.

If it's a disease it's in my blood. Political VD? I don't think they treat that on the NHS. And you and I are dripping with it, along with hundreds of thousands.

BEATY. I hope there are hundreds of thousands.

GAZE. Millions. Many not yet born.

BEATY. If we're wrong –

GAZE. Then I'll cut out my own sex.

BEATY *scoffs.*

Don't you believe me?

BEATY. Oh, I do. 'My love.'

GAZE. Then.

BEATY. Then.

　A silence.

GAZE. Ha!

BEATY. What?

GAZE. 'A sexual thought.'

BEATY. Yes.

GAZE. Both of us naked, touching with our tongues.

BEATY. Yes.

Scene Eight

A gentlemen's lavatory in the Grand Hotel. BEATY, his face wet, as if before a wash-basin and mirror. He has a paper towel. He pulls the skin around his eyes. FEAST comes on, as if out of a cubicle, straightening his clothes. He struggles against drink and fatigue.

FEAST. The sins of the fathers. I feel terrible. Oh.

　He goes off. A lavatory flushes. He comes back on.

　Funny how when you come up north your stool changes.

　He focuses on BEATY.

　Jack?

BEATY *still stares in the mirror.*

　Jack Beaty?

　BEATY *whirls round and stares at FEAST.*

　You O.K.?

BEATY. What's the time?

FEAST. Ah.

He consults a digital watch.

Digitally. Three. Thirteen. A.M. Why do they give tenths of seconds? Who can tell a tenth of a second? These things chop time up. Little bombs. Blip blip.

BEATY. Is Bill Dunn —

FEAST. The Prime Minister is drunkenly asleep. Between two chairs. There is a smell of urine and happiness.

BEATY. Why are you —

FEAST. Hotel's got to me. Corridors. Pipes. We in the middle of a ship? There a night sky up there? Moon? What's that bit in Orwell? The torturer says the sky's just twenty feet above the building. And the stars are light bulbs lit by the Ministry of Truth.

BEATY. Go to bed.

FEAST. Right.

FEAST goes to turn then stops.

Those women.

BEATY. What about them?

FEAST. Do you think about what they said?

BEATY. No.

FEAST. Your face on placards, above mass demonstrations?

BEATY. No.

A silence.

FEAST. Liar.

BEATY. Good night, Bernard.

FEAST (*slurring*). Don't unleash deep-lying social forces. Let deep-lying social forces —

He hiccups.

Lie. Hiccups now. Night time.

FEAST goes off. BEATY, staring at his face.

BEATY. Your dead stand behind you, Jack Beaty. In a lavatory mirror.

Our age began. They divided up the fields. The peasants lost their rights. The human spirit invented Manchester. Or something invented Manchester. The families drifted from the land. The working class found itself born, into a cramped, filthy room. The ceiling as low as a coal-face. The walls screeching with cotton machines. The floor the street of a slum with an open drain. The industrial revolution. A concentration camp in slow motion, decades long. And for basic dignity, against the cruelty of history and the sufferings of daily life – the inmates of the nineteenth century invented Socialism.

Gave you what literacy you have, Jack Beaty. What health. What sense of justice. Right and wrong.

He looks over his shoulder.

Judge, comrades. If I am wrong tonight come out of your graves. Tear my mind to pieces.

Scene Nine

A corridor in the Grand Hotel. A telephone rings throughout the scene. JENNY GAZE *alone.*

GAZE. It's there. A fire. How many floors away? Up or down? A tang in the air, cutting, like acid. They're doing it! Doors kicked in. Drunks and public men choking in the smoke.

She sniffs.

Don't know – that phone! Oh, is it being done or not?

BEATY (*off*). Bitch! Bitch!

GAZE. The years of talk. We've got the arguments but where is the will?

BEATY *runs on, banging against the walls of the corridor. He is soaking wet. He holds a handkerchief against his mouth with one hand, with the other he clutches something beneath his coat. He leans against the wall.*

You're soaked –

BEATY. Sprinkler system. Want me burning, bitch? A human torch, eh?

BEATY *fighting for his breath.* GAZE *shouts.*

GAZE. What happened? Is Bill Dunn alive?

BEATY. Oh, he's alive. With his head half off. He's alive, with his corpse burning.

GAZE. What –

BEATY. His Special Branch bodyguard – wouldn't move! All Ross's creatures. They were ready for the fire, with masks. But they stood and stared. At me! For me to do it!

GAZE. So –

BEATY. So! Smashed the little glass cupboard in the corridor, didn't I. Went in and cut him to bits, didn't I. See?

He opens his coat. He holds an axe. His shirt, arms and hands are covered with blood. He laughs.

Up to now I thought the deadliest political weapon was the telephone.

GAZE. The bodyguards –

BEATY. Promote them! Promote them all! Three brand new Colonels in the brand new Secret Police. We're going to need a brand new Secret Police, aren't we, bitch?

GAZE. For Godsake –

BEATY. Don't worry, bitch. I got to the end of the corridor – and closed the firedoors on them.

They stare at each other. A silence but for the telephone ringing.

GAZE. And the fire alarms –

BEATY. Little stickler in't you?

Ross cut into the circuits. They'll go off when the fire gets hold. Good and true.

GAZE. So.

BEATY. So.

GAZE. The Grand Hotel of government –

BEATY. Is burning down. Good and true.

He begins to weep.

GAZE. Stop that!

BEATY. No –

GAZE. Come here –

BEATY. No –

GAZE. Get all this off –

GAZE, *pulling at his clothes.*

BEATY. A shower before the thirteenth floor caves in?

GAZE. Quickly.

BEATY *grips her.*

BEATY. Come in under with me. Let the tap melt hot metal on us, the water boil us alive.

GAZE, *gripping him.*

GAZE. Listen to me! In the morning people will pick through the ruins. And we'll walk among them, modestly, with serious faces, inwardly screaming with joy.

Fire alarm bells go off. They are gripping each other. A blackout.

Scene Ten

The smouldering ruins of the Grand Hotel. Dawn. Rain. FEAST *and* MURGATROYD *close together, at a distance from* ROSS. ROSS *with a small, black two-way radio set which he holds close to his mouth.*

FEAST *has an umbrella, his clothes are torn.* MURGATROYD *is in his pyjamas, with a coat over them.*

MURGATROYD. I can't stop shivering.

FEAST. What are we walking about in the ruins for? I've been walking about in the ruins for an hour.

MURGATROYD. What?

FEAST. We feel it should be done. Cabinet Minister. Be seen. Give interviews. Go through the cordon – walk in the ruins.

I think I'm still drunk.

MURGATROYD. I phoned my wife. She burst into tears when I told her. I stared at the ear bit. And thought – oh yes, we loved Bill Dunn, and he's dead. I'm in my 'jamas.

ROSS's *radio crackles, the words inaudible. He whispers into it.*

FEAST *glances at* ROSS *then back to* MURGATROYD.

FEAST. What?

MURGATROYD. Why, I'm shivering. Oh my God, what are we going to do? I loved him too. Brutal bugger, but real, heavy with it.

FEAST. 'Years hard.'

MURGATROYD. 'Years hard.'

FEAST. As he said, a hundred times a day.

MURGATROYD. I was close to him, I've got to step into his clothes. And I'm in my 'jamas –

FEAST. Henry, have you seen your Private Secretary this morning?

MURGATROYD. Fly sod's round here somewhere.

FEAST. Mine went from the Hotel before midnight.

A silence.

Without telling me.

MURGATROYD. Before –

FEAST. Before the fire.

A silence.

MURGATROYD. Ha! What are you saying? Rats – a ship?

FEAST. I hope I am still drunk.

GAZE *comes on. She draws* ROSS *aside and whispers to him. He nods.*

MURGATROYD. What's that cow doing here? Inside the cordon –

GAZE *glances at* MURGATROYD *and* FEAST, *goes off.*

Evil-minded whore.

FEAST. Shut up. We've all known for years that woman is Jack Beaty's political wife –

MURGATROYD. 'Political wife'! Funny name for it –

FEAST. Oh, come on. And how is Sally-Ann?

MURGATROYD. Oh –

FEAST. Yes, 'Oh'.

ROSS, *the radio.*

MURGATROYD. He's talking into his walky-talky again.

FEAST. You've noticed that.

MURGATROYD. I've been worried politically before. Worried sick. My ulcers are the scars to prove it. But I've never felt – political fear.

We'll drive. Now. Heathrow in four hours. A plane to the States.

FEAST. No. No – wait for the inner cabinet meeting.

MURGATROYD. Have you been called to an inner cabinet meeting?

FEAST. In the hour –

MURGATROYD. Have you?

A silence.

Have you been called to a cabinet meeting?

FEAST. No.

They stare at each other. A silence.
Suddenly I feel we've got to talk to each other, fast – the next time we see each other may be in a cell –

FEAST. You're having a nightmare, Henry. Wake up.

MURGATROYD. I've always known one rainy dawn I'd not wake up and live on in – the nightmare. Of it all going wrong. (*He scoffs.*) When you've had a job at the heart of government, in the actual pumping, blood and muscle centre – you know how weak it is. How thin the walls –

FEAST. We've only ourselves to blame.

I think there could be –

He hesitates.

An Emergency Government.

MURGATROYD. 'Emergency Government', that the phrase? Coronary of the body politic, eh?

He tries to laugh.

FEAST. That's what the neglect of democracy leads to, has been leading to for years.

MURGATROYD. And who will lead this 'Emergency Government'? That policeman over there?

He gestures at ROSS, *who sees him do so and turns a full circle away, his mouth at the radio.*

That woman? Not Jack Beaty. He'd have nothing to do with it. I mean –

(*He tries to scoff.*) What are we talking about? An armed coup?

FEAST. We think Civil Liberty is as natural as a cow. Standing in a field, glimpsed from a train window. Always there, solid in the rain, chewing the cud. But easily, oh easily, the next time the public takes a train – they could look out and see the field concreted over, blood-stained, the poor beast hacked to bits.

MURGATROYD. What do you know – what do you think you know – Bernard – ?

FEAST. For my sins, I'm close to Jack Beaty. Do you get the impression, Henry, you and I have been allowed, just for a while, to talk together like this?

MURGATROYD. We must – must –

FEAST. What?

MURGATROYD. Save the country.

FEAST. Ha!

MURGATROYD. Appeal?

FEAST. To whom?

MURGATROYD. The people?

FEAST. How?

MURGATROYD. TV –

FEAST. Do you think you and I will ever get near a television
studio again?

And anyway, old friend, what – would – you say? Sorry?

A silence.

MURGATROYD. Sorry.

MURGATROYD *screws his eyes tight and lowers his head.*

FEAST. Sorry you were a young man who believed in Socialism.
And forgot it when you were older.

Sorry you were a minister in a Socialist government – and
became a hatchet man.

Sorry you nailed up lips with threats or promises. Silenced Party
Branches.

Sorry your skull grew thick. Your mind blocked. The hard head
of a hard man, behind the political throne of a hard man.

MURGATROYD (*low*). All right. All right, you bastard.

FEAST (*low*). Walk away now. Through the police cordon if you
can. It's a four-hour drive to Heathrow. I'll put in a word to get
you away.

Go on! Maybe they've not got things tight yet.

MURGATROYD. Comrade –

FEAST. Please. I – don't want your blood on my hands.

MURGATROYD. God, what a thing to say.

ROSS *comes towards them suddenly.*

FEAST. Too late.

ROSS. Gentlemen, you are under arrest.

Scene Eleven

A summer garden. BEATY *and* FEAST.

BEATY. Bernard. It's so good to see you. Come out into the garden.

They walk forward, BEATY *holding* FEAST's *arm.*

FEAST. God.

BEATY. Yes, hollyhocks. Didn't know I gardened, did you?

He giggles.

A Suffolk country garden. See that mulberry tree? A present from the General Council of the TUC.

FEAST. It's –

BEATY. A small tree, yes. A long time growing. When it's grown to maturity we'll all be dead. But what do you expect from the TUC?

Do you mind if I weed?

FEAST. No. No –

BEATY. Ross!

ROSS *glides on.*

A garden trowel.

ROSS *glides off.*

He sleeps with Jenny. You knew?

FEAST. No. No –

BEATY. Ah! You never had intelligence. I mean information. Intelligence of clear thought – that you had.

Still have, no?

FEAST. I've been in prison.

BEATY. Yes. I put you there.

(*He shouts.*) Ross! I called for a garden trowel! To dig up weeds! On the bloody lawn!

(*Touching* FEAST's *arm.*) Don't worry, he'll come with one. Any moment now. Just wait.

FEAST. Jack –

BEATY. Sh.

ROSS *comes on with a brand new garden trowel in a cellophane wrapping. He holds it out to* BEATY.

Gloves, man.

ROSS *takes a pair of kitchen gloves, also brand new, from his pocket.* BEATY *takes the gloves and trowel from* ROSS. *He hands the trowel to* FEAST, *who stares at it.*

No. I'll break the wrapping.

BEATY *stares at* ROSS.

Thank you, Ross. Now go away.

ROSS *turns away, stops, then glides off.* BEATY, *breaking the sealed kitchen gloves and putting them on.*

You know, of course, this country cottage is not what it seems. It is the entrance to a Regional Seat of Government. I move from one to the other of these underground bunkers, with their entrances disguised by English cottage gardens. Did they beat you up?

FEAST. In Brixton Gaol? No.

BEATY. Kitchen gloves. The English countryside is safe compared to others. One poisonous snake. Owls, which can come at your face at night. Wasps, nettles. But nothing that kills. Except for the soil.

FEAST. ?

BEATY. Tetanus.

FEAST. Yes?

BEATY. Lockjaw. What disease can be more fatal for a politician, eh?

He giggles.

Eh?

He nudges FEAST *with his elbow.*

Bernard?

FEAST. What do you want?

A silence.

BEATY. Trowel.

FEAST *throws the trowel away.*

FEAST. I was brought here in a police van. On the way, my bowels opened. Thought I was, at long last, being taken to my death you see.

They're going to do it to me outside London, I thought, looking through the little window.

By the sea, or on a cliff. Or in the countryside, shot in a quarry?

But I was given a bath and these clothes. And pushed into this garden with you. To watch you put on rubber gloves – and weed a lawn.

A silence.

BEATY. Oliver Cromwell was a farmer. Lose yourself in nature? The price of cereals. The annual fix of the Milk Marketing Board. I feel the sense of it, going to kneel on this lawn to dig out dandelions. Over the underground tunnels of RSG number 22. Peace in work.

Looking at his gloved hands.

Henry Murgatroyd is in California.

A silence.

Did you hear from him?

FEAST. In Brixton?

BEATY. You have privileges.

FEAST. A telephone in my cell? A telex? Let alone unopened mail, or visits from my family –

BEATY. You know what I mean.

FEAST. You bastard.

BEATY. You do me an injustice.

FEAST. I do you –

BEATY. Yes. I invite you to my country home –

FEAST. You had me brought here in a black maria! And this is no home. It's a fort. For all the hollyhocks –

BEATY. I think you are under a delusion, Bernard.

FEAST. And what delusion is that, Jack?

BEATY. That you are not free.

FEAST. Oh.

BEATY. The day after the fire – why did you help Murgatroyd get on a plane to America? Bribe an official – spend the last shred of your influence, to free him? And not yourself?

Nothing from FEAST.

Are you in touch with him?

FEAST. I told you, I am in prison –

BEATY. Do –

Do –

You believe there is a class war going on in our country?

FEAST. Yes of course. What do you want, a catechism? I'm still a Socialist –

BEATY. How do you think this class war will –

A flowing gesture with his rubber-covered hands.

Turn out?

FEAST. I hope for the victory of the working class.

BEATY. Mmm.

FEAST. How 'Mmm'?

BEATY. Mmmm, by what means?

See, people demonstrate their support for my government. Every weekend. Streams of banners. TV. Gymnastic displays at Earls Court. Don't you see TV in Brixton? Category 'A' criminal like you?

They've even taken to putting flowers on the spot in that car-park, where you and I met those three women. Carnations.

FEAST. Funeral flower, isn't it, the carnation?

BEATY. No, just expensive. I want you to understand. I want to take you in my arms and love you as a brother.

FEAST. Ross's policemen put flowers in that car-park, every morning. No one else. Admit it. Your regime's a mockery. Oh, parliament still meets, the TV news still comes on, but it's all sham. Mockery. You've subverted everything, admit it, admit it.

BEATY. Yes. We're primitive. Primitive men and women.

He looks at his hands.

Our cruelty. Our personal spite. Our self-loathing. No wonder cripples come to power. Look! My hands are like claws.

FEAST. Christ! You really think you are Oliver Cromwell! One more reluctant axe-man.

BEATY (*low*). What do you mean?

FEAST. All the country knows you killed Bill Dunn with a fire-axe, from a glass panel in a corridor of the Grand Hotel.

Well, the whole of Brixton Gaol knows. As the saying goes, if you want to know the truth about a country, go to its prisons.

Terror bleeds truth, even through prison walls.

BEATY. With every word you say, you become more dangerous. You know that?

FEAST. Ex-politicians become philosophers, confined to their cells. We think a lot about justice.

He laughs.

And come to rule a country, justly. A country three-and-a-half metres long by two-and-a-half metres wide, between a lavatory pan and a steel door with an eye in it.

Closing his eyes and shaking his head.

Tell me – bringing me here to your garden, what do you want? To torment me?

BEATY. It's all right, Bernard –

He puts his arm round him.

Don't worry, don't –

A gesture with his hand.

You made a mistake. 'Murky Murgy' we used to call him in Bill Dunn's time, remember?

He raises a storm in America against everything you and I believe in.

He wants America to send troops. Troops, eh? Landing craft Penzance to Bognor Regis?

Ha! Now the man swims in his element. The 'Free Society' of America. Where pigs can grow fat, snort and churn in the mud. Murky Murgy has become an entrepreneur with a cause – himself. Where did you put my trowel?

FEAST *gestures vaguely.* BEATY, *ripping off the gloves.*

Christ! I'll never make a gardener. An Oliver Cromwell either, eh?

He throws the gloves off.

It's still me, Bernard. It's still Jack Beaty.

FEAST. What do you want from me? Comfort?

BEATY. Work. In my government. As Foreign Secretary. Against Murky Murgy. Against America. To join with the Third World. And at home – to be an honest voice, speaking clearly.

There, you old lag. How does that grab you?

FEAST *weeps.*

FEAST. You want me, just – simply – simply to kill myself –

BEATY. Comrade.

A Revolutionary Government has taken power. Good, I say. It has withdrawn British Troops from Northern Ireland. Good, I say, with all my heart. Cut off links with America. Good, I say. Not become a satellite of Russia. Good. Is working to make a nuclear-free zone in Europe. Do you, as a socialist, disagree with any of that?

FEAST. No.

BEATY. Then – what is your trouble?

FEAST. Prison.

He giggles.

Prison is my trouble.

BEATY. We have legislation in preparation for the workers' control of industry –

FEAST. Ha!

BEATY. Sorry?

FEAST. Sorry to you. What tyranny will ever legislate a democratic institution into being?

He laughs.

Workers' control!

Watch it, Jack, they may vote the Tories back. And American missiles and three million unemployed. And vote you and your mistress and her policeman to hell.

BEATY (*low*). They would be stupid if they did.

FEAST. Oh, agreed. Agreed! Agreed! Agreed! Agreed!

A silence.

BEATY. If you understood so much, why did you help that pig Murgatroyd? You know he is an enemy of everything you believe in. Say 'Workers' Control' to his face and his eye would haemorrhoid.

FEAST. It was just –

He sighs.

Humanity.

BEATY. Ah.

FEAST. I –

BEATY. Ah.

FEAST. He is a pig of a man. In a just world – of no consequence.

And we must act as if the world is just. Else, how can we go on?

Yes. I engineered his escape.

And I stayed saying, yes. I'll serve my country's government. If I am not put in prison.

BEATY. It's wonderful to talk to a good man. Even though I have so greatly – abused him.

Go for a walk.

FEAST. How do you mean?

BEATY. Suffolk. A sunny day. The small fields, like an old-fashioned mattress on a bed, eh? Go to the kitchen. Get a bottle of Chianti, cold, it's my favourite. And go and sit under a hedge, drink wine, think.

Then come back at nightfall. Have supper with Jenny and me. Tell us if you're going to be your country's Foreign Secretary.

FEAST. I'm not in gaol any more? Just like that?

BEATY. Just like that.

FEAST's legs collapse beneath him. He weeps. BEATY cradles him.

FEAST. I can't kill –

BEATY. No, no –

FEAST. Anyone, you see.

BEATY. No, comrade.

FEAST. Human.

BEATY. There there –

FEAST. Not send to their death, at the hands of the police –

BEATY. No –

FEAST. Not anyone.

BEATY. No, no, comrade.

FEAST composes himself. He looks up at BEATY.

It's not manly, is it. To confess. Nor is it manly to be the confessor.

Oh – go into a field and get pissed.

FEAST. All right.

FEAST *stands*.

BEATY. The good are always weak, are they not?

FEAST. Yes, but we must persist.

BEATY. Indeed?

So – off you go.

FEAST. Yes.

BEATY (*aside*). He thinks he is a good man. Oh, help him. Help me.

FEAST. I love you.

BEATY. Ha!

Be back, round seven-thirty, eight.

FEAST *walks off. For the first time we see he has a limp*. BEATY, *after him*.

We'll eat, eh? Roast lamb, baby lamb!

(*Aside*.) Food, talk, in the evening of an English summer day. The fruit of privilege on our plate. Ha! I cut for the guest.

A slow gesture of a knife falling.

The meat dead and still. Yet so fresh and well cooked, to the eater it almost lives.

(*He shouts*.) Ross!

(*Aside*.) I'd like to eat ideas. Chew arguments. Swallow conclusions. Pick my teeth free of little bits of information.

(*He shouts*.) Ross!

(*Aside*.) And wash it down – cold, thick, Sicilian wine of a decision made. Cutting the throat. Making the head – hot.

ROSS *wanders on*.

Take the surveillance team away from him.

ROSS *is about to speak*.

Send two men from the Special Unit. Heavies! Let them catch him by the side of a field. Behind a hedge. Let them bury him, up in the little wood. Reward them – cash from the 'B' fund.

And let them have accidents a few months from now.

Nothing from ROSS, *who turns to go*.

(BEATY *shouts*.) And tell the cook! Tonight, distilled water in the decanters!

ROSS *looks at him then turns and goes off.*

Tonight I'll toast you, Bernard. A glass of pure ideas, raised to the death of a good man.

He giggles. JENNY GAZE *comes on.*

GAZE. I saw Bernard Feast, go by the study window with a bottle of wine in his hand.

BEATY. And how do you think the bastard looked?

GAZE. He limped.

BEATY. Huh. What do you do with a good man who limps? Cut off his leg. Oh, then his body's no good. What do you do with that? Cut that off. Then there's just his memory. Words, he said. So, cut off any tongues that speak them? And bury the lot? Limbs? Torsos? Tongues? Yes! In a little wood, in the countryside! But then the trees will know. In their sap. In their leaves in the spring. Molecules of it, in their fibre. In the juice of it, in the hazels, in the acorns. Then burn the woods, eh? Napalm – bam! Concrete over the little hills. But – the ash. The dust from the fires. In the air! Oh! Into people's lungs. So they breathe – breathe – the words.

Oh, Jenny. We could become the thing we seek to destroy.

GAZE. Stop it. Don't be alone. Keep close, among people –

BEATY. Every thought goes on and on – a bullet that ricochets! Bam! Bam! Bam! On and on, 'til one simple thought means the whole world.

Ha! You look at a weed on a lawn and the jungles of Brazil rise up, growing into your eyes –

GAZE. Stop whirling. Stop. Get something to sleep.

BEATY. You're right. From now on I'll work at night, sleep in the day. A meal at eleven, midnight – start. And come the dawn, let the messages go out. The world of government gone dark to light, light to dark – the Civil Service with their minds torn to bits, eh?

Tea, now?

GAZE. My love, why do we have to think of ourselves as strong? All that matters is what is done.

BEATY *withdraws from her. A silence.*

BEATY. Tea.

Scene Twelve

BERNARD FEAST *alone, with a bottle of wine. He swigs. He sits down, the bottle between his legs. He massages his bad leg.*

FEAST. Two hopes. Two — hopes.

That men and women are not born evil. That's one.

He takes a swig from the bottle. He controls his breathing.

That there is the iron force of reason. With — which — we can make our history. That's s'other.

Mmm.

He pats the top of the bottle with the palm of his hand.

Two hopes. No Socialism without 'em.

We are good. Reason — is strong. Oh help us, help us. Who? To say 'Help' to? God the Father?

He stops patting the bottle. He snorts.

Is it the lot of persecuted revolutionaries, to end up believing in God? Like alcoholics on the wagon? Go away God! Get back down under the hedgerows, with the fungus.

He snorts.

God. And Gods. And magic. Mushroom faiths. We've only ourselves to say 'Help' to. Only us.

He pats the top of the bottle, slows then stops. Two bulky figures in black gear, their faces masked by helmets, approach him. They both carry automatic pistols with silencers. They stand before him. He looks up at them.

Comrades. A beautiful evening. The children will be in bed soon, all — across Britain.

A silence.

A dampness on the ground. Didn't notice, been drinking. But let it come down, eh? Water, steel or fire. I'll be safe in a ditch.

A silence.

Well?

What are you, religious, want my blessing?

He snorts.

You don't have it.

FIRST MURDERER. No. We just enjoy our work.

FEAST. No.

Just – do it.

Don't – bits of me – or –

He flails with his heels to stand up.

Be humane.

Don't.

Look.

The SECOND MURDERER *laughs.* FEAST *stops flailing. He stares one to the other. They advance on him. They put the muzzles of their guns on his kneecaps and other parts of his body.*

FIRST MURDERER. Now comrade, be reasonable.

The FIRST MURDERER *puts his gun at* FEAST's *neck.*

FEAST. Evil. Evil. Oh, what evil.

Scene Thirteen

The cottage's dining-room. A table set for dinner. Candelabra, glass, silver glittering. ROSS *and* BEATY.

ROSS. Like a rabbit.

BEATY. Yes.

ROSS. They said. Transfixed.

BEATY. Yes.

ROSS. They destroyed the face. Tore out the teeth. Cut off the finger prints. Burnt the body.

BEATY. Yes yes.

ROSS. You wanted a full report.

BEATY. What were his last words?

ROSS *shrugs.*

A full report!

ROSS. 'Oh what evil.'

A silence.

BEATY. No, that's not right –

ROSS. The report –

BEATY. No. Bernard Feast didn't believe in evil. That's not right.

ROSS. I assure you, Beaty –

BEATY. He did not say that! I knew Bernard Feast. He did not believe in evil!

He paces. He turns on ROSS.

And I'm not making some schoolboy debating point! Bernard had rationality in his bones.

He wavers.

No, that is not a full report.

ROSS. The bastard's dead. The body unidentifiable.

BEATY. But what got away?

ROSS. What could?

BEATY. Put a guard over the grave.

ROSS. Why?

BEATY. See what comes out of it!

ROSS. What?

BEATY *pushes him in the chest and walks by him.*

BEATY. They will look like animals. Tiny, furry, white mice. But very tiny, tiny, tiny, as almonds.

Slipping away. In the leaves. Out of the wood. Down the hill. Onto the road. To the sea. Along the dunes. In holes along river banks. And into towns. In walls. Cells. Plastered up chimneys. In rotting wood in the roofs.

And breeding. Little nests of chewed up paper!

They stare at each other.

His words.

ROSS. I'll burn the hillside. Will that make you happier?

BEATY. No no. No no.

He smiles and puts a hand on ROSS's *shoulder.*

ROSS. The Ambassador from Chad will be here any moment. His car passed the perimeter five minutes ago.

BEATY. Good good.

ROSS. I'll welcome him? Or you –

BEATY. No, you.

ROSS *hesitates.*

Good.

ROSS *goes off, passing* JENNY GAZE *as she comes on. She wears evening dress.*

GAZE. Go out and meet the Ambassador.

BEATY. Let him come to me. Tonight I'll be the Pope.

GAZE. You neglect things. You sulk.

This man tonight is an Ambassador from the Third World. From a country that has had its revolutionary war. Wake up! We need all the friends we can get.

BEATY. Don't worry. I am briefed. Who is on the side of history, who is not – ha!

BEATY *turns away.* ROSS *comes on with the* AMBASSADOR, *who wears a Mao-like uniform. He is played by the* FEAST *actor, looking exactly like* FEAST.

AMBASSADOR. The Russians put States they help with aid into three categories. We have achieved category 'B'.

ROSS. Which is?

AMBASSADOR. How shall I put it? Railway rolling stock from the nineteen-fifties, but a first-class cossack dancing company.

ROSS *and* GAZE *laugh politely. They all look at* BEATY, *whose back is still turned.*

ROSS. Ambassador, the Prime Minister.

The AMBASSADOR *holds out a hand.*

AMBASSADOR. Comrade –

BEATY *turns. A silence.*

GAZE. Jack?

A silence.

BEATY. Who did this?

AMBASSADOR. I am delighted to meet you.

BEATY. Who?

ROSS. Beaty, what's the matter?

BEATY *crouches.*

Beaty, what's the matter?

AMBASSADOR. Is –

ROSS. The Prime Minister is unwell.

AMBASSADOR (*smiling*). I am sorry to hear it. Leadership demands a heavy price, in human terms. Perhaps statesmanship is a wholly unnatural condition?

BEATY, *backing away*.

BEATY. Un –

AMBASSADOR. I have negotiated in the Kremlin! Believe me I know, in the midst of life we are in death –

He looks from one to the other, smiling.

BEATY (*low, to* GAZE). He's not black.

GAZE. You indulge yourself.

BEATY. He's not, he's not.

AMBASSADOR. ?

GAZE (*to the* AMBASSADOR). Mr Beaty has had fits from childhood. They pass. He insists his official programme is arranged and kept to the letter.

Perhaps we should go out on the lawn? It's a fine night –

BEATY. Tear his face off! Tear it off or I'll tear off mine –

AMBASSADOR (*to* ROSS). Perhaps a ruler. Between his teeth.

BEATY. Oh! A pun, old chum. Ruler – of a nation – me – in my own mouth? You want me to swallow myself?

A silence.

AMBASSADOR (*to* ROSS). I meant St Paul, too, was an epileptic.

ROSS. Yes, of course –

AMBASSADOR. Indeed, to us in the Third World, the victims of Christian missionaries over the centuries, the Pauline faith appears as an ideology conceived in a hallucinatory fit.

ROSS. Yes?

BEATY. So why aren't you black? Why do you stand there with a white face?

A silence.

Well?

ROSS (*gutturally to* BEATY). For godsake, the man's a black African.

BEATY. Then who plastered a white mask on him! (*To the*

AMBASSADOR.) Please, understand. You are either a trick. A ghost. Or madness –

AMBASSADOR (*angrily*). None of those things, Comrade Prime Minister.

I am simply a man from a poor country few have heard of and none care for. I had thought Britain had come to see herself in a similar light. Desperate light? A lonely little island, in a dark and dangerous continent?

BEATY. Whatever you are, I want to kill you.

AMBASSADOR. Huh! Africa has had many of you. Sane madmen. Huh! Now sick Europe is in for its quota.

He points at ROSS.

You!

I want safe guarantees for me and my embassy staff, back to Chad.

ROSS. Of course –

AMBASSADOR. The withdrawal will be complete in forty-eight hours.

ROSS. Yes.

AMBASSADOR (*to* BEATY). Prime Minister.

BEATY. Bernard?

ROSS *and* GAZE *stare at each other.*

AMBASSADOR. What was it your poet William Blake, meant by the saying – 'The cut worm forgives the plough'?

BEATY. Depends. Are you the worm, am I the plough? Or are you the plough and I – the worm?

AMBASSADOR. You, ask me?

BEATY (*chanting*). Get him out get him out get him out –

ROSS. One diplomatic channel –

AMBASSADOR. The Cuban Embassy.

ROSS. Telex?

BEATY. Out! Out! Out! Out!

GAZE *and the* AMBASSADOR *going off.*

ROSS. I will telephone ahead for a motorcycle escort.

AMBASSADOR. Appreciated.

They've gone.

BEATY (*aside*). Nothing wrong.

Actually, if people around me would only concentrate they would see that things, really, are very well.

I am so desperate. Lines go out of my hands for miles, into factories, streets, kitchens, bedrooms. Well – into police stations.

I flap my hands! Make my hands light! Feathers! Light, of no consequence, who doesn't smile at a bird, fluttering, over water, brilliant, blazing, in a moment of no – meaning, power –

No.

Suddenly I understood why dictators have themselves carved in stone, in every corner of a country. Utterly fixed.

He clamps his hands on his knees.

It's because they're terrified to move their hands.

GAZE *and* ROSS *come on.*

ROSS. If you dare to think you're indispensable, if you dare to think that –

BEATY. The history of revolutions is that secret policemen come and go, but what has to be done gets done.

GAZE. Then do it you bastard.

BEATY. I am. Look. I don't even move my hands.

I have subverted – the word? Eaten up – your police force, Ross. Unknown to you I have installed my own command structure. It has taken me many hours, many days, much concentration. But now – you can flap. Ross.

Ha! What are you? A pigeon, standing on my head, shitting down my back?

ROSS *and* BEATY *stare at each other.* GAZE *begins to turn away.*

Scene Fourteen

California, by a swimming pool. MURGATROYD *lies in the sun in large floral swimming trunks. Three women* CIA AGENTS, *one in a jump suit, two in bikinis, sit and lie by the pool. Each wears dark glasses and has a two-way radio to hand.*

MURGATROYD *has a trolley of exotic drinks beside him.*

ROSS *is walking towards him. He stops.*

MURGATROYD. Hello, Ross.

ROSS. Dennis.

MURGATROYD. Welcome to California.

Nothing from ROSS.

I heard you had fallen from favour. The CIA brief me. Sweet
boys and girls. They maintain the fiction I am a king over the
water.

ROSS. Yes.

A silence.

MURGATROYD. So. You turn up by my pool. What do you
want? Go on a phone-in? No, you're a more ambitious political
exile from Red Britannia. Nothing less than the Johnny Carson
Show for you.

He drinks. A radio crackles, one of the AGENTS *lifts the radio
and speaks into it. She catches* ROSS's *eye and smiles.*

Don't look at them! They're CIA agents. What did you think
they were, my whores?

(*He scoffs.*) Something funny's happened to sex in America. Sex
in America isn't about sex at all.

He drinks. ROSS *looking away.*

ROSS. Your wife and your daughters.

MURGATROYD, *still, looks at his drink. A silence. Then he
drains it. He holds the glass out. An* AGENT *comes and fills it.*

MURGATROYD. What – ?

ROSS. They were in a police car. A mob set about it. The car
overturned and was burned.

A silence.

MURGATROYD. Both my girls?

ROSS. Yes.

MURGATROYD. What – were they doing in a police car?

ROSS. Arrested.

A silence.

MURGATROYD. For what?

ROSS *shrugs.*

ROSS. When you start a regiment of Praetorian Guards, Special
Troops, any kind of Secret Police – they all clock on at nine in
the morning. And will find something to do in the working day.
And, in the end, run a country, whatever its hallowed
traditions. I know. I was their chief.

MURGATROYD. So.

He nods.

It's all true. England is a killing ground.

Just like that.

Ha! Hearts of English oak? The valves torn, filled with blood.

ROSS. We can sit here and be maudlin about it. Or we can –

MURGATROYD. We can what?

ROSS. Restore freedom and democracy to the British Isles.

MURGATROYD. Right. OK. Will do. You and me –

He slams his drink down on the trolley. It splashes.

Mr No-name Ross. You're here because Beaty took your police
force away. For his own private use, no?

And you sail to America and go on TV to cry 'Freedom' and
'Democracy'.

Go and wash your mouth out.

ROSS. Like you, with booze?

MURGATROYD. Yes, I am drinking myself to death.

(*Slurring.*) Scientifically.

(*Cheerfully.*) It's going rather well. I'm already getting heads out
of the wall on bad nights. Stalin, Dzerzhinski. Beria. Mine. My
– children's.

He lifts his drink to the sun.

Booze in the California sun.

Light comes millions of miles to what? Splinter in alcohol into
my eye.

And, in a few hours, when the planet turns – to hit the wet
roofs of English towns.

Indifferent. Cold. Light.

ROSS. You disgust me.

MURGATROYD. Don't – that I can disgust you may give me

hope. Dangerous, hope, for bastards like us. If anything's to be done –

A gesture.

'The people' will have to do it. And bleed, bleed.

The despised masses of all the rhetoric, eh?

That human wall we climbed up. Crampons in breasts, faces – and fell from.

Best we don't claw our way back. A kindness. You go and – disappear on the right-wing lecture circuit. Brutal middle-aged American women and college football players – they'll love you. I'll lie down here. Bottom of my bottle.

So let me alone. All of you. (*He waves at the* CIA AGENTS. *They go off.*)

ROSS (*aside*). Six months later I went into a Los Angeles clinic. An inoperable tumour. A week before I died, they gave me the news – Henry Murgatroyd had been found, face down in his pool.

ROSS *goes off.* MURGATROYD *takes a bottle of vodka. He unscrews the cap and throws it away.*

MURGATROYD. Self-destruction. Oh, the luxury of. By my pool of tears. Ha!

He drinks. The vodka runs down his shirt.

Over the sun. I –

BEATY *walks on the water of the pool.*

Walking on the water, Jack? Bloody typical. Do anything now, can you not? God, what gave you the right, the holier-than-thou right, to take everything in your hands, out-manoeuvre and out-do us all?

Don't go, Jack. Invite me back. Give me something to do. I'm a political animal, I can't live without it, the old cut and thrust, the mind-moil, the infighting, public life –

BEATY *walking on.*

You bastard. We were all friends, mucking in. Why did you have to go and spoil it for us all? We ought to have cut you down. Cut you –

He raises the vodka bottle and lunges at BEATY. *He steps into the pool and begins to fall.*

A blackout.

Scene Fifteen

An underground car-park. Carnations. ROSE, CYGNA and JOAN. JOAN, crouched, making a low chant.

JOAN. A spray-can a spray-can –

  JOAN *laughs.*

CYGNA. She'll come with police. Dogs and gas.

ROSE. She said there'd be no guards, there are no guards.

CYGNA. Why believe her?

ROSE. She's a woman.

JOAN. A slogan on a wall, a letter to *The Times.* Swing the duplicator's arm. A pamphlet, a pamphlet –

CYGNA. We must have nothing to do with her.

ROSE. Maybe these people are more tired than we know. And more frightened. Maybe they wither inside, become dry, a shell – which can be cracked, just by a touch.

CYGNA. Wishful thinking, sister.

JOAN. A heckle from the crowd, a stone thrown, a riot – an agitation, a boycott and a strike –

ROSE. I heard her.

JOAN. Millions who say 'No', millions who say 'No' –

ROSE. Come on.

  They withdraw into the shadows. GAZE comes on, her arms full of flowers. She has not seen the three women.

GAZE. I'll put the flowers down.

  A silence.

  I'll put the flowers down.

  She does so. She has a large torch.

  Are you there?

  A silence.

  I'm in good faith. You must help.

  ROSE, *from the shadows.*

ROSE. What do you want, bitch?

  GAZE *whirls round.*

JOAN. One more conspiracy, one more assassination?

CYGNA. She wants us to kill her lover's policeman – and put in hers.

CYGNA *laughs*.

JOAN. Then someone will take power from her. A distant cousin, a lover she doesn't even remember.

GAZE. You've got to help me.

We've been driven into a hole, don't you see? Of having to rule by personal power. No leadership can stand that and be rational, be – humane. And not become distorted and cruel and –

A silence.

It is a matter of cruelty, you see. He can't govern, the cruelty's too much – there'll be disorder and resistance, reaction, we'll lose all we've gained –

A silence.

But we can put it all to rights. Curb powers. Hold shop floor elections.

CYGNA *laughs*.

Talk to community leaders –

The three women laugh.

Learn from past mistakes! Dismantle! Reform! Please –

They stop laughing.

There's a cruelty to yourself, too, you see. To yourself.

ROSE. You were right. We must have nothing to do with her.

ROSE, CYGNA *and* JOAN, *going*.

GAZE. It must be done.

CYGNA. What police state has ever destroyed itself? Said peace and given up?

ROSE. You were socialists and dreamt up tyranny. More dangerous than atomic waste. Better you be buried in glass. Deep. And pray the glass never cracks for twenty thousand years.

GAZE *weeps*.

CYGNA. The bitch weeps.

JOAN. Too late to wake up, Jenny.

ROSE, CYGNA *and* JOAN *have gone*.

GAZE *switches on the torch*.

GAZE. Where are you?

She flicks the beam about the walls.

Nothing. Underground, with flowers. Ha!

She kneels, spreading the flowers.

In a hole? A wide space? Room? A bunker? A field? A wood?
The moon an electric bulb, a bulb the moon.— sh. Sh, woman.
What does it matter to you, my love? Me, my love. Let me talk
to you, love. And you tell me little jokes and stories about who
killed who. What have you done to yourself? I can't feel you,
come down here, with me. In a room, in the grass, in a field, in
a wood, in a cupboard, in a hole.

A light change to moonlight through moving branches.
Night sounds.

Scene Sixteen

Woodland. Night. JENNY GAZE *is scrabbling at the earth.*
JACK BEATY *comes on with a two-way radio.*

BEATY. Where?

The radio crackles.

In the trees, where?

He sees GAZE.

Oh God.

He watches for a moment. Then he speaks into the radio.

All the cameras — all that spying, lying junk. Smash it.

The radio is silent.

You hear me? Not one of you look.

At her, like this.

He lets the radio hang from his wrist.

What are you doing up here, Jenny? Don't you know men —
watch you everywhere in this wood?

She continues to scrabble in the earth.

Stop that! He's not buried here anymore. I had his body, him, it —

A gesture.

You always hated Bernard when he was alive.

She stops.

What have you taken?

GAZE. What's done is done.

BEATY. I can call a doctor, if you say.

GAZE *clutches her stomach.*

GAZE. Oh! Oh! Oh! Oh!

She stops, breathing heavily.

BEATY. Please, let me call them —

GAZE. Don't — be — sentimental.

BEATY. You're right. Good. I'll help you kill yourself. That way we'll be a modern couple to the end.

GAZE (*scoffs*). You'll have to leave me. I've got to fall asleep. The pills will — damage me, if I don't fall asleep.

BEATY. Oh Jenny, eat something — grass — be sick —

GAZE. You were always like a dog, frightened 'cos I'm strong.

BEATY (*low*). I loved you.

GAZE. You did not.

BEATY. How can you say that?

GAZE. You never fought me. Lovers must fight! If they don't, their bed's a nightmare, spooks and graves.

BEATY. Ah well, there was time. But —

GAZE. No, no, no, no you don't. Sentimental lover, bastard man. Tyrants make the countries they rule one vast panorama of their private lives. Well, look about you —

She laughs.

BEATY. Jenny —

GAZE. I must go to bed now. To bed, to bed, to bed, to bed.

She curls up and is still. BEATY waits, then stands and walks away. He stops. He speaks, low, into the radio.

BEATY. This area. No one comes near. No one sees.

Scene Seventeen

A bunker beneath Whitehall.

Above, in two blows, the clamour of riot and the smashing of steel doors.

BEATY, *alone.*

BEATY. I believed in so much. I wanted so much.

The clamour. He laughs.

What is my experience in Government? That authority is not loved. But, you want to make history, then be prepared to be a part of history. Even if that's a corpse in a ditch.

That is my contribution, my decisive contribution. A skeleton along the road, the shining road, the way forward.

He grips his fist.

To the future – the garden – the –

The clamour again. The ghosts of FEAST, GAZE, DUNN, MURGATROYD *and* ROSS *appear in the shadows. He does not look at them.*

But what do you expect? Someone must take it up. Authority, the banner, the will. You want universal justice, the common good? Well, the unjust, you know, aren't going to say 'Fine. Great. Here's our money and our houses and our banks, oilfields, all our revenues and power and very lives.' Oh no. You're going to have blood on your hands. You're going to have your dead. Eh, comrades?

People find it hard to believe in ideals, you see. Very hard. They'd rather believe in human nature – and that it's bad. Despite all the evidence, all the evidence to the contrary.

That we're good. And on a long high road. Ha! I don't believe in the conspiracy theory of history. I should know – I am a great conspirator.

So don't look for conscience, comrades. There is virtue in me. I did not corrupt it.

The ghosts begin to fade.

Take what analysis you fancy, off the shelf of the ideological supermarket. A Socialist Government that foundered on the usual rocks. A command economy. Food prices held down artificially. With that, corruption. Black marketeering. And the

people, sullen, angry, self-destructive. And government –
blocked. In the mind, in the mind.

Gripping his fist.

Block-age. A blocked age. Rage, blocked.

But then! Every single hope of mankind is a bloody business, eh
comrades? Eh?

The ghosts begin to leave.

So what does it matter, what does it matter? If good comes of
it, the dead are forgotten. A century on and all will be well. All
manner of things.

The figure of STALIN walks through the shadows.

*A blackout as the alarm goes off. ROSE, CYGNA and JOAN,
in the dark. They have torches.*

ROSE. Switch that alarm off! Someone switch it off!

CYGNA. Must be on another circuit.

ROSE. Get it off –

The alarm stops.

Going right through me.

JOAN. The smell down here. Something burnt.

ROSE *coughs.*

CYGNA. Must be something still smouldering – ow!

JOAN. What?

CYGNA. S'all right, firebucket. (*She throws sand about.*) It's hot,
it's hot. Hot.

JOAN. All this metal.

ROSE, *coughing.*

ROSE. It's electronics. Smashed up – careful, there may be
something still live –

CYGNA's *torch flicks over a dummy of a withered corpse in
BEATY's chair.*

CYGNA. Eh! It's him, it's him! He's all – burnt.

They burst into laughter.

It's the War Room. We've gone and blundered into the War
Room.

They hold each other, laughing. Then a silence.

JOAN. Maybe he smashed it all up down here. All his telephones. Maybe he wanted people to pull it all to bits.

ROSE. What's it matter?

She gestures at the stage with her torch. She switches it out.

It's just underground. Let's get back up, and breathe.

CYGNA. I know. In the light. And celebrate and have a holiday – and swim, and talk, and think –

CYGNA *and* JOAN *switch their torches out. A blackout and –*

Epilogue

*In the darkness, the crash of waves on a beach. Lights up. JENNY
GAZE and JACK BEATY are walking along a beach, well
wrapped up. BEATY has a lame leg and walks with a stick.*

BEATY. How – are you listening?

> *They stop.*

> How could a hit over the head, make a leg go like this?

GAZE. Well, you've talked about it.

> *She turns away.*

BEATY. You don't think, when someone gets hit – 'bout injury.

GAZE. No.

> *A silence.*

BEATY. All right! All right!

GAZE. I think we should just have this holiday, don't you? Since
the Ward had a whip round to send us on it.

BEATY. Oh yes we are local heroes of a punch-up with the local
fascists. Ha! First day it's not rained. Out of season two weeks
the back end of Christmas. Thank you, comrades.

GAZE. Don't – let's – moan.

BEATY. No.

GAZE. Cold comfort, love.

BEATY. I s'pose so.

> I dreamt something, after the punch-up. When I was out.
> Funny, I feel it's the dream that's done my leg in, not the fight.

GAZE. Dream of what?

BEATY. Peace, funnily enough.

GAZE. I dreamt that, in a way.

BEATY. After a nightmare.

GAZE. Funny how we can't actually describe peace.

BEATY. You can bugger your leg up for it though.

GAZE. Yup.

> *She picks up a stone.*

BEATY. But then, peace is not a personal matter, is it?

GAZE. No.

> *She is about to throw the stone. A blackout just before it leaves
> her hand.*

THE GENIUS

To Jane

The Genius was first performed at the Royal Court Theatre, London, on 8 September 1983, with the following cast:

LEO LEHRER, *a professor of mathematics*	Trevor Eye
GILLY BROWN, *a student of mathematics*	Joanne Whalley
RICHARD WEIGHT, *a university vice-chancellor*	Clive Swift
GRAHAM HAY, *a university bursar*	Hugh Fraser
VIRGINIA HAY, *a statistician married to Graham*	Anna Nygh
ANDREA LONG, *a student*	Alyson Spiro
TOM DICKS, *a student*	Paul McGann
CLIFF JONES, *a cycling lecturer*	Alan David
A SKELETON *playing the violin*	Sue Latimer

Directed by Danny Boyle
Designed by Peter Hartwell
Lighting by Gareth Jones
Sound by Patrick Bridgeman

ACT ONE
Scene One: The Prize-winner
Scene Two: Equations in the snow
Scene Three: Theories in a wood
Scene Four: Crisis in a garden

ACT TWO
Scene One: An accident
Scene Two: State moves
Scene Three: Treacheries
Scene Four: Embassy
Scene Five: Peace moves

ACT ONE

Scene One: The Prize-winner

A blackout.
A low electrical hum. The hum rises slowly to a thunderous noise.
The noise rises in pitch to —
A second of silence.
Then with a loud, sharp explosion a blue flash crosses the stage in mid-air, giving the audience this retinal image —

After the flash, in the blackout, the sound of wind and rain. The lights come up slowly.

Campus grass.

A rainy, windy, grey early autumn afternoon.

A small, pink umbrella, turned inside out, is blown onto the stage.

LEO LEHRER *walks on. He is thirty-six. He holds the lapels of a short jacket to his throat.*

LEO. Exile. To an English university in the Midlands. Jesus, look at it. The edge of the Holy American Empire. Concrete in the rain.

GILLY BROWN *runs on for the umbrella. She is eighteen. She carries a large, old brown suitcase. She drops the suitcase and runs to the umbrella, which she picks up.*

GILLY. Do you know where E-Block is?

Nothing from LEO. *She tries to put the umbrella to rights.*

My Mum's. She's had it twenty years. First time her daughter leaves home, what does she do, warn me about the wicked world? No, she gives me her pink umbrella. I'll have to tell her on the phone tonight it's bust. She'll cry, I know. The waterworks. Do you know where E-Block is?

LEO *stares at her.*

Well thank you. Thank you very much.

GILLY *picks up the case and goes off.*

LEO. Exile.

He looks about him.

Late twentieth century style. The Romans used to send their bad boys – lovers of the Emperor's wife, dirty poets – off to little islands. Maybe they did the same for their scientists.

He laughs.

A Roman engineer gets ahead. Invents the steam engine, two thousand years too early. The emperor has him dragged before him, in chains. 'OK Albertus Einsteinus,' says the emperor. 'Steam engines do the work, whadda the slaves do? You wanna wreck the empire's economy? You wanna get us all killed? So long, smart guy, enemy of the state. Go sit in a puddle and count your abacus in Lowland Britain.'

He puffs his cheeks and blows out.

Jesus, am I jet-lagged.

RICHARD WEIGHT, *aged sixty-two, the* VICE-CHANCELLOR *comes on with* GRAHAM HAY, *aged forty-five, the* BURSAR. *The* VICE-CHANCELLOR'*s hat is blown across the stage.*

VC. My hat!

The VICE-CHANCELLOR *and* GRAHAM *laugh.* LEO *runs at the hat and catches it with a forward roll, skilfully coming to his feet again.*

GRAHAM. It's Leo Lehrer.

VC. Really?

The VICE-CHANCELLOR *fumbles glasses suspended round his neck from beneath his coat and peers at* LEO.

So that is the radical and mathematical young lion. Doesn't look much. I'd better do the honours.

GRAHAM. I'll introduce you.

GRAHAM *goes towards* LEO, *hand outstretched.*

Leo. You got to us early.

LEO. Hello Graham.

GRAHAM. We weren't expecting you 'til next week.

LEO. I got itchy. Got on a flight.

GRAHAM. This is a good chance. Leo, this is Dr Richard Weight, the Vice-Chancellor of the university. Vice-chancellor, Dr Leo Lehrer.

VC. Who has my hat at first slip.

LEO. What?

GRAHAM. Cricket.

The VICE-CHANCELLOR *and* LEO *shake hands,* LEO *limply.*

VC. I followed all the to-and-fro-ing. Getting you out of the Massachusetts Institute of Technology was like staging a robbery of Fort Knox.

His joke falls flat. Polite smiles. LEO *wants to withdraw the hand, the* VICE-CHANCELLOR *does not.*

Forgive me if I be the cat that's licked the cream. But vice-chancellors the length of the land will tear out their eyes when they know we have a Nobel Prize-winner.

LEO *turns away.*

LEO. A third. A third of a Nobel Prize. And we were lucky.

VC. Ah, the collective 'we'. Never the personal 'I'. We measure out our lives in democratic verbal twitches. Even in academic life there are trots. But we chairpersons stumble on, squelching in our consensus wellies.

LEO (*to* GRAHAM). What are wellies? What are trots?

GRAHAM. Rubbers and trotskyists.

LEO. My God.

VC. I must tread the mud of committee language, the dreary art of saying nothing so that only the right people know what you mean. So – you lighten our darkness, Dr Lehrer! The trots will go mad to hear it and I get blood in my administrative wellies – but, in the end, the glory of a university is the exceptional, individual brain. The individual human being.

LEO. Shucks.

GRAHAM *shakes his head at* LEO.

VC. There will be a more formal do to welcome you. But since we've bumped into each other let me say I hope you take part in the general hurly-burly of campus life. Birmingham is a car drive away, but that city is hardly the Florence of the English Midlands. So we amuse ourselves. I have a little thing in mind. A vice-chancellor is a gargoyle set in the concrete architecture, but underneath I am an Arts Man. Shakespeare was my field. Did an image count. On average Shakespeare has 24.7 images every hundred lines, twice that of any of his rivals. Not many know that. Anyway – here is my little thing. Why don't we give a public talk together? We'd take a general theme – 'The nature of creativity', nothing too taxing. Do it in the Arts Centre. That's –

He points.

The monstrosity with the pop art tower. They're always desperate for something to put on over there. I even thought of a title – 'The marriage of Art and Science?'

A silence.

LEO. Mr Vice-Chancellor.

VC. Dick –

LEO. Dick.

He pauses.

All I want from you is computer time. That's what got me here. Computer T – I – M – E. Written in my contract. OK celebrate, you landed a Nobel Prize-winner. Go print a picture of my arse on top the university note paper. You want anything more – call my lawyer in New York.

A silence.

VC. Tea-time. We are on our way to the Senate House. Join us?
The first muffin of autumn?

LEO. Go fuck yourself.

GRAHAM (*low*). Leo, calm down!

VC. Well. See a lot of you, no doubt. When you're settled in.

Nothing from LEO.

Exit pursued by an American bear. My hat?

LEO *gives the* VICE-CHANCELLOR *the hat*.

But think over our public talk. 'The marriage of Art and
Science.'

The VICE-CHANCELLOR *nods and smiles and walks away
with* GRAHAM, *who glances at* LEO *angrily*.

LEO. Vice-Chancellor!

The VICE-CHANCELLOR *and* GRAHAM *stop*.

They got divorced. When Galileo sold out to the Inquisition in
1633. Three hundred and fifty years ago. Didn't you notice?

The VICE-CHANCELLOR, *not smiling, turns away again*.

VC. The radical and mathematical young lion is a prickly little
shit.

GRAHAM. I'll pour oil.

VC. You had better. You twisted all our arms to get him. Hope
he's worth it.

He goes off. GRAHAM *hesitates then goes to* LEO.

GRAHAM. What are you trying to do? You may be a film star of
the academic world but there's no need to come on like Jane
Fonda on a Vietcong tank.

LEO *is looking away*.

Leo?

LEO. Who are they, over there. Students?

GRAHAM *looks*.

GRAHAM. Oh. No. Townies.

LEO *doesn't understand*.

Kids from the city. They come up and bum drinks in the
student bars. There are thefts and there are fights. But – this is
meant to be a people's university.

LEO. Some o' Britain's legendary unemployed, eh?

GRAHAM (*calling out*). Er – on the path, please.

A silence.

The path.

A VOICE, off.

VOICE. Fuck off!

GRAHAM *looks away with a sigh.*

LEO. Hey Graham, we are on the grass.

GRAHAM. But we are members of staff.

LEO. Got you.

GRAHAM. Leo, this may not be the time or place. But when you want to say something serious in England it never is the time or place.

He hesitates. LEO *turns and looks at him.*

LEO. OK, OK, Graham, burst all over me.

GRAHAM. I feel I got to know you while we were negotiating your famous contract. And you well know that is a hell of a contract – copper-bottom protection for a programme of pure research. Fine. Fine. We all pay lip service to pure research in a university, 'being for pure research' is like being for life and against death. But actually we loathe it, because we all know, in our tiny souls, that real mathematics, science, pure knowledge aspires to the condition of music. And a university is paid for – by a government that wants weapons, a car industry that wants the petrol-free engine. And who is going to fight a war or run a car on a bloody string quartet? It doesn't concern you and I don't want it to concern you, but I nearly went to the wall to get you here. Don't be fooled by the VC dribbling on about muffins: university officials are professional politicians, their apparent senility is a rhetorical ploy. The VC can talk about blood in his administrative wellies, mine are full of broken toes. If I go down you will need that fabulous New York lawyer.

LEO, *a shrug, hands held out.*

All right all right! I can handle the politics. I know who is carrying knives in the university Senate against your professorship, I will strangle their togas around their old-school ties. You will never know the murder that was done on your behalf. That's my life! I go to many meetings, to me an agenda glitters with razor blades. I look at my fingers making notes on a report and know they are podgy. Nervous over-eating is a bureaucrat's disease. But I persist. You see, though I am embarrassed to say it, I believe in the university. Learning. Free thought. Not a factory for careers but a place for true, human experiment. So! I could do with a little – grace, Leo. Not for me personally, but for some grist to throw into the wheels within wheels. A little human grace? After all, we are the angels. Our cause is purity.

LEO. Purity.

He laughs.

You got any idea what you been stripping your stomach wall for, Graham? You got any idea what my research is?

GRAHAM. Unified Field Theory?

LEO. Yeah? And what is that?

GRAHAM. You want me to blind myself with your science? I'm just another arts graduate, with a PhD on the more boring bits in William Blake. It's up to you to know what you're doing. Presumably you do know what you're doing?

LEO. Yes. Or no. Or – too much.

He laughs.

No calculation is pure, Graham, no calculation is pure. Mathematics, the mother of machines and bombs?

GRAHAM. Leo –

He hesitates.

Around MIT, when I was over haggling for you, there was a rumour. Hardly anything – just the rattle of ice in the dry martinis. But it was hinted the reason MIT were willing to let you go –

He hesitates again.

LEO (*low*). Oh Jesus.

GRAHAM. Vague, it was very vague, but it said you soft pedalled on something. A project, financed by the Pentagon? And that, by letting you come to us, you were being punished.

LEO (*low*). Jesus.

GRAHAM. Is there anything, Leo?

He pauses.

That I should hear?

LEO. What do you want to hear? OK you've been sold a dud,

'old chap'. My lack of human grace is brought on by a dose of the post-Einstein clap. Real guilt and dread. I had the new E equals MC squared but flushed it down the john. I feared it would burn the world. But Spiderman crashed in through the men's room window, dived down the pan and rescued the magic maths for the Pentagon. That kind of thing happens all the time at the Massachusetts Institute of Technology.

GRAHAM. Why is the American sense of irony like a kick in the head?

LEO. No irony. I am kicking you in the head.

GRAHAM. The rumour was true? You refused on some work?

A silence.

Can you tell me what it was?

LEO (*shouts*). How the hell could you understand it if I did?

A silence.

Sorry. I'm sorry.

He laughs.

Wrote about little lambs, didn't he, William Blake? How the hell can a poem about a little lamb equip you to understand the mathematics of modern physics?

GRAHAM. It may, morally.

LEO. Bullshit.

GRAHAM. Yes.

A nervous laugh.

The great divorce.

During LEO's *speech* VIRGINIA HAY, *aged thirty-nine, comes on.*

LEO. Don't worry, Graham. I am intact. You'll get what you paid for. Your hick computer is going to wonder what has got it by the balls. I am still an all-American boy – give me ego and fame and money and get me laid. What do I do about a screw around here, by the way?

GRAHAM. Whatever you do, don't touch the students. You can bite off more than you can chew.

VIRGINIA *has seen them. She comes downstage.*

Oh, darling.

LEO. Hello.

GRAHAM. My wife, Virginia. Virginia –

VIRGINIA. Leo Lehrer. I've seen your photograph.

LEO. I hear we tread the same muddy pool.

VIRGINIA, *with a glance at* GRAHAM.

VIRGINIA. Yes, I was a mathematician. Before I gave birth to children. Statistics. Behavioural psychology.

LEO. Counting rats in mazes, ringing bells?

VIRGINIA. That kind of thing.

GRAHAM. Leo's dodged having tea with the VC.

VIRGINIA. A coward.

GRAHAM. But must come to supper.

VIRGINIA. Must.

GRAHAM. Really Leo, anywhen. Just drop round.

VIRGINIA. Ring the bell.

LEO. I'll do that.

GRAHAM. Um –

He looks up, raising his umbrella.

Rain again.

VIRGINIA *joins him under the umbrella. He puts an arm about her waist.*

Welcome.

LEO *nods, looking down.* GRAHAM *and* VIRGINIA *turn and walk away.*

He's stoned, he's stoned. I know he's stoned.

They go off. LEO *pulls his jacket up above his head, his arms held out by the tightened sleeves.* CLIFF JONES, *aged fifty, comes on, riding a bicycle. He wears cyclist's yellow bad-weather clothing, his head is bare. He sees* LEO.

CYCLIST. Bloody awful weather. But, on the other hand, we could all be dead. See you.

He cycles off. LEO *begins to spin slowly. At the back two students,* ANDREA LONG *and* TOM DICKS *come on. They carry leaflets.* TOM *has his beneath a coat.* GILLY *comes on, still carrying her suitcase and umbrella.*

GILLY (*to* ANDREA *and* TOM). Scuse me. Could you tell me where E two-six-eight is?

TOM. Student Residential Block E. Door two. Floor six. Room eight. Is – that hunk of concrete.

He points.

Not that hunk, not that hunk, but that hunk.

GILLY. Thanks. I've been wandering about.

ANDREA. First year.

GILLY. Yes –

ANDREA. You're soaked. Come and have coffee in the Union. Then we'll take you over to E-Block.

TOM, *looking at the spinning LEO.*

TOM. Who's that idiot?

ANDREA. Don't know. I'll do him. (*To* GILLY.) Don't go away.

ANDREA *goes quickly to* LEO.

TOM (*to* GILLY). You too.

He takes the leaflets from beneath his coat. It is a large sheaf and disordered. He hands GILLY *a selection.*

For a happy start to university life, get your left-wing literature down you.

GILLY. Oh. Thanks –

ANDREA (*to* LEO). Oy. You in there.

LEO *stops spinning. She holds out a leaflet. He does not take it.* END.

LEO. EN what?

ANDREA. Campaign for European Nuclear Disarmament.

A silence. Then LEO *sinks to his knees giggling. He speaks gutturally.*

LEO. Nuc – lear – Disarm – a – ment. Nuc – lear Disarm – a-ment.

ANDREA. CND? 'Ban the Bomb'?

TOM. Come on, Andrea!

ANDREA (*to* LEO). What's so funny?

LEO *gestures her toward him. He points. She looks where he is pointing then back at him.*

?

LEO. Spiderman!

He rolls over, foetus-crouched, laughing.

ANDREA. Get lost.

> GILLY, *holding the leaflets out to* TOM.

GILLY. I don't want anything to do with politics. I'm here to study mathematics.

> *A moment still –* GILLY *holding the leaflets out to* TOM, ANDREA *holding the leaflet out to the rolled up* LEO. *A blackout.*

Scene Two: Equations in the snow

Snow. Brilliant light. Gog Hill. Boxing Day. GILLY *wanders on. Like everyone else in this scene she is wrapped up against the cold. She wears mittens. She carries the pink umbrella, furled. She also carries a loose-leaf binder under her arm. She tramps downstage, preoccupied. She stops.*

GILLY. 'Fury said to a mouse
That he met in the house
Let us both go to law; I will prosecute you – '

> *She opens the loose-leaf binder and looks at it. Then snaps it shut. Then speaks the second verse, drawing mathematical symbols with the tip of the umbrella in the snow.*

'Come I'll take no denial;
We must have a trial;
For really this morning I've nothing to do.'

> *The* CYCLIST *comes on, puffing. He carries his bicycle over his shoulder.*

CYCLIST. Merry Christmas.

> GILLY *stares at him.*

Don't think I'm mad, climbing up a hill in the middle of a field with a bicycle on my back. My eight-year-old son is down the bottom. He bet me I couldn't ride my bike down Gog Hill on Boxing Day. So here I am. Didn't think it would bloody snow.

> GILLY *stares.*

Well. Here I go.

> *He runs with the bicycle across the stage, mounting it at the last*

moment. A silence, then a distant yell, that fades. GILLY *waits, then looks back at the snow. She writes with the umbrella again, the equations spreading across the stage.*

GILLY. 'Said the mouse to the cur
Such a trial dear Sir,
With no judge and no jury would be wasting our breath.'

The VICE-CHANCELLOR *walks over the hill. He has a large, knobbly walking stick.*

VC (*humming*). Pom pom pom, pom-pom pom pom.

He sees GILLY.

Merry Christmas.

He waves his stick in the air to the tune.

Pom pom pom. Bach's 'Musical Offering'. The great theme, layer on layer. Balanced. Pom-pom pom pom.

GILLY *stares.*

You are?

GILLY. Gillian Brown.

The VICE-CHANCELLOR *is stranded.*

First year maths.

VC. Ah. Happy with work and play?

GILLY. Don't know –

VC. Boxing Day beer for me. Over Gog Hill to the pub, far beyond. Know what this little hill is?

GILLY. Yes.

He ignores that.

VC. A Norman keep. Wholly artificial. But before that, a Roman fort. See!

Stick pointing.

The Fosse Way, great Roman road – the jugular artery of Roman Britain, running through the fleshy Midlands to go 'blip' and dodge around this bump. No doubt the hill was here before they made the road. A Celtic site. Before that, a neolithic burial mound? Layer on layer! Balanced! And on top the snow, the cowpats and us.

GILLY *stares.*

On now. A pint of Greene King by lunchtime.

He waves the stick.

Work and play.

He goes off. GILLY *takes off a mitten and gets a ball-point pen from a pocket. She writes in the binder.*

GILLY. 'I'll be Judge, I'll be Jury
Said cunning old Fury:'

She looks up, thinking. Then –

'I'll try the whole cause and condemn you to death.'

ANDREA *half walks, half runs on. She is in the middle of a row with* TOM, *who runs on after her. He carries a half-drunk litre bottle of cheap red wine.*

TOM. But why? Why resign?

ANDREA. Because I'm tired, bored, sick and tired, tired, tired – of men shouting at me about the Vanguard Party.

TOM. What a deeply, deeply –

He shouts.

Stupid remark.

ANDREA. There, you shouted at me!

TOM. You can't resign. No one resigns, they just change sides. We're all locked in a room together. There's only one way out and that's called death.

ANDREA. Oh thank you, thank you. One more male thought to make me feel bad. (*To* GILLY.) Hello.

GILLY. Hello.

GILLY *continues to look at her binder.*

TOM. You've not got into Rad. Fem. anti-marxism. Not that.

ANDREA (*to* GILLY). What do you think?

GILLY. A lot. But not all the time.

TOM. Jesus Christ! If I were an ideological agent working for the CIA trying to invent a creed to fuck the Far Left, I think I'd dream up Rad. Fem. anti-marxism. Divide the socialist camp down the old sex war lines. Get at the reds in their beds. Andrea, infantile, bloody infantile –

ANDREA. Oh! Oh! Infantile. Trigger word. 'Cos Lenin said it, didn't he. 'Infantile disorders'. Only Lenin meant anarchists, you mean women. I do believe communism to be sharing, dignity, the hope of the world – but why does it look like a conspiracy of men? Very old men, on a balcony, with all the guns and all the police. Vanguard Party?

GILLY. Get off!

ANDREA. The English revolution in male mouths begins to sound to me – just like football. Something men shout about down the pub, getting into the class war and the Greene King. Big cocks and big ideas, killing people.

GILLY. Get off my sum!

ANDREA. What?

She looks.

Oh. What is it?

GILLY. Told you. A sum.

TOM. I mean –

He waves the bottle.

Universal education! Literacy!

ANDREA (*to* GILLY): Do I know you?

GILLY. I'm first year maths.

ANDREA. Yes?

GILLY. I met you first day of term. You gave me a leaflet. Don't you remember?

ANDREA. Sorry.

TOM, *turning, the bottle held high.*

TOM. The ghosts of Chartists, old socialists and reformers, haunt the concrete university. They gave their lives so we could read. And what is the most read magazine in the Students' Union? The *Beano*. Back in your graves, comrades.

He wanders backwards into GILLY's *figures.*

We are good, middle-class children, squandering two hundred years of socialist agitation –

GILLY. Get your feet off!

TOM. What?

ANDREA. You are trampling on her mathematics!

TOM. ?

He looks down.

Oh.

GILLY. Go away. You talk too much. Clack clack. That's all I hear from people like you. Clack clack. So go away.

TOM. There you have it! Authentic, pig-headed, ostrich in the shit heap, anti-intellectual apathy.

ANDREA. Ostrich with a pig's head?

TOM. I know, I know, the wine's run out, the metaphors are mixed and I need the pub.

He jumps clear.

ANDREA (*to* GILLY). He thinks International Capitalism is making him an alcoholic.

TOM. Right!

He cartwheels.

Ph! Come my mid-twenties, will I still do that? Andrea. Pub. Please.

He backs away.

A pint of Green Worker, then.

ANDREA *and* TOM *eye each other. Then he turns and runs off.*

ANDREA. Don't think too badly of us, Ms Workhead. Think, what if we're right, we left-loonies, and there is a 'Great It' running our lives? Down to you doing one and one are two in the snow.

GILLY. You're still talking.

ANDREA *nods, backing away.*

ANDREA. OK.

She smiles.

Just don't work too hard for the bastards.

ANDREA *turns and walks off quickly.*

GILLY. Work. Words. Clack.

She holds the binder between her knees and demonstrates with her hands.

There are no layers. Only one thing, passing through itself. You think you see different things – there, there and there. But – blink blink blink. It's just one thing you've seen, one force, one whole –

She is dead still, in mid-sentence.

Oh, I can do the work but I can't do the words. Clack clack!

She turns her hands over and stretches them above her head.

After six – no, it's weekend rates on Boxing Day – anyway, I'll ring my mother and tell her I've done a really good bit of work. And she'll have the waterworks, 'Why didn't you come home for Christmas, first time ever not, you're making Daddy ill.' 'I told you, Mum, I'm doing this work I – I – I've got to do this work.' 'No I'm not on drugs, no I'm not catching VD with a man, I'm doing a calculation! A sum! And you'd clash with it you see, Mum, your voice, you, the way you fill up the air, the look on your face, that funny little hair on your nose, it would all go out of my head because the sum is very beautiful and you – are – so – very – ugly. Mum.'

Her arms flop down, the binder slips from between her knees. For a moment she is still, then she brightens.

Oh well! Pick yourself up and dust yourself off.

She picks up the binder and her umbrella, opens the binder and wanders away.

Wish I had a new binder, this one's getting chewed up.

She goes off. The stage is empty for a moment, then LEO *and* VIRGINIA *come on. They walk slowly, relaxed, six feet between them, hands in their pockets.* LEO *spins once, looking around.*

LEO. Is Graham –

VIRGINIA *points into the distance.*

VIRGINIA. A dot upon the white. Talking to the vice-chancellor. A little university politics in the snow. Like a little dog 'Oh look. The VC is in that field, walking to the pub' and he's off, all waggy tail.

LEO. My flesh crawls when you bad mouth him.

VIRGINIA. Shall I tell him about us?

LEO *stops walking, she continues.*

LEO. OK.

She stops.

Tell him every time he looks the other way you screw his best friend.

VIRGINIA. OK.

They look at each other. Then they laugh.

We are not great and good lovers. It would be wonderful if we were, but we are not.

LEO. No way.

VIRGINIA. He's off to Paris next weekend after all. The UNICEF Conference – on the world shortage of school textbooks.

LEO. Why don't they just spend the money on the books?

VIRGINIA. Why protest? We can go to bed.

They look at each other.

It's still the school holidays. I'll send the children to his mother.

LEO. You are a ruthless woman. I look Graham in the eye in the Staff Club and think – don't you know your marriage is kind of damp? Like in bed with come from me and your wife?

VIRGINIA. Don't try to shock me. Leo. I've given birth to two children, I'm nearly forty and married to an Englishman who loves his mother. I can't be shocked. I am at a dangerous age. Either I live it or I don't.

Suddenly she is upset.

LEO. Hey Virginia –

VIRGINIA. No!

She tries to laugh.

I do keep on having baths. I'm terrified he'll smell us.

LEO. You Europeans begin to get to me. Can't you people have a good time without pain?

VIRGINIA. Pain in love is a great European tradition.

LEO. Learn the trick from the American way of life – don't give a shit. Once you don't give a shit you can be kind, gentle, whatever you want. Just like –

He clicks his fingers.

That. Don't give a shit.

VIRGINIA. All right. Let's make love in the snow.

A silence.

LEO. Why not? Babylon is my home town.

They hesitate. Then giggle. Then he goes to her and rumples up her skirt. She counters by pulling at his trouser belt.

Look, er –

VIRGINIA. Don't worry. I've decided to be a sucker for experience.

She pushes his trousers down.

LEO. Virginia, we going to do this?

He looks around.

Britain is a densely populated island.

VIRGINIA, *sitting down on the snow, pulling off her tights.*

VIRGINIA. What's the matter, Mr American Macho? Can't you live it?

Her tights catch on her boots. She tears them from her heels and throws them away. She sits back, looking at LEO.

LEO. Oh shit.

VIRGINIA. Shit you too, citizen of Babylon.

LEO. OK! OK.

He pushes his trousers down his legs. They catch on his shoes. He falls over in the snow.

Jesus Christ it is cold!

VIRGINIA. Come on.

She holds her arms out. He squirms in the snow, kicking his trousers off. He crawls to her. She turns him over and lies on him.

LEO. Hey. Wow. We getting into birch twigs later?

VIRGINIA *kisses him lightly.*

VIRGINIA. Leo – why –

A kiss.

Aren't you –

A kiss.

Using the computer?

LEO. All this and you want pillow talk too?

VIRGINIA. I was over there, Christmas Eve. They said there's been no work from you since you got here, at all.

A kiss.

Zero.

A kiss.

Zilch. What do you do all day, Leo? When you're not taking the jeans off some little student?

A finger on his lips.

You stare at the wall, don't you. Leo, your clothes smell of hash. Your eyes drift. You soften.

She caresses his hair.

You are rotting away.

LEO. It's like this.

He pauses.

I feel, I feel – like a snowball's been rammed up my arse –

He rolls over. They fight and laugh.

VIRGINIA. Leo –

LEO. Come on, let's go all the way, let's strip –

They roll pulling at each other's clothes.

VIRGINIA. You've got to start working.

LEO. I am, sex and science – a new equation of the flesh –

VIRGINIA. Calculate again, Californian –

She pushes snow up his shirt front.

LEO. Hey! Wow! Ow!

VIRGINIA. Madness, madness oh madness –

They have rolled to where GILLY *wrote in the snow. He sees the figures. He is dead still.* GRAHAM *walks on. He, too, is still.*

GRAHAM. Is it me? Something about me? Personal, something in me, you want to destroy?

VIRGINIA (*to herself*). It has happened, it has happened.

GRAHAM. Some mannerism of mine?

LEO. Who did this?

GRAHAM. Something private, something deep, that you hate?

LEO *stands.*

LEO. Who did this?

GRAHAM. That you want to tear out, dig out of me, my bowels and burn them?

VIRGINIA. Graham, very, very quietly, just – go away.

GRAHAM. What if I'd come up the hill with the VC? What? How could we go on, I –

LEO (*to* VIRGINIA). You do this? Some crazy practical joke? You sneak out in the snow and get me up here, and aim to ball me on it, give me a lift, a bad time, all the nightmares?

VIRGINIA. What are you talking about?

GRAHAM. I suppose we're going to be adult about this! Bloody, bloody adult!

LEO. That!

He runs up and down the equations, still with his trousers off.

VIRGINIA. What is it?

LEO. You don't know?

VIRGINIA. No.

With a finger she points through the figures.

GRAHAM. I'm spinning. It's my life. What about the children? What about me?

LEO. Only a fragment of it but it's right! It's right!

VIRGINIA. A fragment of what?

LEO. What I ran away from, there in the snow.

He scans the landscape, shouting.

Who are you? Come on! Show yourself!

VIRGINIA, *still at the figures.*

VIRGINIA. Amazing.

LEO *kicks into the snow, destroying the equations.*

LEO. It's on snow, on grass, on a hill.

VIRGINIA. Leo –

LEO. Water and ice. It goes. It'll mulch back down, mud and grass. Hey, but –

VIRGINIA. ?

GRAHAM. ?

LEO. Aerial photography!

VIRGINIA. ?

GRAHAM. ?

LEO. Something drawn on snow! That leaves an impression on grass? Like archaeology? See it, on the ground? We got to burn this, bonfires –

He scrabbles at the snow and earth.

Rake the ashes, dig it in, dig it in –

He stops, crouching, head down. He begins to shake.

Oh God, God.

GRAHAM. I wait for someone to make a remark to me. I don't expect an apology, an insult will do.

VIRGINIA. Shut up Graham, you're pathetic.

GRAHAM. Thank you, darling.

Near tears.

You're so kind, so kind.

He floods with anger.

(*To* LEO). You bastard!

LEO. Who cares?

GRAHAM. You say something to me?

VIRGINIA. Please, it is Christmas.

GRAHAM. I said, you say something to me?

LEO. Who cares? Join in 'old man'. Let's all screw ourselves into the surface of the planet. What's it matter, when the whole globe, ye olde spaceship earth, is going to burn?

He laughs. A gesture at the churned-up patch of snow.

We're all going to burn, shouting at each other about who fucks who.

GRAHAM. You two-bit ageing hippy. I trusted you and what do you do? Cock your leg up on everything, my trust, my marriage. I'm going to kick your teeth in.

LEO. Old fellow, I am in better shape than you –

GRAHAM *falls on* LEO, *who hits him in the stomach. They roll grunting.*

VIRGINIA. For Godsake stop it! You're intellectuals. The humanist tradition and look at you –

GILLY *runs on. She stops.*

GILLY. How many more of you?

They stop fighting and look at her.

Coming up, messing me up.

LEO. You –

GILLY. It's not fair. Lucky for you I've got it written down, in my binder.

She walks, then runs off.

LEO. Hey!

He tries to stand but GRAHAM *holds his leg.*

Virginia, get her!

GRAHAM *bites* LEO's *leg.*

You stupid bitch, get her!

GRAHAM *bites* LEO's *leg again.*

Ow!

He hits the back of GRAHAM's *neck.* GRAHAM *grunts and loosens, unconscious.*

VIRGINIA. You hit him in the head.

LEO *(shouting over the landscape, turning)*. Come back! There's more! There's more! Come back, I'll show you!

VIRGINIA. You hit him in the head! LEO. You know her? That little girl, that little fool, you know her?

A silence. They stare at each other.

Don't you understand? The ground has opened up under my feet.

VIRGINIA. You bastard. How can we be safe from people like you?

Still for a moment. Then a blackout.

Scene Three: Theories in a wood

A wood. Moonlight. LEO *and* GILLY.

LEO. Gillian.

GILLY. Hello.

A silence.

LEO. Had to bullshit my way into the university Senate House to find you.

GILLY. Oh? Why?

LEO. The files. You know they've got a file on every student over there, with a photograph?

GILLY. I got my 'photo done on Euston Station, one of those machines for passports. Behind a little curtain. You worry drunks are looking at your knees. I'm talking too much 'cos you're famous.

A silence. She takes the binder from beneath her coat.

LEO. Is that it?

GILLY. Maybe.

LEO. Can I look?

GILLY. Why don't you want me to show it to anyone? And why write me a letter, why not come round to E Block?

LEO. Have you shown it to anyone?

GILLY. And getting me out here. Daffodil wood. This place has got a bad reputation.

LEO. Have you shown the equations to anyone?

GILLY. No, actually.

LEO puffs his cheeks and blows out.

LEO. Where you from, Gillian?

GILLY. Watford.

LEO. What's Watford to go and warp the universe?

GILLY. A place.

LEO. You still want the City of Watford to turn with the planet? You still want there to be a planet?

GILLY. Don't know.

LEO. You don't know.

GILLY. I don't know what you're talking about –

A cycle bell rings. The CYCLIST rides on, the lights on his bicycle shining over the stage.

LEO. Get down.

GILLY. What?

LEO. Off the path.

The CYCLIST gliding past.

CYCLIST. Evening boys and girls in the bushes. Snow has

gone, soon be bluebells. Take precautions, don't get
pregnant.

He rings the bell and has gone.

LEO. Who is that guy? I see him in the staff club. He drinks eight
  pints of beer a night.

GILLY. Don't know.

LEO. Creepy.

*They are still squatting. He puts out a hand. She is still, then
she hands him the binder. He opens it, takes a flashlight from
his pocket and reads. He turns one page, he turns another.*

*A solo violin begins to play the theme and three part invention
from Bach's 'The Musical Offering'.*

*The stage darkens to a blackout. LEO and GILLY still squat,
LEO reading the binder by flashlight.*

*Towards the back of the stage a SKELETON glows faintly. It is
playing a violin.*

*The SKELETON becomes brighter, the music louder, rising to a
fearful pitch of distortion.*

The SKELETON lifts the bow, sharply. A second of silence.

An explosion as the

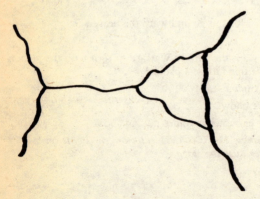

flashes across the stage.

The SKELETON disappears. LEO reads on.

Slowly the moonlit wood returns to the stage.

Then LEO *switches the torch out and closes the binder.*

A silence.

LEO. All right. Where did you steal it?

GILLY. What do you mean?

LEO. Off one of your teachers?

A silence.

GILLY. No!

LEO. Who then?

GILLY *shakes her head.*

Some smartarse graduate? What, he screw you? You pick this off the bedroom floor and walk out with it, to give him a lift?

GILLY. Why do you think a man had to write it?

LEO. A woman then –

GILLY. Why not? A woman, a beautiful woman, with beautiful thoughts –

LEO. You saying this maths spewed out of some kind of lesbian scene?

GILLY. You've got a sick mind.

LEO. Whoever did this –

He slaps the binder.

Has got the sick mind.

GILLY. It's brilliant!

LEO. Who wrote it, Gilly? Give me her, give me his name.

GILLY. Me! Me! I did, said Gillian, with my little – I did.

Both still for a moment. Then LEO *flips open the binder, takes out a pen and switches on the torch. He scribbles.* GILLY *looks away, upset. He finishes then pushes the pen and binder at her. He tosses her the torch, contemptuously.*

LEO. Answer that.

GILLY. A test?

LEO. Yup.

GILLY. Get lost.

GILLY glares at him but then puts the binder on the ground, angrily. She holds the torch and looks at what he wrote, sucking the top of the pen. Then she writes fast, at length. She stops abruptly, looking at it, then pushes the binder, pen and torch into his lap. He looks at it.

LEO. Jesus fucking Christ.

GILLY. It's not like being St Joan and hearing voices.

She laughs.

Angel coming down and telling me what to write. Well, not exactly!

She thinks, then –

It's more like knowing a piece of music by heart, without ever having heard it before, or read the notes. You just sit down at the piano, play and the air remembers the music, and there it goes, out of the window.

She laughs.

No, music you can play wrong, wrong key, it jars. Music's got something inside it that says it's right or wrong. But maths hasn't, has it? It's the funniest thing about it. You can't prove logically that maths is logical!

LEO. Godel's inconsistency theorem.

GILLY. Yes.

LEO. When did you understand Godel's theorem?

GILLY. When I was about nine.

LEO. Nine.

GILLY. I didn't know what it was called then, of course. Didn't have the books! Enid Blyton is a bit thin on the philosophy of mathematics.

LEO. When you were nine, you understood the fundamental inconsistency of mathematics.

GILLY. Why not? There a law against it?

LEO. How do your teachers handle you? Arc welding mask and asbestos gloves?

GILLY. Oh, I don't let on.

LEO. How d'you mean?

She shrugs.

GILLY. I do bad work deliberately. Just enough, so they won't realise.

LEO. Why do that, Gilly?

She shrugs.

Because it scares the shit out of you?

GILLY. No!

LEO. It does. I know the signs. The 'take this cup of sick from me' look in the eye.

GILLY. I'm just frightened at being so good at it. Hang over from your school, I s'pose. Y'know, in school, you get a reputation for being weird, liking books or something, and you get your head put down the toilet. I think that goes on, out of school too. You can get called a fraud, or people tell lies about you and twist everything you do. Mess it.

She pauses.

Like when you know a beautiful tune and someone sings it horribly. So horribly, the tune sounds rubbish.

LEO, *looking away.*

LEO. What you trying to say, you're some kind of fucking artist?

GILLY. I'm brilliant at mathematics. I didn't ask to be, but I am and that's that. What I believe is, when we're born, we know everything. All maths, all science. We can't say it, we can't really think it, it's an 'isness' – is, is, *wis*dom, you see it when a baby looks at you. A baby in a pram is happy being alive, happy with – oh, with genes wriggling in our cells, happy with things about nature the adult world won't discover for a thousand years, if ever – happy.

LEO. 'Til it shits itself.

A silence, GILLY glaring at him. Then she snatches at the binder.

GILLY. Give it to me.

He wrenches the binder away, standing.

You'll twist it, you'll – it!

He throws the binder away, upstage into the darkness. He pulls his jacket up around his head and spins.

LEO. The cradle is full of shit, Gilly. Oh boy, you have not a blind idea of what you have done.

GILLY. Tell me then, big American.

He stops spinning.

LEO. What do you want? Me to teach you? I don't want to teach. Grin to the class, in pretence that all is fine and in harmony? All the teaching you need is — go away and blow your mind to bits, little girl.

GILLY. What did you get me out here for then?

LEO. Bad conscience. No, too fancy. Terror Gillian.

He pauses.

Terror.

GILLY. Of what, Mr Nobel Prize-winner?

LEO. OK.

He pauses.

OK. OK. It is time to teach, it is time to pass the poison on.

He pauses.

You got any physics?

GILLY. Didn't do physics at A level. It's numbers I love, physics — ugh. All metal and iron.

LEO. Oh sister, you really are some kind of child of nature. Out o' some kind of backwoods of the world called Watford and you have written out — the pure mathematics — for the unity of the four forces of nature.

GILLY. That what I done? News to me.

LEO. OK student. Four forces of nature, what are they?

GILLY. Earth? Air? Fire? Water?

He laughs.

LEO. Medieval, honey, medieval. Still, teacher must not despair. Even Isaac Newton believed in magic.

He rips off his jacket.

I give you the first force of nature —

He bundles his jacket into a ball and throws it up. It falls before him. With a mock bow.

Gravity. Attraction of two bodies, my jacket and me to the planet. Infinite in range. The binder of stars. Nothing escapes it, not a feather, not the planet Saturn, not you not me, not a particle of atomic dust, drifting in space.

He picks up the torch.

The second force of nature.

He switches the torch on.

The electrical force. Binds atoms to atoms in molecules, gives light out the socket for your TV – lightning, God in the sky?

He flicks his finger.

Come here. C'mon! Get your pop science down you, you want to know how the ugly old world is made.

He grabs her round the waist, holding her tight.

The strong nuclear force. Binds particles in the nucleus of the atom. Give me your bag.

GILLY. What?

LEO. Your shoulder bag.

GILLY. You want some funny business mister, I'll scratch your eyes out.

LEO. Fourth force of nature. Weak nuclear force.

They spin, he whirls the bag around their heads.

Responsible for radiation!

GILLY. Ow!

LEO. Wonders of nature! Force on force! Brutality in balance, harmony o' good old fucked creation –

GILLY. Bastard!

She gets a hand free and hits him on the side of the head, they stumble and fall. They roll and then sit up.

LEO. Shucks we just had a nuclear explosion.

GILLY. That your idea of teaching? With hate?

LEO (*low*). What are the four forces of nature?

GILLY *at once.*

GILLY. Gravity. The electrical force. The strong nuclear force. The weak nuclear force.

She pauses, then again effortlessly.

Gravity, the attraction of bodies with any weight?

LEO (*low*). Mass.

GILLY. Mass. The electrical force, binding atoms in a molecule. The strong nuclear force, binding particles in the nucleus of the atom. The weak nuclear force, responsible for radiation.

She shrugs.

So?

LEO. So, Gillian.

He pauses.

So under the farmlands of Illinois, there is a machine. Fermilab. It is a tunnel, in a circle, four miles wide, along its rim magnets of enormous power. A circle around which they smash bits of atoms. A particle accelerator. Europe has one, outside Geneva, so big it swings across the border into France. The Soviets have one, in Serpukhov, Siberia. The only secrets are nature's, the only secrets are nature's.

He laughs to himself, then continues.

Millions of dollars, millions of roubles to smash bits of matter near the speed of light, round and round under the grass. Looks kind of innocent – mankind playing on the beach with grains of sand. That is how it is presented to the public – for the love of it, the love of knowledge. That's how you talk about your maths, Gillian, like it's love.

He pauses.

But the machines in Illinois, Geneva and Siberia are not for love. In this world, millions of dollars and roubles are not spent for love. They – are – spent – for – power. What they want to do, is prove that the four great forces of nature are, in truth, one force.

He pauses.

To see them as one force. In truth.

GILLY *to herself, demonstrating with her hands as in Scene Two.*

GILLY. Like you think you see different things, there, there and there. But – blink blink blink. It's just one thing you've seen, one whole, one –

She hesitates on the word.

Force.

LEO. What's the matter, sister? Suddenly seen a gleam of darkness in the middle of all that light?

GILLY (*to herself*). Patterns.

She holds up her hands, fingers splayed, one behind the other.

If you can see two different patterns, the right way round –

She reverses a hand.

You see one pattern.

LEO. Yup! It's called the Gauge Theory.

GILLY. I know all about that, mathematicians have been doing that stuff since the nineteenth century.

LEO. Yup! We been doing all kinds of stuff, for centuries. Like we are all programmed? All rushing to one great rational conclusion? Like by force of brain, becoming God? Early in 1983, in the Geneva machine, they did one million experiments, to prove that the strong nuclear force and the weak nuclear force, are one and the same.

He pauses.

Thirteen times out of the million, they got it right.

GILLY. That all?

LEO. It's enough. All they need now is the mathematics.

He turns on her.

They need the mathematics, student! Time and time again some mathematician sits down and for the sake of purity, love? Writes out some elaborate pattern. Hell, when we work out what quarks are, the mathematics were those of a Frenchman, Evariste Galois, who wrote down all his ideas the night before he was killed in a duel in the eighteen eighties. Like you, sitting down in the snow, one Christmas vacation?

GILLY. But it's wonderful.

A silence.

What I wrote could help scientists?

A silence.

You had better tell me why it's not wonderful.

LEO. Albert Einstein said that, if he had known that his 1905 paper on Special Relativity was to lead to the atom bomb, he'd have given up mathematics –

GILLY *(together).* And made
LEO   cuckoo clocks –

GILLY. Didn't though, did he! Come on teacher, 'teach'!

LEO. I'm cold.

He wanders over to his jacket and puts it on as he speaks.

I did the same work in America. It hit me like it hit you. Pur – it – y. The world in a grain of sand, under your fingernail? I had all that innocence. Arrogance.

A silence.

Then I was on a beach. Californian holiday? Up came an individual and sat down beside me. Blue eyes, the body of a surfer. The Government, Gilly, the Government of A – mer – ik – a. And it began.

GILLY. What did?

A silence.

LEO. Everything. The threat in a smile. The offer of power. A lead role in a cage.

He puffs his cheeks and blows out.

They wanted the work and they wanted me, for Uncle Sam, the free world, for weapons research, for – a – bomb. That's what it means, the tune you and I scrawled out with our ballpens. You describe how something lives and dear old human kind will use your words to kill it.

He shakes his head.

Oh boy, the consequence of describing life is death?

He laughs.

I am not a hero, I am an American boy who wants to get laid. I was made for fame and sex not paranoia in a lonely room, out of my mind that the phone is bugged. So I said – OK, no calculation is pure. Therefore calculate no more. I gave up, Gilly, I closed down, I exiled me into my own head. If you are shit scared of the damage you can do, do nothing, eh?

A silence.

In the end they let me alone. And let me hide, here in England. Then you walked out in the snow one morning.

GILLY. But you can't not think.

LEO. No? Try it.

GILLY. A thought is a thought. You can't not have it –

LEO. Don't you know how fucking naive that is? How fucking young?

GILLY. No I don't!

She looks at her hands.

The – equations are as natural as –

She searches for the phrase.

A tree. If a murderer ties someone to the tree and kills them, or if lovers lie down and make love under its leaves, the tree doesn't care! And if men with blue eyes in America do something horrible with the equations – I don't care. I can't. What I think is me and what I write is me and that's that. And you've not stopped thinking, have you? Closed down on the outside, but inside, you can't stop, can you? And you didn't tell them, the blue-eyed men. You're even a hero, though you don't want to be. You can't stop it, you can't stop nature –

LEO (*shouts*). Right! Right! Little Miss Light from the cradle, happy on Mother Nature's tit.

He runs into the darkness and comes back with the binder.

I'll show you, I'll show you.

He opens the binder on the ground.

Look! Look!

She kneels down and opens the binder. They work.

Birdsong. The stage begins to brighten. Dawn, a fine sunny day. The shadows of trees and branches across the stage.

They finish work. GILLY closes the binder. They are very cold. LEO stands and shakes his clothes. He offers GILLY a cigarette, lights it for her. They smoke.

GILLY. That's how they'll do it.

LEO. Yup.

GILLY. It's only – thirty sheets of paper. Like watching you – build up – crazy towers, a mile high from it. All metal and iron.

LEO. Yup.

GILLY. Bomb. Bomb.

LEO takes a deep breath, breathes out.

What do I do? Have breakfast? I don't think the egg on the plate will look the same. Ring my Mum? 'I know how they can make a new generation of weapons, Mum! Isn't that wonderful?'

She smokes. She laughs.

OK. Let's burn it.

LEO. 'Til the next –

GILLY. Bright kid from Watford, yes. We got it wrong, haven't we, there must be something wrong in the physics –

LEO. You got the physics all the way.

GILLY. Just two clever shits like us?

LEO. You'll go over it all the time. Welcome to insomnia, sister.

GILLY. Just play the piano. The air will know the tune. But I can't now. The tunes will burn the air. It's unfair! Doing maths – was a joy.

LEO. Galileo said one day, scientists will come forward overjoyed with a new discovery to be greeted with a universal cry of horror.

GILLY (*giggles*). Another clever little shit, was he?

They pause.

Do you want to do it?

LEO. You.

She throws back her head, takes a deep breath and lets out a long scream, quiet at first but rising.

The birdsong swells. The lights fade as the Bach theme is heard.

Scene Four: Crisis in a garden

A summer garden. Sunlight dappling the stage. A table covered by a white cloth, upon it opened bottles of wine and wine glasses. All wear bright summer clothes –

But for GRAHAM, who is in a pair of trousers from an old suit, sandals without socks and a dirty white shirt, sleeves rolled up. He is discovered walking upstage to the table. He picks up a bottle. He looks at the label.

VIRGINIA *comes on.* GRAHAM *does not see her.*

GRAHAM. Are we all now to drink Californian wine?

VIRGINIA. What to some is truth, to others is a drink of piss.

GRAHAM. True, true.

He pours a glass, puts the bottle down and turns. They look at each other.

VIRGINIA. I didn't know Leo had invited both of us. Otherwise I would, or would not, be here.

GRAHAM. G – g –

VIRGINIA. What?

GRAHAM. Gang bang!

VIRGINIA. Sorry?

GRAHAM. Maybe that is what he has in mind.

VIRGINIA. Graham –

GRAHAM. Summer party? End of term. It is warm. The sun is at

its highest arc above the English Midlands. The young we seek
to teach come to a zenith in their lives. Career dreams and
dreams of love, lock. Now middle-aged lecturers hope to find
themselves naked with their students in high, green bedrooms.

He sips wine.

VIRGINIA. Why are you stuttering?

GRAHAM. I'm n – not.

VIRGINIA. You can't go on, sleeping in the caravan, parked slap
in the middle of the campus!

GRAHAM. A touch of squalor in the academic paradise.

VIRGINIA. The university won't put up with it.

GRAHAM. I am the university, I'm the bloody b – bursar.

VIRGINIA. All right, go potty. But beware – the English love
eccentrics, but turn on them when they become insanitary.

GRAHAM. Don't worry. I go over to the staff club to use the
gents.

VIRGINIA. I need a drink.

GRAHAM. How –

VIRGINIA. Don't ask me how the children are, don't, or I'll
scream.

GRAHAM. Do –

VIRGINIA. No longer. Our American sexual Odysseus has begun
to work hard. He rows with the computer people day or night.
He is also, day or night, with a little student from E Block.
Didn't you know?

GRAHAM, *a quick shake of the head.*

GRAHAM. Out of t – touch.

He pauses.

Can I get you that drink?

VIRGINIA. No.

GRAHAM. Don't want – near me?

VIRGINIA. I'm afraid you'll smell.

Lower.

Smell.

GRAHAM *pulls at his shirt sleeve, looks at it, then sniffs his
armpit.*

GRAHAM. Sexual Odysseus?

He nods.

He's cruel too. See, he's put us in his garden and changed us into p – pigs.

He walks away. VIRGINIA *looks away, then goes quickly to the table and pours herself a drink.* ANDREA *and* TOM *come on.*

Hello Tom. How's Trotsky?

TOM. Pissed off, bursar. How's caravaning?

GRAHAM. Smelly.

TOM laughs.

Don't you laugh. You too will come to middle age, bad teeth and arm-pitty shirts.

TOM. Not me, bursar.

GRAHAM. Expecting early death?

TOM. Why not?

GRAHAM. By nuclear holocaust or by alcohol?

TOM. Get stuffed, Graham.

GRAHAM. I've tried that. Tried that.

TOM (*to himself*). Fucking hell.

TOM *goes to the table and picks up a bottle of wine and drinks from it.* VIRGINIA, *giving* ANDREA *a glass.*

VIRGINIA. I shouldn't know and I shouldn't tell you. Do you want to know?

ANDREA. I sort of know, anyway.

VIRGINIA. You got a first.

ANDREA. Yes.

VIRGINIA *sips her wine.*

VIRGINIA. What will you do? Stay on and do an MA?

ANDREA. I am going to work as an orderly in a mental hospital.

VIRGINIA. I see.

ANDREA *sips her wine.*

For the young or old?

ANDREA. How do you mean?

VIRGINIA. I don't know much about it, but I imagine the old and insane are really disgusting.

ANDREA. It is a hospital for old people.

VIRGINIA. The men must be worst.

ANDREA. There are men.

VIRGINIA. The sexual drive of insane, old men. A real purgatory for a young woman with a first class degree. You make me very angry.

ANDREA *sips again and says nothing. The* VICE-CHANCELLOR *comes on. He carries a shooting stick.*

VC. Ah junketing, junketing. To slurp the cup of summer.

TOM (*to* ANDREA). Uh uh, the heavy mob.

GRAHAM. Oh! Vice-Chancellor!

The VICE-CHANCELLOR *ignores him, planting the shooting stick and sitting on it. He looks around and chooses* VIRGINIA *to talk to.*

VC. Virginia, my dear.

VIRGINIA. Hello Richard.

He kisses her on the cheek.

VC. Is mine host to be seen? I rang the doorbell but there was nothing, so round I came to the garden.

VIRGINIA. Yes, where is Leo?

VC. Nice to see you here with Graham.

VIRGINIA *takes a step back.*

VIRGINIA. Red, white or rosé?

GRAHAM *is shaking his head, moving his hand, as if talking to himself. The* VICE-CHANCELLOR *looks over at him. Suddenly they are all looking at him.*

VC. It is extremely tedious, Virginia, when senior members of the staff will not keep their bodies under control.

Nothing from VIRGINIA.

A glass of white wine, please.

TOM. A glass of wine, a glass of class, a nod a nonce. The English intelligentsia are in their garden.

ANDREA. Oh shut up.

She turns away from him.

TOM. No sweat, 'doll'! The flowers grow. Anything wild and wonderful is called a weed and pulled up by the root. Red moles under the lawn are dug out and gassed, the turf put back, smoother than before. All the little talents are in a row in the sun, happy with their prizes. Sprayed to kill off any harmful insects, y'know, the odd marxist idea? So sip, sip! Never mind the wind is American and, just over the hedge, there are bodies on the barbed wire. (*To himself.*) In a way, I like it, in a way it is right. It is what I know. Believe what you want, do what you want, we are all licensed killers walking among the flowers. Well I am, I am.

TOM *swigs from the bottle. As he spoke a bundle of papers, print-outs and notebooks,* GILLY's *binder among them, bound with a big red bow and flowers has been lowered down about them, jerkily.*

GRAHAM. There's something coming d – down.

They all look up.

VC. Ah. Rag time?

ANDREA. It's from the tree.

VC. I do believe the string leads to that window.

GRAHAM. He's right. it goes over a nail.

VIRGINIA. For Godsake.

She shouts.

Leo.

TOM. What is all this?

He goes to the bundle. GRAHAM *stumbles to the bundle, pushing* TOM *aside. He ruffles through the papers, helplessly.*

GRAHAM. It's mathematics.

VIRGINIA *takes the papers from* GRAHAM *and walks away with them, her back to the company.*

VC. Party game? Clues, paperchase, crock of gold at the end?

GILLY *walks on. She is horribly burnt all over her body, the burns fresh. She is hairless and naked but for a few traces of charred rags. She is blind, her eyes bloody pits. She carries a silver tray, upon it champagne glasses, filled. They all stare at her.*

TOM. Er –

GRAHAM, *a loud giggle.*

GRAHAM. Hahahahahahaha!

A silence.

VC. What a pity no one told me it was fancy dress.

GILLY *turns aimlessly, stumbling, the champagne glasses chinking.*

VIRGINIA, *reading upstage, sinks silently to her knees.*

ANDREA (*to* GILLY). What do you want us to do?

TOM. Looks like champers.

He strides to the tray. He takes a glass, drinks liberally from it, holds the liquid in his mouth for a second then sprays it out and bends double.

Ahhh!

LEO *walks on.*

LEO. We did her up, best we could, first degree burns? The epidermal layer, what we call 'our skin', gone? The blood vessels beneath, exposed? And blinded, if not by the flash, by photothalmia? Ultra-violet light? The ozone layer stripped away, ten minutes outside, and – eyes gone?

VC. Ah!

He slaps his thigh.

CND. Touch of street theatre? Very jolly.

TOM, *holding his throat.*

TOM. Ahhh!

GRAHAM. What was in the glass?

LEO. Hydrochloric acid one, twenty megaton bomb on Birmingham, that is something like what it would do to us, in this garden.

GRAHAM. For crying out loud he said he drank –

LEO. Hydrochloric acid, so what, the worst we can do to each other? Serve acid in a garden, nothing, twenty megaton bomb, nothing, there is more horror to human intervention than we can dream.

All still for a second. He shouts.

Dream!

GRAHAM. B – b – b – b – b – bloody irresp – p – p – p – p – ponsible –

ANDREA. Get a drink of water!

She runs to the table. The VICE-CHANCELLOR, *rising from his walking stick.*

VC. If this is to go too far, if you have gone too far –

LEO. OK, it is not HC1, no one's throat will burn and Gillian, that is a swim hat, paint on it, not a burn from the flash fire of Birmingham, England, nuked.

TOM. And I tell you that weren't fucking champagne.

LEO. A little human piss with Alka Seltzer for the bubbles.

TOM *swigs at the wine and splutters.*

TOM. I mean why me?

LEO. Why any one of us, man?

VC. Your champagne turns out not to be hydrochloric acid, merely urine. We must be grateful for small mercies. It is the end of summer term, one tolerates the odd collapse into bad taste. Nevertheless, perhaps an explanation? The university does expect more from its Nobel Prize-winner than a glass of pee – with or without bubbles.

VIRGINIA, *still kneeling, laughs.*

VIRGINIA. Love it, love it. I love it. Oh you clever bastards of the world.

She stands, the bundle in her hands.

You are very bright and golden, Leo, and you? (*To* GILLY.) A little girl fresh from her comprehensive, lit up like a light bulb and wrote it in the snow? (*To* LEO.) For you to fall over. I love it. The great leaps of science, Copernicus, Newton, Einstein and the last great leap? A low farce.

GRAHAM. But what? What have they done?

VIRGINIA. Nothing a mathematician with a good, first class degree, could not grasp. (*To* GRAHAM.) But have you got a degree in mathematics? (*To the* VICE-CHANCELLOR.) Have you? (*To* ANDREA.) You? (*To* TOM.) You? No. Good, educated people, with no hope of ever knowing how the world is made. That's part of the farce.

TOM. Elitist bullshit. What are you, a priesthood, with secrets to hide?

VIRGINIA. That is what we are. (*To herself.*) I tried to leave, denounce my vows.

She lets the bundle of papers and notebooks fall to the ground.

VC. The young man has reason. I am an Arts man. The simplest long division and I go down with brain fever. But I have a layman's picture of the atom. Little balls going round big balls? Therefore explain, explain!

GILLY. There –

She pauses. They all look at her.

There are four forces of nature.

LEO *puffs his cheeks and blows out. Then –*

LEO. What are they? Someone answer before the bell goes clang.

ANDREA. Earth, air, fire, water?

VIRGINIA. Clang.

LEO. Would that not be beautiful? Back in the middle ages, yes, the world was made of earth, air, fire, water. But for us?

GILLY, *sing-song.*

GILLY. The four forces of nature are the strong nuclear force, the weak nuclear force, the electrical force – and gravity.

LEO. When we say force, put no pictures in your head. There are no pictures. What you see in the pop science programmes on TV, atoms like (*To the* VC.) your balls going round balls – forget it. All the pop science is propaganda, to say all's right with the world and Mother Nature loves us. There are no pictures of existence. Mother Nature is blind.

GILLY. What Albert Einstein tried to do, for forty years, after he did what made him famous was write –

She pauses.

Write a series of equations, uniting – the four forces of nature into one. One force, one whole. He knew that if he did that, it would be like writing out – the secret name of God.

LEO. Einstein didn't make it because the schmuck was a moralist. He wanted to believe in God too much, the eye in the sky. He threw up when the mathematics wanted to say 'Blind, it's blind'.

He pauses.

I am no moralist. I don't give a fuck. I sat down and wrote out the equations in America. That.

He points at the bundle.

And I looked upon all my works and – threw up. I ran. Hid. Tell them why, Virginia.

VIRGINIA. Any mathematician sees it at once.

GRAHAM. Oh G – God, they said at MIT. (*To* LEO.) M – m – military work? Classified material? That is c – c –

LEO. Yeah yeah, what the Pentagon wanted, Captain America will be zapping out a' the trees any moment now.

GRAHAM, *free of the stutter*.

GRAHAM. Leo! The grossest irresponsibility, abuse of academic behaviour, all trust –

ANDREA (*to* VIRGINIA). A bomb.

VIRGINIA. 'Yup'.

TOM. Yip, yippee –

LEO (*to* GRAHAM). It's trust we want from you. All of us in this garden, like it or not – we are the children of Galileo. And look what the old bastard's given us to handle. OK! Gilly's tried to do the shock stuff, let me try the reason. Here we are, teachers and students. Help two of your number deal with the product of their – twisted, bloody, clever clever brains. Protect us. Help us deal with what we've done. Be a university.

GRAHAM. Vice-Chancellor –

VC. Yes, I think I have to intervene, would the undergraduates present please leave, there may be a matter for Senate here –

GRAHAM *throws the tray down on the ground, smashing the glasses.*

GILLY. They'll never understand. They'll twist it. They'll destroy it. They're stupid, they're all dead.

She scoops up the bundle of papers in her arms.

It's – time – we – got – out – of – the – pram.

All freeze for a moment. Then GILLY turns and runs. A blackout.

ACT TWO

Scene One: An accident

Night. The path through the wood. The CYCLIST *rides on, lamps lit. He rings his bell.*

CYCLIST. Out my way foxes, out my way, little furry animals!

GILLY *runs on still in the make-up of the garden, straight at the* CYCLIST. *She knocks him and the bicycle over. They both go sprawling. He sits up.*

My clips. One's popped off. I don't want to lose my clips.

He looks at her.

What in heaven's name have you done to yourself?

GILLY. They say you're a communist.

CYCLIST. I beg your pardon?

GILLY. That's the gossip. 'Mong the students.

CYCLIST. Nothing broken.

The CYCLIST, *standing.*

GILLY. They say you go to Moscow.

CYCLIST. Cast as resident red mole am I?

GILLY. See, I thought 'write it on the walls, stick it on trees' – or let it run down drains, in the sewers and in the rivers, out to sea, washed up on beaches, all gluey, stuck in sea gulls' feathers, or! Throw it in reservoirs, let it come out the taps and everyone drink it, like a drug!

CYCLIST. Goodness. Everyone drink what?

GILLY. The secret of the world.

CYCLIST. You working up a fever?

GILLY. But now I think 'Give it to Russia'.

CYCLIST. A high old fever. Better get you to the students' nurse, hot drink and wrap up.

GILLY. No listen, what the traitors did with the atom secrets? Maybe they were right and heroes.

CYCLIST. Kim Philby and Co., heroes of the revolution? I always thought they were a bunch of upper-class wankers. Here, have my coat.

GILLY. No!

CYCLIST. Now you listen to me. All you are is a stupid, spoilt, know-nothing child, messing about in a wood. Knock me off my bike, prattle about communism? You want to go to the Soviet Union, take a package holiday. Can you stand?

GILLY *backs away.*

GILLY. You're like all the rest. Crows on the wire, on the barbed wire fence. All the teachers, all the mums.

CYCLIST. Don't run off!

GILLY. I want to tear your eyes out. Blind you. So you don't see me, so you sit on your fence blind and never see what I do, what I see.

She runs off.

CYCLIST. Come back here! Oh buggeration, buggeration.

He gets on the bicycle and rides off. The stage darkens. In the distance POLICE *with lights and a dog, barking.* VOICES *calling –*

VOICES. Gilly! Gilly! Gilly!

Scene Two: State moves.

A small room. The VICE-CHANCELLOR *and* GRAHAM. *The* VICE-CHANCELLOR *in a luxuriously covered armchair. A drinks cabinet, in the wall.*

VC. Any sign of her?

GRAHAM. No.

VC. Looked on the Senate House roof? Students on the blink often go up there, to throw themselves off. Half a dozen in my time. I talked them all down, but for one. He is now a paraplegic, in Cheltenham. Sends me a card every Christmas.

GRAHAM. We've searched the roofs.

VC. One ends up hating the young. The endless repetition of telling them what the world is like. The waiting for them to believe it when they're thirty.

He pauses. GRAHAM *shifts.*

And the American? Presumably in a narcotic haze somewhere?

GRAHAM. The police say he left the search and went home.

VC. With your wife?

GRAHAM, *a little jerk of the head but says nothing. The* VICE-CHANCELLOR *drums bad-temperedly on the arm of the chair.*

Running, running.

GRAHAM. I'm sorry.

VC. This business, running away, out of our hands. Events are in train. As an administrator I have always disliked 'events'. In a big institution, it is an essential condition for progress that nothing happens.

He stops drumming and stares at GRAHAM.

How long have you known that I'm dying?

GRAHAM. I –

VC. Come on! We discuss matters of high state. Let's not waste time over my disease.

A pause.

GRAHAM. Eighteen months.

VC. What, sneaked a sight of my medical report? A nod to a secretary, the slide of a filing cabinet drawer and behold – cancer.

GRAHAM. Richard, I am really horribly sorry.

VC. Be horribly glad! You are ambitious. Pour me a scotch.

GRAHAM. Should you?

VC. Oh fuck you, fuck you rotten!

GRAHAM *pours him a drink and hands it to him.*

It is late at night, let us be naked. I want you to be Vice-Chancellor of this university. Not some clapped-out Tory ex-minister, come to cut everything in sight. I have groomed you, I have conspired for your cause. You have not helped. The wobble in your married life.

GRAHAM. I am through that.

VC. And now our wayward American.

GRAHAM *pauses*.

GRAHAM. Yes.

VC. It's down to you. You got him here, you watered him, now you —

A gesture.

Snip him off. Preferably at the root.

The VICE-CHANCELLOR *slouches back in the armchair, the whisky to his lips*.

Train him up the wall. With all the other colourful personalities.

GRAHAM. It may not be a matter of personality.

VC. I lose faith in you, Graham — everything is a matter of personality.

GRAHAM. There are great causes.

VC. Nonsense. There is only self-interest. Self-interest is another phrase for 'being alive'.

GRAHAM. That's cynical.

VC. Not cynical at all. Honest. Graham, after all the American has done to you in your private life, I do believe you still want to be a martyr for his science.

GRAHAM. He is a bastard. But — a bastard who is trying to talk about whether or not we are going to blow ourselves to bits.

VC. Nonsense again. He is talking about the size of his own ego.

GRAHAM. The nuclear holocaust isn't a matter of a personality disorder.

VC. That is exactly what it is. CND? Ban the Bomb? The whole thing is a middle-class neurosis that is in danger of becoming hysterical.

GRAHAM. Richard, in the Science Block of the university you and I run, there are smartarse graduates dreaming of stripping genes from the nuclei of human cells —

VC. Don't slander my Science Block. That is my pride and joy.

That Science Block gets this bloody place funded.

GRAHAM. But to do what? There are mathematicians over there calculating how to fracture matter itself. We administer that, we mild, decent men. We administer the nuclear holocaust.

VC. Hysteria! It is not going to happen.

GRAHAM. How are you so sure?

VC. Because people like me are not going to let it happen!

GRAHAM. But you're dying, you old fool!

A silence.

Sorry, but I'm not going to apologise for that.

He pauses.

Probably your counterparts in the Soviet Union are dying too. The structure of matter, life itself is in the hands of foolish, sick, old men –

VC. Calm yourself, Graham.

GRAHAM. No, I won't calm myself! People like me keep on calming down in this bloody country and we do no end of harm. The work Leo has done and is now, in his confused way, trying to make amends for – we should protect it.

VC. Indeed. But is that not a good argument for putting the whole thing into the hands of the Ministry of Defence?

GRAHAM. Vice-Chancellor, have you not heard a word I have said? Did nothing that Leo and the girl did, in that rather puerile but desperate display in the garden, touch you at all?

VC. One is always pleased to see passion in the academic world, which is actually about academic work. Most of the passion round here goes on who is getting what salary.

GRAHAM. It is more a question of vision.

VC. Vision? Oh, vision. Now that can be tiresome –

GRAHAM. Vision of what a university can be –

VC. You're getting out of your depth, Graham. It's down to 'people like you' to run this place, not to ask what it is for.

GRAHAM (*low*). Disgraceful –

VC. What?

GRAHAM. That is a disgraceful remark!

VC. Oh don't be a pompous ass.

A silence

GRAHAM. You know what our problem is here?

VC (*to himself*). I do, actually.

GRAHAM. Genius.

VC. Oh? Whose, yours? Sorry.

GRAHAM. We can't handle it. It seems the last place intellectual brilliance can prosper is a university. We must understand Leo Lehrer, if we can't, here, who will? We – must become like a monastery, in the dark ages. Keeping alive the secret of writing. Hiding the books in the cellars from barbarians.

With a flick of the head.

I propose we set up a Research Institute. We take no government or commercial money to finance it. We investigate Professor Lehrer's work – in secret. We find out if his fears are justified. Will his work lead to a knowledge of nature which will endanger nature itself? We answer that.

The VICE-CHANCELLOR, *with a sigh.*

VC. And if the answer is 'yes'?

GRAHAM. Then –

He pauses.

Then we bury it. In the cellars.

VC. Like an illuminated manuscript of the true gospel? Away from the gaze of the Viking hordes.

GRAHAM. Y – es. And we turn the university into a centre for Peace Studies. We win moral authority in the world –

The VICE-CHANCELLOR *with a sudden snort.*

VC. Ha ha! Sorry again. Like so many idealists you are so second rate, Graham, because you are hopelessly romantic.

He stretches himself in his chair.

Now I have to tell you, that Professor Lehrer's work is no longer our concern.

GRAHAM. What do you mean? It is our main concern –

VC. I said! Events! Running! Out of our hands!

GRAHAM. What have you done, you old fool, whom have you told –

VC. You are the fool.

He calls out.

Mr Dicks, would you come in?

TOM *comes into the room. He stands respectfully, smiling at* GRAHAM.

GRAHAM. I don't think a student should be present –

VC. Mr Dicks is a student, but that doesn't mean he is a student. He is a very bright fellow indeed. (*To* TOM.) Drink?

TOM. No thank you, sir. May I –

VC. Do.

TOM. Bursar?

TOM *takes out a paper and pen and holds them out to* GRAHAM.

GRAHAM. ?

TOM. You can sign it in London, but –

He shrugs.

GRAHAM. London?

TOM. I've got to drive you down tonight.

A silence.

Better. This way, you'll be back lunchtime tomorrow. No one'll know you've been talked to. I mean, you've got no one at home at the moment, have you?

GRAHAM *hesitates.*

GRAHAM. No. Wh –

TOM. Official Secrets Act. You can sign it in London, but do it now and you'll feel happier, talking in the car.

GRAHAM. You sp – spy? On – your fellow students?

His voice cracks.

On our teachers?

TOM. I love good old squidgy England, don't you?

He pushes the paper and pen into GRAHAM's *hands.*

Sign it Graham.

GRAHAM *does not move.*

VC. Sign it man. Why do the educated classes insist on seeing the world as something complex, when all the time it is brutally simple? Like – you are loyal to your country or you are not. And is England so bad? Walking in the autumn woods with your feet warm in your wellies. And your garden? House? Job? And a little malt whisky, late of a night?

He scoffs.

I mean, are you going to turn on all you believe in? Be photographed jumping the Berlin wall the wrong way – at your age?

They are all still. Then GRAHAM scribbles fast, the paper held against his knee. He pushes the paper at TOM, who dangles car keys.

TOM. OK. Off we go.

GRAHAM. I feel weakened.

TOM. Coffee and sandwiches in the car. OK?

GRAHAM *looks at the* VICE-CHANCELLOR *then goes, quickly.* TOM *turns to the* VICE-CHANCELLOR.

All good gardening, sir?

TOM *goes.*

VC. Garden. Grow. Achieve. Finance, build. Library extension, Olympic standard swimming pool, opportunity, the young in one another's arms, brave new world.

He pauses.

Dust, all dust. And a sip of malt.

Scene Three: Treacheries.

Wood. Early afternoon. LEO *walking slowly, alone. He stops.*

LEO. You want to be quiet. Talk in a whisper. And what do you do? Open your mouth and scream.

He looks about him.

You want a swim in clear, cool, calm water. What do you do? Set off a tidal wave and drown all the swimmers in sight.

He pauses.

And here I am now. A walk in the woods, an afternoon among the trees. To think. Hey hey, careful man! A thinker round here, that's a human flame thrower. One thought, all the trees will be on fire.

He stops.

Oh shit. I have that feeling that they are watching you – when they are watching you.

He turns on the CYCLIST.

You have something to say to me?

CYCLIST. Have you to me?

LEO. No.

CYCLIST. Are you sure?

LEO. I keep on seeing you around. What is it with you?

CYCLIST. One strives to be a presence in the lives of the great and good.

LEO. Oh yeah? Why count me in their number?

CYCLIST. Don't go modest on me, Mr American Scientist. An American affecting modesty really takes the pip.

LEO. What do you teach here?

CYCLIST. A load of rubbish called the History of Fine Art. The Government has so far failed to notice my department exists. When they do it is bound to be cut. Actually, it is not by accident I bump into you this afternoon. I have noticed you come to this wood now and then. No doubt for assignations of your choice.

LEO. What is that to you?

CYCLIST. Oh a great deal. You are a problem in my life, Mr American Scientist. For I do have something to say to you.

LEO (*to himself*). And you are going to say it, aren't you chummy.

The CYCLIST *pedals, glides and brakes near* LEO.

CYCLIST. You see, I doubt your prediction of highly radioactive isotopes from elements of low atomic weight.

LEO *stares.*

Within certain conditions of a unified field, which you postulate.

LEO *stares.*

Well I say 'I' doubt it, truer to say there are they who doubt it.

LEO. Why do they?

CYCLIST. Ah, now, there you have me by the short and curlies.

LEO. 'They', 'they', who is this 'they'?

CYCLIST. The word bothers you?

LEO. It splits my arse, Mr Fine Art.

CYCLIST. There is always a 'they', is there not, Mr Scientist?

LEO. That is my experience.

The CYCLIST *pauses.*

CYCLIST. You must have known this would be said to you, once in your distinguished career. Now it is being said. I give you the greetings of Professor Abelski and his wife Irena of the Leningrad Institute for the Advancement of Science. A delightful couple, though with something of a shared drink problem – I believe you met them in Los Angeles?

LEO. Oh wow.

CYCLIST. He has written you this letter.

He produces a long envelope from within his saddlebag. LEO does not take it.

LEO. Wow.

CYCLIST. A purely technical letter, detailing recent work he has done that may interest you. However, Professor Abelski wishes you to know that the facilities of the Institute are at your disposal. The Socialist Peoples hope you will join them to work for world peace.

LEO. Wow.

He spins.

Wow wow.

He stops spinning.

I always thought you people would what, hit me with heavies in black coats, from a black limousine? Or a blonde in the bathroom of an International Hotel, offering to suck me off? Not some freak who scours the English landscape for the Kremlin, on a push bike.

He laughs.

Oh wow.

He collects himself.

What do I do now? Weep? Mess my pants?

CYCLIST. That is up to you. We are all masters of our fate.

LEO. You believe that?

CYCLIST. Utterly. I get bloody irritated with intellectuals who do not.

LEO. I thought you commies were historical determinists.

CYCLIST. I don't think you want to get into a dialectical discussion with me, sonny boy, I will have you for breakfast.

LEO. Bullshit.

CYCLIST (*to himself*). Oh dear oh dear, how your kind do bring out the worst in me.

LEO. Thinking about it – I'll mess my pants.

CYCLIST. That is a sort of reasoned response.

LEO. Reasoned? Oh yeah, you are an apostle of reason, being a communist. That's why I see you in the staff club, out of your head on eight pints a night.

CYCLIST. There is a strain, when you believe what I believe in this bloody country. I do not deny that. You take what relief is on offer, though it be pissy beer the profits from which fill the coffers of the Tory Party. But if personal habits are the matter of debate, shall we get onto yours? Cocaine and other men's wives?

LEO. I don't see there's any debate between us. I get the impression I am talking to a closed mind.

A silence.

CYCLIST. Yes, my mind is closed. I slammed the door on everything you represent, years ago. Ha! Thirty years in the Party, pushing pamphlets in the rain and now I do this. Probably the most important thing I will ever do in my life. You will find it bizarre, but I hope to retire in the Soviet Union. My wife and I are building a house there. We do it bit by bit, every summer holiday. Last trip, the border police found a load of copper piping T-joints under the back seat, for the plumbing. That cost me two hundred American dollars in backhanders. Next summer it'll be an English lavatory pan – that will be a heavy scene. You see, for all the horrors, the Socialist World is my 'they'. I know where I belong. Do you?

LEO (*to himself.*) Belong. Belonging.

The CYCLIST *offers the letter.*

CYCLIST. Do you want this?
LEO *takes the letter.*

LEO. Just for the science.

CYCLIST. Yes of course, the science, the bloody blood-stained science.

He cycles a circle.

If you want me, I am aways over the hedge.

He cycles off with a spurt of speed. LEO *holds the letter up, looking at it, then rips it open. There are thin sheets of paper. He flips through them, fixes on a passage then laughs.*

LEO. My God, are they that desperate?

GRAHAM, *drunk, and* VIRGINIA *come on at the back. They are in mid-argument,* VIRGINIA *holding his arm, he pulling away from her.*

GRAHAM. No, I bloody well will not!

VIRGINIA. Oh you will!

GRAHAM. I will or I will not do what I will!

VIRGINIA. When, Graham?

GRAHAM. When I will.

They struggle. LEO, *aside, waving the letter.*

LEO. Hey hey, a bribe from the East with promise of glory in history. And here comes the West, with sex and drink and the bitchiness I know and love. It is a very tasty world.

He laughs.

GRAHAM. You laughing at me?

VIRGINIA. Go away, Leo.

GRAHAM. He is laughing at me.

VIRGINIA. Please Leo.

GRAHAM. I want to know why your lover is laughing at me.

VIRGINIA (*to* LEO). We are negotiating the sale of our house. Or at least I am. Please have the decency to go away and leave us alone –

GRAHAM. Can't walk away from each other!

VIRGINIA. Oh no, no.

She walks a distance away and stops.

LEO. Where you been, Graham? I called you.

VIRGINIA. We would all like to know where he has been. And, indeed, where he thinks he is now.

GRAHAM. All right all right, you want my fingernails? Take 'em.

Offering his fingers.

One to ten, all the way!

LEO. Is he smashed?

VIRGINIA. Am I my husband's keeper?

LEO. What's the matter, Graham?

GRAHAM. Matter, matter, atomic matter, with me?

He giggles.

LEO. You've got to get over me and her.

Indicating VIRGINIA.

I mean, old man, it was only sex. We're all happy dogs in the park getting up each other, why make a big scene?

VIRGINIA. How charming, how beautiful, how lyrical. If there is going to be talk from the male jockstrap I am going –

GRAHAM. No.

He blocks her way. A silence.

No. I – was down in London. All night.

A silence.

Taken, to London. And questioned. (*To* LEO.) About you. So please. Neither of you – go. Or speak loudly to me any more. I –

He looks down.

Have been badly frightened.

LEO. Jesus Christ.

GRAHAM. As a young man said to me, last night – 'We are all locked together in a room, no one can leave!' (*To himself.*) Had a feeling he'd said that to others before me. It had the feel of a truth worn smooth (*To* LEO.) He said it to me in a car, on the motorway, I looked at the car door, thought 'Can I throw myself out, like in the films? Roll away in the dark, to fanfares . . .'

VIRGINIA. Graham –

GRAHAM. No, don't touch me! I am holy. Member of a holy band. Who have been canonised to the sainthood of our times – those who have been in the hands of the secret police. English, but nevertheless, secret police.

He laughs.

Know what? They're all old Etonians. It really is amazing to discover your country is a totalitarian state, run by old Etonians. (*To himself.*) In a big room with carpets and a big fireplace.

VIRGINIA. I don't think this country is a totalitarian state, it's just a squalid mess. I'm sorry, but run by men like you, Graham.

GRAHAM. Think I'm exaggerating? That's because they've not touched you yet, 'darling'. (*At* LEO.) Or him. Oh no, not the glamorous prize-winner. It's decent little runts like me that get the horrors.

LEO. If you fool around with a secret of the universe, the local cops are bound to call. What do you expect, old man?

GRAHAM. I do not expect to be interrogated. About you. Threatened! I mean, we've all got our lives and they really are rather p – precious to us. I mean, I will go to the wall with the rest, under the mushroom cloud, but alone? With young men in sm – smart suits, sneering at me?

LEO. It is cruel to say this, Graham – but you had better tell me what you told them.

GRAHAM. I had better not.

He looks at his hands.

No, I told them the lot. Your hands look the same. Air, going up your nose, feels the same. I am so scared.

LEO. You told them –

GRAHAM. Yes yes yes! The rumours about you in America, you and the girl's work, the rumours in the staff club about your druggy habits, all that you've been up to. Yes! And –

He pauses.

You and her. (*Meaning* VIRGINIA.) Yes!

A silence.

Utter betrayal. Ut – ter nakedness. What I regret is that I was not stripped naked, put up against a wall, in a filthy cellar, cold freezing water, I am ashamed that I was not.

LEO (*low*). You little shit.

GRAHAM. More of that, please, if you can. It is very sweet to me. Leo –

He pauses.

It's the girl they want. You, they think they can handle. Perhaps they're confident your pleasures will bring you to heel? But little Gillian – oh dear, the chip off a fallen star, the meteorite, your little skirt with the goods, eh?

He giggles.

She really bothers 'em. Female, genius, state secrets? Chaps
know chaps will, in the end, do what chaps should. Shut up.
Pull together. But little Gilly? Different animal. Not got a chap's
tackle between the legs, chaps get very jumpy indeed. For all I
know, when they find her they'll put a bullet in the back of her
neck. Tell me where she is.

He pauses.

Friend.

He slurs.

I feel disgusting. I studied William Blake, revolutionary
visionary. I think I'd better sit d —

He plomps down.

LEO. I've no idea where Gilly is, tell them that, no idea.

GRAHAM. Please, you must. While I was being questioned — I
wet myself, out of fear. That is not an English experience — I
never want it in my life again.

LEO. I told you old son, she's gone.

GRAHAM. I have destroyed myself for you. Argued for you. Do
this for me.

LEO. How can I?

GRAHAM. They won't do anything to her. Just take her in hand.
Rap her over the wrists.

VIRGINIA. Steal her mathematics?

GRAHAM. Just nail her down to the floor! It'll be all very British.
They'll give her a grant or something. But one way or another,
nailed to the floor she will be! We must all be nailed to the
floor! Where we belong!

LEO. I can't do anything for you, Graham. As you once said, our
cause is purity.

GRAHAM. He refers to his science. His true love. Quote!
'You love the world that I hate.
Thy heaven's doors are my hell gate.'
That's Blake.

He hiccups.

More or less. Which gate does your science go in, eh Leo?

LEO. You podgy little Englishman, what are you moaning about?
You think that purity, a pure thought, a pure line through the

mindmoil will not cost? I've had the gremlins out of the wall for me, too. Take my advice. Carry no baggage. No friends. Fuck if you must, but don't make love. Be light!

GRAHAM. Ha!

A silence.

Ha. I could never take that about you. Your freedom and b – beauty. The person who throws off all human feeling is *so* free, so beautiful, real people like me, we bumblers, we sweaters, we can't handle the chaos. Therefore –

He struggles to his feet.

I am ditching you. I am withdrawing my love. Divorce my wife, name you –

VIRGINIA. Oh! Thank you very much.

GRAHAM. And I will have you out of the university in a year. Batter my way, back up. I'll be Vice-Chancellor by the time I'm sixty. If I be not burnt to a crisp in your Third World War. Eh?

He looks from one to the other. They do not laugh.

Eh? Eh?

He lurches away.

LEO. See you at the gate.

GRAHAM *stops, not looking at* LEO.

GRAHAM. Don't think so. I'm going to Heaven. 'Friend'. So sod the both of you.

He lurches away and goes off.

VIRGINIA. Do you enjoy effortless, personal cruelty?

LEO. Yup.

VIRGINIA. Cold – as – ice.

LEO. That is me.

VIRGINIA. Your cause is purity.

He looks at his watch.

Seeing you destroy my husband in that cause – well, I suppose it was an interesting insight into the men's locker room. The patterns on the wall look quite pretty – 'til you realise they're made with blood. What are you up to, Leo?

LEO. How d'you mean?

VIRGINIA. You're waiting for someone.

Nothing from LEO.

I know it can't be the girl.

LEO. How do you know that?

VIRGINIA. Because I am hiding her.

A silence.

With a friend. Never mind who. Should I have told you?

LEO. Dunno.

A silence.

You didn't tell your husband.

VIRGINIA. To put him out of his agony.

LEO. No.

VIRGINIA. No.

LEO. See what it does to you, Vee? You too grow cold.

He pauses.

Is she OK?

VIRGINIA. What you mean is 'are the mathematics OK?' The little squiggles. The 'ideas'. Has she gone off her head, left them on a bus, in a railway station ladies loo, put them in a bottle and thrown them in the sea?

She pauses.

The mathematics are OK. As for Gilly, she thinks you are a hero.

Nothing from LEO.

I said she —

LEO. I heard you.

VIRGINIA. She wants to see you.

Nothing from LEO.

I said she —

LEO (*shouts*). You did!

A silence.

VIRGINIA. What are you doing Leo, why are you waiting here while we all wash in blood around you? You won't see her?

Nothing from LEO.

You taught her.

LEO. It was never my intention to teach anyone.

VIRGINIA. Oh?

LEO. Or to remake the world at large. All I am is a kid who was
in love with numbers. The bitch with numbers is – they add up.
And the totals are not wholly numerical. They are a British kid
running out of a garden. You. Graham out of his mind. Some
room with carpets in London. Letters from the East. Threats
from the West. Trees on fire. But what is all that to do with
me? I feel like a singer, who sings a note in innocence and all
the glass in the windows smashes. Is the consequence of what I
think down to me or not? I say – not. I am sick of being some
kind of moralist by default – all because I was in love with
numbers.

VIRGINIA *stares at him. Upstage the* VICE-CHANCELLOR
comes on with TOM, *who stands a few yards away. The light is
now that of a golden late afternoon.* VIRGINIA *turns and sees
the* VICE-CHANCELLOR. *He smiles.*

VC. Good evening, Virginia.

VIRGINIA *whirls on* LEO, *who does not look at her.*

LEO (*low*). Just go home. Run a bath. Put on the TV. Then,
whatever you've got in the house to blow your mind, use it.

VIRGINIA (*low*). You American bastard. What have they offered
you?

She pauses, then turns and runs off. The VICE-CHANCELLOR
and TOM *come down to* LEO, *slowly,* TOM *keeping his
distance.*

LEO. I want you to think very carefully how you speak to me,
because I may suddenly throw up on you.

VC. Understood, Professor Lehrer.

LEO. This –

He takes a key out of his pocket.

Is a key to a locker on Birmingham Railway Station, there you
will find all the material, from me, from the girl, with a
breakdown of the work you will also find in the university's
computer.

VC. Ah.

A silence. Then LEO *throws the key into the air.* TOM *takes a
few steps back and catches it. The* VC *and* TOM *relax.*

You –

He pauses.

Bumped into our resident red mole earlier this afternoon.

He pauses.

Dear old Cliff Jones, you know he is trying to build a house somewhere in the Urals?

He laughs.

A real local character is Cliff. Of course I am doing everything to stop his department being cut, but – Fine Art? In these harsh, utilitarian times? Particularly when it's Fine Art run by an alcoholic Marxist-Leninist –

LEO (*shouts*). All right! (*Low.*) All right.

He takes out the letter and holds it up. TOM *comes forward and takes it, deliberately.*

TOM. Do you know where the girl is?

LEO. I said be very careful how you talk to me –

VC. There are –

He pauses.

Her parents to think of. The university is responsible for the children in its care –

LEO. No!

A silence.

VC. No matter. All will be well. Now that we are at peace. I know you want nothing said. An act of conscience is a lonely thing. Best resolved at the soul's still centre? All I will say is –

LEO *closes his eyes.*

I find it rather wonderful that an exile from your country has given us all a lesson in patriotism.

He holds his hand out to shake. LEO *vomits, crouching.*

My dear fellow –

TOM *touches the* VICE-CHANCELLOR's *arm and shakes his head. They walk away. The* VICE-CHANCELLOR *stops and looks back at* LEO.

VC. One is tempted to say 'And we did not even have to show him the instruments of torture'. Young man, I will buy you a drink in the staff club.

They go off, the VICE-CHANCELLOR *helped by* TOM's *arm.* LEO *alone. The stage darkens. Moonlight.* LEO, *still crouching,*

sniffs cocaine. He grunts, he breathes deeply, he coughs. GILLY,
VIRGINIA *and* ANDREA *come on. They do not see* LEO.

GILLY. Leo? Leo?

VIRGINIA. Gilly this is wrong –

GILLY. He'll be here.

ANDREA. With policemen watching –

GILLY. Leo?

VIRGINIA. God I hate being frightened, I hate it.

GILLY. He – will – be – here!

ANDREA. Aren't you sick of dangerous men by now?

GILLY. He's not dangerous, just too clever, too bloody clever by
half!

She runs forward.

Where are you? Clever teacher!

VIRGINIA. We've got to stop here –

ANDREA. Just let her, let her.

GILLY. Let me see you, clever man, clever, clever man.

She sees LEO *and approaches him.*

Why?

She pauses.

Why?

She pauses.

Why?

LEO. Let – us – say –

He pauses.

That I have exchanged a walk-on part in the war, for a lead
role in a cage.

He giggles, coughs.

Isn't that from a pop-song somewhere? Y'know, you grasp at
splinters. As they fly past in the air –

He wipes his nose with his sleeve.

GILLY. You've given it all to them?

He stares at her.

LEO. Yeah, 'the discovery', the 'great work', yeah I've given them
the whole kerboodle. You want some of this?

The cocaine. GILLY *ignores it.*

GILLY. You showed me how they can make new weapons. Out of what you and I wrote down, on thirty bits of paper. You were brilliant, in six hours, you showed me the physics, out of pure numbers – like a terrible web, spinning out. When you finished I screamed, I screamed, I still am screaming inside. And after doing that to me, you turn round, like a traitor – (*Low*). I believed in you.

LEO. Mistake. If there is one thing we have to do, it's to learn not to believe in each other.

GILLY. No?

LEO. No. None of us can take the strain.

GILLY (*shouts*). Tell me why you did it!

LEO (*shouts*). Because!

He shakes his head, he blinks his eyes.

Because I despair. Right? I despair. That is the personal bullshit.

He pauses.

As for the intellectual bullshit – the ideas, Gillian. The ideas do not love us. I have come to the conclusion that all the investigations into the atom, discoveries, calculations, formulations, nearer and nearer to the description of the force of nature – the scientific quest of the century – is fundamentally malign. All the technology that has flowed from it, atomic fission, power stations to bombs, the actual material – is malign.

He laughs.

Get your head round this one, philosopher. What if the most *un*natural thing our species can do, is to understand nature itself? Malignity! In the ideas, in the idea of the ideas. if I were religious – and thank the fuck I'm not – I'd start talking about evil.

VIRGINIA *and* ANDREA *come on at the back.*

VIRGINIA. Gilly?

They see her and stop.

LEO. Yup! If I were the Pope, I think I would announce that we are forbidden to know the true nature of gravity, electromagnetism and the nuclear forces. But – too late, holiness. We're never going to dig that knowledge out of our lives, out of our thoughts, out of our machines. Yup! As Pope I think I'd burn myself at the stake. Did you say you wanted some of this?

The cocaine. She hits him once, very deliberately on the side of the head. He laughs.

VIRGINIA. Gilly, they're probably watching him. Come on.

GILLY. Thank you – for teaching me – the physics.

Near tears, she runs to VIRGINIA *and* ANDREA. *They go off quickly.*

LEO. What about you, then? Walk-on part in the war?

He looks about him.

Gilly?

He pauses.

Where are you?

He pauses.

Where you gone?

He pauses.

(*Slurred.*) Well am I right or not? Look –

He pauses.

Let's calculate it through 'til come the rosy dawn.

He pauses.

Float away, come the rosy dawn, do some maths.

He pauses.

This time you show me, eh? You pass me the poison. Teach the teacher.

He pauses.

Eh? (*Low.*) I need you, student. Where are you?

Scene Four: Embassy.

In the blackout, the low electrical hum, building up to a screech, then a second of silence –

The lights come on, brilliant all over the stage. The hum returns.

GILLY *walks forward. She is dressed in soiled, outdoor clothes. She bends under the weight of a large hiker's back-pack, messily put together, a rolled sleeping bag hangs from it.*

GILLY'S MOTHER *walks with her, played by* VIRGINIA, *who is in lumpy, winter clothes, a middle-aged woman's coat, holding the pink umbrella to obscure her face.*

GILLY. Don't go on, Mum. I got to get up this hill.

MOTHER. I don't know why you hurt me and Daddy –

GILLY. Why do you always call him 'Daddy'?

MOTHER. Living in filth and dirt. I worry so much about how you live –

GILLY. I worry about you too, Mum.

MOTHER. Like that time I found pills under your pillow and was worried sick you were on drugs –

GILLY. They were aspirins, Mum. I was twelve. I had my first period.

MOTHER. Things I don't want brought into the house. Like that poster on your wall of a bomb going off –

GILLY. But the poster means don't let the bomb go off!

GILLY *slips the back-pack off.*

Please, I'm so tired.

MOTHER. You're our only child. We had you late. You don't realise. When the back extension roof went and damp got in I couldn't sleep for months.

GILLY. I'm tired.

She sits, leaning against the back-pack.

MOTHER. All the terrible things in the world. What if Daddy got sick? If we lost the house we'd have to sleep in a hole in the ground, all because of you.

GILLY *closes her eyes.*

GILLY. Don't want you to live in a hole in the ground, Mum.

MOTHER. Blowing people up, going to prison, men in the parks and little girls, guns, pornography, oh, that poster looks communist, Gilly, Daddy's ever so upset.

GILLY. Sorry Mum, did I bring the nuclear bomb indoors?

VIRGINIA. Gilly wake up!

GILLY. But the bomb's in you, Mum.

VIRGINIA. Gilly!

GILLY. In you! It'll go off in you!

VIRGINIA. Gilly, for Godsake!

GILLY wakes up with a start.

VIRGINIA lowers the umbrella.

The light changes to a drab, London afternoon. It is raining. At the back, the dull, smeared green of a park. The hum changes to the sound of traffic.

Don't go to sleep. There's a policeman looking at you.

GILLY. My mum never wanted it in the house.

VIRGINIA. Gilly, get up.

GILLY. Oh yes.

She stands, stiffly.

VIRGINIA. You just plomped down on the pavement and went to sleep –

GILLY. Yes.

VIRGINIA. We're so tired, so –

ANDREA runs on.

ANDREA. I got inside. There was a man in a shabby suit, in front of a TV screen. Opening letters. I couldn't make him understand.

VIRGINIA. What did he say?

ANDREA. 'No.'

VIRGINIA. 'Niet.'

She scoffs.

ANDREA. It doesn't look like the Russian Embassy. Just any old big house, behind any old hedge. Except for the cameras on the walls.

GILLY. We've got to see him.

VIRGINIA. They are not going to pay any attention to us Gilly. Look at us. Three tramps. Cranks in the rain.

ANDREA. Gilly wants to do this. Let her.

VIRGINIA. Madness.

GILLY. We've got to see the ambassador.

VIRGINIA. A naive gesture. And I'm not even sure it's right –

ANDREA. Shut up Vee.

VIRGINIA. All right, I know I am the older woman on this escapade. I mean, I think she was dreaming I am her mother!

GILLY. I'll go in.

ANDREA. The man in the shabby suit told me to leave. They won't let you in.

GILLY. Then I'll post it through the letterbox.

VIRGINIA. Oh for crying out loud.

GILLY. It's in my back-pack –

VIRGINIA. Don't –

But GILLY is pulling at the back-pack.

That policeman's looking at us again. He'll think you've got a bomb in there.

ANDREA. Gilly does think she's got a bomb in there.

GILLY pulls out a big envelope and her binder.
She pauses.

GILLY. I'm doing this because there must be no more secrets.

A silence.

I won't be a mo.

She runs off.

VIRGINIA. Look at us. We're like refugees.

ANDREA. That's what we are.

VIRGINIA. No country?

She laughs.

The anarchy, the squalor. I never thought 'protest' would be this – grubby.

ANDREA. Who was it said 'The only country I have is the people I love'?

VIRGINIA (*low*). Come on, come on.

A silence.

Refugees.

A laugh.

But what's the war? Against men, against the East, against the West, even against ourselves? Or just against death, jolly old mother Death?

ANDREA. Father Death?

GILLY *runs back on.*

GILLY. Plop. Just like that. There was a cat, sitting up in the ivy, by the steps. She blinked at me and said 'Meow! What have you done?' 'Done something at least, my dear' I said.

A blackout and —

Scene Five: Peace moves.

The Bach Theme is heard, played, undistorted, by the violin.

In the blackout the sound of strong wind and rain begins and grows.

The lights come up to an ugly grey dawn before layers of wire fences that recede into the distance. The wire on the fences rattles and hums in the strong wind.

Large sheets of mud-streaked polythene flap on the stage before the fences.

Four POLICEMEN, *played anonymously by the* VICE-CHANCELLOR, GRAHAM, TOM *and* CYCLIST *actors, stand amongst the polythene sheets. They are in bad weather capes and each has a walky talky.*

The SKELETON VIOLINIST *sits to one side, playing, A woman — she wears a fisherman's hat against the bad weather.*

VIRGINIA *and* ANDREA *are moving plastic bags and rucksacks about from beneath the polythene, taking no notice of the* POLICEMEN.

The noise of the wind, that is of wind machines in the wings, the rattling of the fences and flapping of the polythene, is almost too much for speech to be heard.

LEO *and* GILLY, *both well wrapped-up, are downstage. She carries the pink umbrella, again blown inside out, and a large cake tin. She is struggling to open the tin.*

GILLY. My mum sent me a cake!

LEO. You what?

GILLY. Cake! Can you open it?

LEO. Yeah, cake –

GILLY. I expect it's bloody sponge!

She holds the tin, he pulls at the lid.

Do you want to see Vee? She's over there.

LEO. I turned up. Had no idea you were here. Don't you get pneumonia?

GILLY. What?

LEO. Pneumonia.

GILLY. Never healthier.

LEO. Here we go!

The cake tin lid comes off.

GILLY. I've done more work! On the equations! You?

LEO. Yeah, it don't stop –

GILLY. In my head, all the time – hey it's fruit!

LEO. There's a note – hey!

He stops it blowing away. He gives GILLY *the note. She turns against the wind and reads it.*

LEO. Have the planes come in?

   GILLY *laughs at the note.*

They said in the press, anyday, the planes come in.

GILLY. My bloody mother says she's proud of me and sent me a cake! My bloody mother!

LEO. This is what I done recently!

He takes a brown envelope from beneath his coat. In the distance, the sound of planes approaching.

GILLY. I got something too, here!

She zips open the front of her coat. A binder. She holds it out.

New binder! The planes with the missiles will be Galaxy transporters. We're going through the wire, onto the runway. Swop?

They swop envelope and binder. The noise of planes and wind rising. They laugh. They embrace. ANDREA *and* VIRGINIA *turn and run at the wire,* VIRGINIA *making a hold for* ANDREA's *foot. She climbs up the wire. The* POLICEMEN *run at them. They freeze.* ANDREA's *fingers in the wire, the* POLICEMEN *crowded in,* LEO *and* GILLY *embracing. The lights go down. The noise ceases. There are a few notes further from the Bach Theme.*

BLOODY POETRY

The People in the Play

BYRON

Lord George Gordon Byron was born in 1788, of 'Mad Jack' Byron, a
Captain in The Guards, and Catherine Gordon, a Scottish heiress descended
from James I of Scotland. At birth his right foot was deformed, a disability
he fought against all his life with violent exercise. Described by a lover,
Lady Caroline Lamb, as 'Mad, bad and dangerous to know', he was the
most fashionable and commercially successful poet of his day, earning
huge sums for his long poems *Childe Harold* and *Don Juan*. To his
contemporaries he was both idol and bogeyman, a profligate talent with a
rakish reputation — he once said 'What I earn by my brains, I spend by my
bollocks'. Like Oscar Wilde eighty years later, he was the victim of a sexual
scandal, a love affair with his half-sister Augusta Leigh. Because of it he left
England in 1816 and never returned. That year he met Shelley for the first
time at Secheron on Lake Geneva, Switzerland. A rebel by temperament
rather than by intellect, he died in 1824 of a marsh fever at Missolonghi,
while organising a brigade in support of the Greek forces in the ultimately
successful Greek Revolution against Turkish rule.

BYSSHE

Percy Bysshe Shelley was born in 1792 the son of Sir Timothy Shelley, a minor aristocrat and country squire. With, for some, the exception of John Milton, he is the greatest poet in the language after Shakespeare. He was educated at Eton, where he fought remorseless bullying with ferocious fits of temper. In 1811 he was sent down from Oxford University for writing a pamphlet, *The Necessity of Atheism*, with his friend T.J. Hogg. In 1812 he travelled to Dublin where he published his *Address To The Irish People*, a tract against British rule in Ireland. His early poem *Queen Mab*, though it sold less than two hundred copies in his life-time, became an inspirational text for early trade unionists and the Chartist Movement. Among his major poems are *Hymn To Intellectual Beauty* and *Mont Blanc* (1816); *Julian And Maddalo* (1818) which dramatises an argument with Byron about human nature; *Prometheus Unbound* (1818-19) which rivals *Paradise Lost* in ambition and breadth of vision; *The Mask Of Anarchy* (1819), written in protest at the Peterloo Massacre; *Epipyschidion* (1821), a complex personal meditation on love, and the unfinished allegory *The Triumph of Life* (1822). He was drowned in a boating accident in the Gulf of Spezia, Italy, on 8th July, 1822 — he was twenty-nine years old. His body was recovered and burnt on the beach in the presence of a few friends, Byron among them.

MARY

Mary Godwin was the daughter of Mary Woolstonecraft, the author of *The Vindication Of The Rights Of Women* and William Godwin, the author of *Enquiry Concerning Political Justice* — it was a famous family of radical political thinkers. Mary's mother died giving birth to her: her father doted on his daughter obsessively. Mary met Shelley, then married to Harriet, in 1813: she was the first to declare love. With Claire, they eloped to the continent. William Godwin's wrath at this out-break of 'free love' amongst his family, the preaching of which he preferred to the practice, was abated by a series of loans from Shelley which he, in turn, had to borrow money to pay. She was the author of *Frankenstein, or The Modern Prometheus*, a profound parable attacking some basic beliefs of the Romantic Movement, which has been sadly travestied by 20th century horror films. After Shelley's death she gradually became estranged from Claire and Shelley's friends, who accused her bitterly of suppressions and omissions in her publications of Shelley's work. Nevertheless her notes to the poems are a lucid and militant defence of the poetry and their life together. She died in 1851.

CLAIRE

When the play opens Claire Clairemont is eighteen. She was christened Jane, but changed her name to Claire because it means 'light'. Her mother married William Godwin in 1803, his second wife — she and Mary Godwin were therefore sisters by marriage. The passionate, volatile triangular relationship between Claire, Mary and Shelley began at the same time Mary and Shelley became lovers. Claire's mother believed that Shelley had seduced Claire with Mary's connivance. Claire was a free-thinker and a utopian who wanted to create what she called 'The subterranean community of women'. Her surviving letters do not do justice to the tenacity and optimism with which she lived her life. Her affair with Byron began in April, 1816 — their child Allegra was born the following year. A year after Shelley's death she travelled to Russia, taking a post as a governess in Moscow. She never married and died, in genteel poverty, in Florence in 1879. Her refusal in old age to give Shelley's love letters to an intrusive American academic inspired Henry James to write *The Aspern Papers*.

HARRIET

Harriet was the daughter of John Westbrook, a retired merchant and coffee house proprietor. She met Shelley through her friendship with his sisters. In 1811, when sixteen years old, she eloped to Scotland with the nineteen year-old Shelley where they married against her father's wishes. She accompanied Shelley to Dublin and helped him distribute anti-British, pro-Fenian material. The marriage came under strain on the birth of their first child, Ianthe, in 1813. Shelley left her for Mary Godwin when she was four months pregnant with their second child, a boy, Charles, born in 1814. She fought fiercely to save the marriage, travelling to London to confront Mary, then for her young family threatening Shelley with a private prosecution for atheism if he did not increase the allowance for the children. In the summer of 1816 she sent the children to the country to be looked after by a clergyman and cut her ties with her family to live with an army officer. When he was posted to India she found herself penniless and pregnant. She drowned herself in the Serpentine, London, in December 1816.

POLIDORI

Doctor John William Polidori graduated from Edinburgh University at the age of nineteen with a degree in medicine and a fluent grasp of French and Italian. He accompanied Byron on the flight to Europe in 1816 as his secretary and personal physician. At the same time, without asking Byron's permission, he accepted 500 guineas from John Murray, Byron's publisher, to write an account of the journey. A vain, highly strung young man, he became the butt of Shelley, Mary and Byron's at times cruel sense of fun. He wrote plays which they mercilessly ridiculed. He was accident prone — paying court to Mary one day he fell over and broke his ankle. Biographers are in his debt for his sensational account of the night of 18th June, 1816, when talk of ghosts and Byron's reading of Coleridge's *Christabel* induced a violent fit in Shelley. Mary, with some malice, used his name for Frankenstein's evil teacher — perhaps out of revenge Polidori claimed, untruthfully, to have given her the plot in the first place. He shot himself in 1827, because of gambling debts.

Bloody Poetry was commissioned by Foco Novo Theatre Company and was first presented at the Haymarket Theatre, Leicester on 1 October 1984, with the following cast:

PERCY BYSSHE SHELLEY	Valentine Pelka
MARY SHELLEY	Fiona Shaw
CLAIRE CLAIREMONT	Jane Gurnett
GEORGE, THE LORD BYRON	James Aubrey
DR WILLIAM POLIDORI	William Gaminara
HARRIET WESTBROOK, later her GHOST	Sue Burton
VOICE	a member of the company

Director Roland Rees
Assistant to the Director Marina Caldarone
Designer Poppy Mitchell
Costumes Sheelagh Killeen
Composer and Musical Director Andrew Dickson
Lighting by Richard Moffatt
Sound by Paul Bull

This production transferred to the Hampstead Theatre, London, where it was first performed on 31 October 1984.

The play takes place between the summers of 1816 and 1822 in Switzerland, England and Italy.

'Shelley's life seems more a haunting than a history.'
Shelley: The Pursuit, Richard Holmes

ACT ONE

Scene One

BYSSHE
Flickering shadows, the window of a coach.

BYSSHE. The Alps. Switzerland. The coach. Aching bones.
   Dirty clothes.Hotel rooms we cannot afford. Above us —

   Far, far above, piercing the infinite sky
   Mont Blanc appears, — still, snowy and serene —
   Its subject mountains their unearthly forms
   Pile around it, ice and rock; broad vales between
   Of frozen floods, unfathomable deeps,
   Blue as the overhanging heaven —

   Bump, bump, bump — dejected thoughts. In exile.

   He laughs.

   The flight out of England, Mary! With little William, and
   Claire, what an unholy, holy family! We little band of
   atheistical perverts, free-lovers, we poeticals — leaving England.

   England, England.
   A people starved and stabbed in the untilled field.
   Rulers who neither see, nor feel, nor know
   But leech-like to their fainting country cling,
   Til they drop, blind in blood.

   Bump, bump, bump —

   Men of England, wherefore plough
   For the lords who lay ye low?
   Wherefore weave with toil and care
   The rich robes your tyrants wear?

   Bump, bump, bump, bump, bump, bump!

   The living frame which sustains my soul
   Is sinking beneath the fierce control
   Down through the lampless deep of song
   I am drawn and driven along

   Bump bump, wave on wave —

   This world is the mother of all we know,
   This world is the mother of all we feel —

Waves.

The shore of Lake Geneva. The 25th of May, eighteen hundred and sixteen.

Scene Two

Beach. Lake Geneva. BYSSHE, MARY *and* CLAIRE. MARY *and* CLAIRE *looking out.* BYSSHE *pacing back and forth at the back.*

CLAIRE. There!

In that boat! His head against the light.

BYSSHE *stops, looks briefly, then continues to pace.*

The head of a god, the head of Lord Byron.

MARY *winces.*

MARY. It is the head of a local fisherman, out for the fish that will be fresh on the menus of expensive restaurants tonight. I do not think the Lord Byron is out catching with his own hands what he may well pay excessively to eat.

A silence.

CLAIRE. It was you and Bysshe who wanted this meeting. It was you who encouraged me to engineer it. It was you who wished to throw yourselves at the feet of England's greatest living poet.

MARY *glances at* BYSSHE *who snorts angrily.*

I knew he would come to this hotel. It was I who sat up late last night, and heard his coach.

MARY. His Lordship's coach. It is — an ostentatious vehicle.

CLAIRE. I have ridden in it. It has a bed!

MARY. For two, of course —

CLAIRE. Shelves lined with books and is, naturally, very well stocked with wines.

MARY. Naturally. A library, bedroom and bar-room on wheels. What more could a poet desire?

CLAIRE. I — sent him a letter. At two o'clock this morning.

MARY. Claire, you did not —

CLAIRE. I sent a letter to my lover, yes.

MARY. Oh Claire my dear, my dear.

CLAIRE. I am not ashamed.

MARY. No.

A silence.

No, you are not.

CLAIRE. I told him Bysshe and we were here.

MARY. He did not rush to meet us at breakfast.

CLAIRE. His footman said he had gone into Geneva, to shop.
For —

She picks at her nails.

For his dogs.

MARY. For dog-food?

CLAIRE. But if we walk on the beach he will come off the lake.
I saw him, putting out in a boat. He will come off the lake,
he will!

MARY. We wait ten days for him in a hotel, at a ruinous price.
The Olympian god of English poetry arrives, ignores us and
goes to buy dog-food —

CLAIRE. He is most anxious that, after a journey, his dogs be
fed fine meat.

MARY sighs and looks out over the lake.

Mary?

Nothing from MARY.

This is not like you, to be so — uneasy.

MARY. I —

CLAIRE. What?

MARY. No matter.

CLAIRE. What?

MARY. I — still have dreams of the journey here.

CLAIRE. The mountains were beautiful.

MARY. They were desolate.

CLAIRE, *irritated.*

CLAIRE. Oh we must not — ! Be dejected, spiral down, fall into dejection and — hurt each other, we must not.

MARY. No.

A silence.

No.

CLAIRE. We are privileged to make this journey. We are privileged to stand on this beach, and see George Byron and Bysshe Shelley meet. It will be history!

MARY. Well. We will all write it up in our diaries, surely. And read each other's accounts, secretly. What else is there to do?

Looking out over the lake.

Drifting across Europe. Spying on each other's confessions.

CLAIRE. The two poets meet on a beach. Light blazes off the water, behind them. In their exile, they embrace. It will be like a statue. And I have been the lover of one, and am the lover of the other.

A toss of the head.

All of us, we will become magnificent. The men and the women of the future will thank us. We are their great experiment. We will find out how to live and love, without fear.

MARY. If the money does not run out.

CLAIRE. Your sarcasm's horrible Mary, I hate it, I hate it, I have never heard it before.

MARY. I told you — the journey has made me — cold. Inside.

CLAIRE. Horribly unfair! When you heard that George and I —

With a toss of her head.

The Lord Byron and I had made love, your first thought was — 'Oh good. Claire will arrange a meeting between Bysshe and him.' No, 'sister'? Did you not have, at once, that scheme? In your notoriously strong, womanly mind —

MARY. Forgive me Claire. Yes.

CLAIRE. Yes! Then keep in mind, I lifted my skirt, for this.

Bitter, suddenly near to tears.

In a hotel room, ten miles from London, I lifted my skirt. For

the good of English poetry? Long live poetry, yes, Mary? He
has very bad teeth, George Byron, you know. His teeth they
are not good. And he has the scar marks of boils on his body,
from something he caught from little boys in Turkey, he
told me.

MARY. Claire, I do want them to meet, I want us all to meet.
The attraction is too strong, a like-mind. In England they want
to hang us all. Bad reviews are not good enough for our
enemies, they would like a public execution.

She looks at CLAIRE.

You do know that the Home Office has set up secret
committees. That they are investigating Bysshe.

CLAIRE. Oh, he'll love that (*To* BYSSHE.) You'd love to be
last seen, shouting before a firing squad on Tower Hill.
Wouldn't you Bysshe!

BYSSHE *turns away.* CLAIRE, *quoting:*

We tread
On fire! The avenging Power his hell on earth hath spread!

MARY. Quite. They want to hang, draw and quarter what
we stand for. And the loneliness is great, is it not, my
dear. So —

A shrug, a laugh.

Let us play at gods and goddesses, moving in brilliant light on
a beach by a lake, in dresses of white silk flowing about limbs,
we statues. But we must not forget that statues — do not eat,
they do not have bank accounts overdrawn by thousands of
pounds, they do not —

With a glance at BYSSHE.

— have lungs of mucus and blood, they do not —

She looks at CLAIRE, *pauses.*

— have women's wombs.

CLAIRE. I don't care, I don't care, I don't care.

MARY. Nor do I.

They glance at each other, a giggle.

CLAIRE. I am going to live it.

MARY. Yes.

CLAIRE. I am going to be loved, happy and free.

MARY. Yes.

Depression.

Yes.

CLAIRE. Let us draw courage from our appalling reputations. How the world sees us is, like it or not, how we are condemned to live. I think we have no choice in the matter. Good I say, good, good!

She laughs.

Remember what the *Daily Mail* called us?

MARY. All too well.

CLAIRE. 'Shelley's ball girls? Quote — 'Mr Shelley is a bad poet. Like a bad tennis player, his verses forever smash into the net and fall to the ground. But Mr. Shelley is lucky. Two beautiful girls crouch on the sidelines, waiting to pick up his balls'.

MARY. Gutter journalism.

CLAIRE. The real world.

BYRON, *shouting at the back.*

BYRON. Damn you sir — your destiny may be to be eaten by crabs and fishes, but mine is not sir! You are no sailor sir!

The weak voice of POLIDORI *is heard.*

POLIDORI. My Lord I do protest —

BYRON. Blast you, do you — there are people of quality upon the beach, go off sir!

POLIDORI. My Lord!

BYRON. Go off and drown, damn you! I will have none of your damn foolery!

BYRON *storms down up onto the stage. He limps. He turns and shouts.*

Off! T'Neptune! A watery trident up your arsehole sir!

Turns to CLAIRE. *Charm.*

Claire my dear.

CLAIRE *and* MARY *curtsey.* BYSSHE *stands his ground at the back.*

CLAIRE. My Lord —

BYRON. No request, no word! I am lathered, horribly.

Eyeing MARY.

CLAIRE. Mrs Mary Shelley. Mary, My Lord Byron.

Another curtsey from MARY.

MARY. My Lord.

BYRON. Mrs Shelley.

Takes her hand and kisses it.

I am cursed with a fool of a boating companion. The Lord keep us from the fantasies of our sycophants. There are some people who are like leeches, they hang on, you flick at them to brush them off, but they stick!

CLAIRE, *looking round for* BYSSHE, *who hovers as far away as he can, glowering.*

CLAIRE. And my Lord, this —

BYRON. Yes.

BYSSHE *and* BYRON *stare at each other.*

A younger poet.

A horrible silence. MARY *and* CLAIRE *attempt to intervene.*

CLAIRE. ⎱ We —
MARY. ⎰ Mr Shelley —

BYRON *ignores them.*

BYRON. What do you write on?

BYSSHE *about to reply, but —*

I write on gin and soda water. At night, 'til dawn. Damn important to pace yourself, I find. As the sun riseth so doth the gin in the glass.

A silence.

CLAIRE. Mr Shelley does not drink.

BYRON. Not another damn Wordsworth. I do distrust a sober poet who writes of nothing but ecstasy. Like a virgin writing hymns about the delights of a brothel. God's teeth! Bysshe

Shelley the wildman does not drink? What do we scribbling poets have in common?

Sir, you are silent.

A silence.

Sir, I do not know whether you are beginning to bore me, or to make me laugh.

A silence.

Sir, I have met this silence from fellow scribblers before. It usually means they think I am a bad poet. If that is why Miss Clairemont has affected this introduction then — I thank you for your spite. As a satirist, spite and hatred are meat and drink to me —

BYSSHE (*interrupting*). My Lord, you are a great poet.

MARY *and* CLAIRE *start and glance at each other.*

But you are an abominable sailor.

BYRON. Sir, what do you mean by that?

BYSSHE. I cannot see why you abandoned your barque in the hands of a fool.

BYRON. Ah. Ah. *That* — does call for an explanation.

Looking out.

That is my official biographer. Foisted upon me by John Murray, my publisher. Is Murray touching your stuff?

BYSSHE (*clipped*). No.

BYRON (*airily*). He will, he will. Commerce in the end hath every talent, raped up against a wall. Particularly when the talent is in the throes of divorce proceedings. A predicament that, I gather, is familiar to both of us?

BYSSHE. I do not hold with . . .

BYRON (*shouts out over the lake*). Polidori! Polidori!

(*To the company.*) The young shit hath a wonderfully ludicrous name, no?

(*Over the lake.*) Polidori!

(*To the company.*) He is also my personal physician. I am his sole patient. He has killed off all the others.

(*Across the lake.*) To the bottom, sir! Let the mermaids chew your bollocks off!

POLIDORI (*off, at the back*). I am trying hard, My Lord —

BYRON (*to* BYSSHE). Are there?

BYSSHE. My Lord?

BYRON. Are there mermaids in lakes?

BYSSHE. If a rhyme is needed, no doubt there can be.

BYRON. Indeed.

He laughs.

Indeed! I see I am talking to a fellow professional! So, you sail?

BYSSHE. Yes.

BYRON. Well?

BYSSHE. Yes.

BYRON. Excellent. You swim?

BYSSHE. Yes.

MARY starts.

BYRON. Well?

BYSSHE, *a shrug.*

Excellent.

They stare at each other.

You called me great. One is always pleased to receive a good review. For writers in our position, a good review is as rare as a double-yolked egg at breakfast.

BYSSHE (*bitterly*). For me, yes, but not for your Lordship —

BYRON (*the airy wave*). The praise of critics is bought, bought and sold. It is all to do with fashion. When you have some fashionable reputation with critics, cash it in. Foist an outrage on the bastards. It may, sir, come as a surprise to you that —

BYRON *looks down, thinking. Then continues.*

That the epithet 'great' is contrary to my nature.

MARY *scoffs. They all stare at her.* BYRON, *with a bow.*

Madam?

MARY. I am sure, my Lord, that no one of this company is
foolish enough to confuse 'greatness' with 'arrogance'.

BYRON. Ah. I will think on that.

A sexual look at MARY *from* BYRON. CLAIRE, *trying to
get over the hiccup.*

CLAIRE. But there is a touchstone. Shakespeare was 'great'.

BYRON, *up again.*

BYRON. I am loathe even to apply it to Shakespeare. A
grotesquely talented little shit in the pay of royalty. (*To*
MARY.) And yes, yes, I am in the pay of my publisher,
Mr Commerce.

The look from BYRON *again,* MARY *dead still.* BYSSHE *sees
nothing of this. He flares.*

BYSSHE. Shakespeare did not go far enough! Further than any
of us can go, but not far enough! King Lear himself,
not Gloucester, should have been blinded, and by his own hands.
Then in his darkness he should have turned on God himself.

BYRON. But at least the bugger wrote a great deal! The greatest
sin in a poet is anal retention.

BYSSHE. Explain —

BYRON. I have heard of this habit that certain madmen have
from the pathetic Polidori. (*To* CLAIRE.) It would seem that
some mad people are obsessed with their own shit.

CLAIRE, *mouth open,* MARY *takes a step forward but she
says nothing.*

(*To* BYSSHE.) They tighten their arseholes day and night, to
retain their turds. Which they do, for weeks.

BYSSHE, *enthusiastically.*

BYSSHE. I have heard of this too! What could release them from
the infirmity, is the shock of electricity —

BYRON, *ignoring this.*

BYRON. Yes yes, but certain poets are turd retainers. When, after
months, their bowels squeeze open, all they lay is a turd.
Which they invite the public to see as a fertilized egg. With the
purity of pure hatred, shall we name names?

BYSSHE. Why not?

BYRON. William Wordsworth!

Robert Southey!

We all, of course, write for love. But love can be a soggy dough. A little hatred is yeast and salt —

BYSSHE. You are wrong about Wordsworth.

BYRON. Yes yes, it is boring to be so wonderfully wrong about so wonderful a poet. I hate his guts. But — I give up. He has sold too many books. The poison of his works has, irredeemably, infected the bloodstream of our literature. You disagree. You know his poems, no doubt by heart.

BYSSHE. Those written before 1802 —

BYRON. Ah! Before reaction got him! Before he went religious. The rats! The rats! The rats that leave the revolution's ship! For the comfort of the Church, or some concocted mysticism, or good reviews in the *Times Literary Supplement*, or the Oxford Chair of Poetry! Sir!

He stares at BYSSHE.

You are serious. But a bit of a bitch too. There may be something in you. Dinner! Tonight!

Turning.

All of us, in my rooms.

CLAIRE. George —

BYSSHE, *over her.*

BYSSHE. Thank you, my Lord.

BYRON. Eat fish, d'you? Being vegetarian?

BYSSHE. No.

BYRON. Damn pity. Hired a man to catch trout in the lake for you. The lazy fella's at it now out there, if Polidori's not scared all the fish to death. No matter. (*To* MARY.) Maybe the women'll fancy a peck at it.

MARY *curtsies.*

MARY. My Lord.

BYRON. My dear Shelley you may have all the nuts and broccoli you can devour.

He pauses.

I have read you, sir.

BYRON *extends his hand. He and* BYSSHE *shake.* BYRON *holds on to* BYSSHE'*s hand.*

I particularly admire your entry in the register of the hotel. 'Name: Percy Bysshe Shelley. Profession: Democrat, Philanthropist and Atheist. Home address: Hell'. I know you wrote it in Greek, but do you want to be eaten alive?

BYSSHE *wants to withdraw his hand, but* BYRON *still holds it. Then* BYRON *kisses* BYSSHE'*s hand.* BYSSHE *recoils.* BYRON, *bowing to all in turn.*

My dears! Dinner! Dinner! Dinner! Tonight, tonight!

A gesture at the lake.

If my biographer's body is washed up on this beach, drowned, send it back to England, suitably decomposed.

He has a hip flask in his hand. He strides away, drinking from it. CLAIRE *runs after him.*

CLAIRE. George, my dear —

BYRON, *viciously, into her face.*

BYRON. Dinner, dinner, at dinner!

They stare, faces close. MARY *and* BYSSHE *have seen and heard the exchange.* BYRON, *airily to them.*

Life goes on!

He goes off. CLAIRE *at the back, looking at the ground.*

MARY. Drunk.

BYSSHE. Brilliant.

MARY. Brilliant.

BYSSHE. Drunk.

MARY. And silly.

BYSSHE. But himself.

MARY. And —

A nod at CLAIRE.

Brutally cruel.

BYSSHE. But we have met.

MARY. Yes! Now it has happened we can make it all mythical!

BYSSHE. Quite! We met naked —

MARY. At sunset —

BYSSHE. Maidens twined flowers about our hair —

MARY. Autographs were given to mermaids —

BYSSHE. Byron left on the back of a dolphin —

MARY. And Shelley?

BYSSHE. Ah! Shelley — erected an electrical machine and sucked the soul of Byron into a bottle! Screwed tight! Which he then did mix with a magic liquid, and drink, so Shelley too could have fame and money —

MARY. Embellish the scene!

CLAIRE turns, flushed.

CLAIRE. Did you see how he did love me, wonderfully?

A silence.

BYSSHE. Claire —

MARY. My dears, I think it best in matters of love, that —

She pauses.

That we have a good time? Introduce pleasure, and who can tell the taker from the taken?

CLAIRE. Mary, sometimes you are most matronly and sensible, at others you are a dirty-minded bitch —

BYSSHE. The school rhyme! We heard the children sing!

They look at each other, then come together and embrace in a triangle, dancing round, chanting.

All. 'Oh Lord Byron loves his sister
His sister his sister
What a dirty mister, dirty dirty mister
Lord Byron loves his sister
And they both lie *down*!
Oh —'

POLIDORI steps up onto the stage, soaking wet. They stop in mid-song looking at him.

POLIDORI. Ah! Mr Shelley. I — er — have read your *Queen Mab*. Some of it is very well done, some of it slapdash.

A silence. Then SHELLEY whispering inside their circle.

BYSSHE. A critic! A critic!

CLAIRE. Ugh! Ugh!

BYSSHE. Ugh! Ugh!

CLAIRE. A slimy thing.

BYSSHE. Out the slimy sea.

CLAIRE.
and   } Ugh! Ugh! Ugh!
BYSSHE.

MARY (*through giggles*). Doctor Polidori, sir?

POLIDORI. Madam — I — who the pleasure — do I —

CLAIRE. We are Mr Shelley's concubines, sir.

BYSSHE. Run sir, these women have drunk the milk of paradise!
No man's spunk is safe!

POLIDORI. Indeed —

MARY. Forgive us sir, our high spirits —

She leaves the circle.

POLIDORI. At once madam, of course. Though it is not advisable
to cavort so on a public beach.

He looks around.

There are tourists with spy-glasses. Er —

He puts a hand out.

William Polidori.

MARY. Miss Claire Clairemont.

CLAIRE *curtsies.*

Mr Shelley.

BYSSHE *walks away.*

POLIDORI. I seem to have —

He shakes his arm, it drips water.

CLAIRE. Lost Lord Byron?

POLIDORI (*turning in panic*). Oh my Lord!

And BYRON *limps and stumbles back on. He ignores*
POLIDORI.

BYRON (*to* BYSSHE). This damn hotel — we will move! I will

take the Villa Diodati. The poet Milton stayed there, perhaps the wallpaper is conducive to good verse. There is a smaller house, five minutes walk away. I suggest you, Miss Clairemont and Mrs Shelley take it, that Polidori here will do the business arrangements, a summer lease —

BYSSHE. I —

BYRON. No no no, we will summer together! It has hit me sir, an idea sir, we will all go communist. We are upper class renegades, we can afford it. More tonight! Plans, plans, of changing the world, of ripping human nature apart, love and summer, tonight! At dinner!

He turns to go.

POLIDORI. My Lord you abuse me.

BYRON. My abuse is a gift. It will enrich your diary.

He goes off.

POLIDORI. I share his Lordship's confidence, you see. I do share it. Anything you wish of him — ask me.

Going off.

My Lord —

And he's gone.

CLAIRE. Can we — afford a house?

MARY. No.

BYSSHE. No.

MARY. But we will! Life —

CLAIRE. Goes?

BYSSHE. On! On! On!

They move toward the circle again.

Scene Three

— But BYSSHE *walks away between the two women and goes off.*

Bright sunshine, green leaves. Pathways and vines between the Villa Diodati and the small house, Montalégre.

MARY. You were with him, last night, up at the big house?

CLAIRE. Oh yes!

MARY. Slept with him?

Nothing from CLAIRE.

We go back and forth upon these paths between his Lordship in Milton's old house and our — modest abode, every time of the day. But what do we say to each other?

CLAIRE. It is lovely this summer! It is lovely!

MARY. Have you told my Lord Byron?

Nothing from CLAIRE.

Have you told him you are to have his child?

Nothing from CLAIRE.

Claire, my dear, my darling, your mother married my father. That makes us sisters, yes. Also we are in love with the same man —

CLAIRE. Mary, now —

MARY. You deny you slept with Bysshe?

Nothing from CLAIRE.

You deny you still sleep with him?

CLAIRE. You — are with him every night!

MARY. But we all walk out, in the daytime, in the fields, along the shore, in an infinite combination of couples —

CLAIRE. Yes!

A silence.

We make love in the open air. Among the vines. On the stones. Or no, Bysshe and I do not make love, in the open air, among the vines, on the stones.

MARY. All I want to say is that, because of the higgledy-piggledy jumble, tumbled confusion of the state of our affections — I do not think I can bear — to have to be your mother too, my dear Claire.

They look at each other. Then laugh.

CLAIRE. Mary, Mary —

They embrace.

MARY. He —

CLAIRE. He? Which 'he'?

MARY. George Byron. He is the father of your child?

CLAIRE. Oh yes!

Realises.

Oh yes, Mary.

MARY. Tell him.

CLAIRE. I will.

MARY. Then claim the child.

CLAIRE. Oh no. George Byron will make me his wife. I will claim *him.*

A silence.

MARY. Claire, claim the child. For his or her sake, for your sake.

CLAIRE. But he will marry me!

MARY. How do you know that?

CLAIRE. Because of the manner in which I oblige him.

MARY. Claire, Claire —

CLAIRE. You will see tonight, at dinner, how his affection hath deepened.

MARY. How we do trust 'our affections'.

CLAIRE. What else can we do, all of us, in our predicament?

MARY (*to herself*). He hath no affections.

CLAIRE *withdraws.*

CLAIRE. Do not speak of George that way.

MARY. No I do not mean George Byron.

CLAIRE. Who then?

MARY. A figure.

CLAIRE. Mary, what is the matter?

MARY. Nothing it's silly, silly. I am writing the story of a monster. Very very silly!

CLAIRE. Monster?

MARY. He lives up in the snow, in the mountains.

CLAIRE. And he does not love us?

MARY. No.

CLAIRE. Maybe we will summon up your monster tonight, after
   dinner! Or Bysshe will, with electricity!

MARY. Or — he will come of his own accord.

CLAIRE. Mary! How beautiful you are, beautiful and strange.

   They link arms, and —

Scene Four

Night. Lightning, thunder, rain.

*Then, with candelabra standing about the stage, BYRON,
BYSSHE, CLAIRE and MARY lounge on the big cushions.*

*BYRON has a large brandy glass and decanter, which he dangles
and pours from throughout the scene. MARY and CLAIRE drink
wine. BYSSHE drinks water. BYSSHE is reading. He knows it by
heart, and looks up after a few lines, to give himself time to think
of what they say.*

BYSSHE.
   There was a time when meadow, grove and stream
      The earth and every common sight
         To me did seem
         Apparelled in celestial light,
   The glory and freshness of a dream.

   A silence.

   It is not now as it hath been of yore; —
      Turn wheresoe'er I may,
         By night or day,

   A silence.

   The things which I have seen I now can see no more.

   Shades of the prison house begin to close
      Upon the growing Boy,
   But he beholds the light, and whence it flows,
      He sees it in his joy —

   A silence.

   At length the man perceives it die away,

And fade into the common light of day.

BYSSHE *closes the book, pushes it from him. A silence.*

Whither is fled the visionary gleam?
Where is it now, the glory and the dream?

A silence.

BYRON. Yes yes yes, yes yes yes — *but*!

He pours a large brandy.

God's teeth Bysshe, must you after every dinner, dish me out these great slabs of Wordsworth? Like the slap of a cold fish in the face?

MARY. It is your medicine, my Lord.

BYRON. S'truth, I love they who love my health, but it is hard to take. Why? Why do you admire this dry-arsed poseur's lines so greatly? You are a publicly declared revolutionary. A communistical personality if ever I met one —

A wave of the glass at MARY and CLAIRE.

Willing to share your all, with all and sundry —

CLAIRE. | George —
MARY. | My Lord I do not like that —

BYRON. Brandy, brandy, brandy talking, no offence, *but*!

Charm. Smiles.

This is ridiculous. I sit here in the company of this rabid, militant personage, and he quotes England's most reactionary poet into my face. (*To* BYSSHE.) You admit the poem you quote is of defeat?

BYSSHE (*carefully*). Wordsworth does not think it is — but, yes, it is a poem of defeat.

BYRON. No no no, I'll pin you down. Are not the lines you just quoted aching with a middle-aged regret for the loss of youth's fire?

BYSSHE. Yes.

BYRON. You realise the poem argues that a five-year-old knows more than any twenty-five-year-old, let alone a thirty-five-year-old. Did Socrates talk rubbish from when he was six?

He groans.

I can even quote the bloody thing now from heart.

Trailing clouds of glory do we come
    From God, who is our home:
Heaven lies about us in our infancy!

A silence.

Why do you not throw up? It is nonsense! I am agnostic, but you are an atheist. It denies experience, the maturity of manhood —

Another wave at MARY *and* CLAIRE.

And womanhood —

MARY *and* CLAIRE, *nod, at each other.*

CLAIRE. Thank you very much sir —

MARY. Very very much, sir —

BYRON (*with malice*). You do know about Willy Wordsworth, don't you, you know he was a Jacobin, that the light shone from Robespierre's arse for our William, when *he* was young? That he was in Paris, at the height of France's revolution, and thought the Terror a wonder of human excellence? *And* while there, got a girl pregnant, in the shadow of the guillotine? Met her once. Thin, long dank-looking black hair, horribly attractive actually, her name was Annette. And the child? Ah! Ah! Ah! If you want to utterly destroy William Wordsworth in conversation, ask 'Where are the children of the Revolution now?' — I did. His eyeballs burst with hate and guilt. What, what, what do you admire there?

MARY. Feeling.

BYSSHE. Yes. Song.

A silence.

BYRON. You defeat me.

MARY. The poem's argument is wrong, but its song is true. Truer than its argument. So why is there any difficulty — in singing it?

BYRON. Ah! Ah! Ah! Romanticism rears its ugly, look-both-ways, have-it-both-ways head! Though something be nonsense, feel the feeling.

MARY. But you have been called Europe's greatest Romantic poet.

BYRON. Slander! Slander!

He looks at his glass.

It may sell books, but slander! My favourite poet is Alexander Pope.

BYSSHE *about to explode.*

BYSSHE. Unreadable! Unspeakable, rhyming tinsel to flatter the ruling class, against life, I mean, I mean — the language deformed, prostituted, stuck in obscene corsets —

BYRON, *airily.*

BYRON. Read him every night myself. To clear the air. Yes, he was a deformed little dwarf of a man — but honest to himself. To what he knew.

BYSSHE. So is Wordsworth, in tonight's poem! Honest to himself! Are you?

A silence.

BYRON. Ah.

MARY. No, Bysshe.

BYSSHE. In what you write tonight, will you be honest to yourself?

A silence.

BYRON. I do not know, Bysshe. What I write tonight will, I am afraid, write itself. I will not know its worth, let alone its honesty.

A silence.

But if you write tonight, you will. My dear Bysshe, my dear, dear Bysshe Shelley. True poet.

He raises his glass.

But I do wish you were a fellow piss-artist. Drunkenness would give you a flair for publicity, if nothing else. And you would not drink water and quote Wordsworth late at night. Eh? Eh?

He looks around at them. They are all looking down.

God, you radical communards. I fumble a compliment to the poet among you, and I do not know if you be offended, indifferent, or moved. What matter, what matter.

CLAIRE. Moved. We are moved.

MARY, *looking up.*

MARY. But what matter?

BYRON *and* MARY *look at each other.*

BYRON. Perhaps, in the end, nothing. Or everything. I could end up believing not this, not that, but that *everything* is true. 'Everything is true' – what, pray, is that philosophy?

BYSSHE. Liberalism.

BYRON. Am I that ill?

MARY. You have symptoms, My Lord.

BYRON. A political pox, eh?

CLAIRE, *looking down.*

'Everything is true'. But for tyranny. Against that, I will take up the gun.

BYSSHE. I know you will.

BYRON. Mm. Mm. Mm, mm! I begin to enjoy myself greatly with you lunatics.

They all laugh.

Claire, my dear?

CLAIRE *crawls to* BYRON, *they put their arms around each other.*

'Crawling between Heaven and earth'. The shitty Shakespeare's line.

He pauses.

'Crawling between Heaven and earth.'

The line is meant to be a horror, but it is strangely comforting. I do not know why.

MARY. Because it sings.

BYRON. Ah.

A silence.

I do believe I have just lost a literary argument.

BYSSHE, MARY *and* CLAIRE *glance at each other.*

(*To* MARY.) Madam, last time such a thing happened to me, I fought a duel! Pistols, dawn, a secret field, all formality!

MARY. Name your weapons.

BYRON. Mm — rhyming couplets?

MARY. Refused.

BYRON. Your choice.

MARY. Wait

She thinks.

Home truths.

BYRON. I — am dead.

They laugh. Thunder, lightning. POLIDORI *comes on. He stands, swaying over the lounging group.*

POLIDORI (*aside*). I entered the drawing-room of the Villa Diodati. Outside, there raged the storm. No. Outside the storm raged. No. Outside, the storm abated. No. Outside, the storm I had just left, rolled around the gloomy house. No. No. I was wet and miserable.

He looks around the group. BYRON *and* CLAIRE *kiss passionately.* MARY *shifts toward* BYSSHE, *turning the pages of the Wordsworth. They do not respond to* POLIDORI's *presence.*

In a flash I saw them, a flash of lightning. The air in the room was heavy with their illicit sexuality, they had been at it, I knew it, I knew it, I knew it! They had thrown their clothes back on, the minute I came to the door! No. The two great poets, were, I observed, in contemplation, the women observing a discreet silence.

MARY *turns, she and* BYSSHE *kiss passionately.* POLIDORI *flinches.*

No. The profligate would-be poets and their, their whores, lounged upon the floor, and felt disgraced at my entrance, for I brought with me the wind and the rain.

He looks from couple to couple.

No. I am so lonely. Why do they assume I am second rate, when I am, not! When I am not second rate? I mean, has Shelley ever had a good review in his life? As for my life, I have never done one thing that is not decent, to anyone; or going on middling to decent! And look at them. Byron is an overweight alcoholic, Shelley is an anorexic, neurotic mess! The planet is bestrewn with their abandoned children, lovers of both sexes and wives! Shelley has tuberculosis, Byron has syphilis, and these are the men whom the intelligent among us worship as angels of freedom. No. It was a privilege to be the friend of those two young, beautiful men, in the heyday of that summer. No. Yes. After all, I am paid five hundred pounds, by Byron's publisher, to write a diary of this summer. Dreadful time, no! Time of my life. My decent life. So!

The couples finish their kisses.

I entered the living-room of the Villa Diodati, that stormy night.

BYRON. Polly, Polly, Polly Dolly dear, have a brandy.

POLIDORI. Lightning! Over the lake!

BYRON. What, sir, are you watery again?

POLIDORI. I was in it!

MARY. The lake or the lightning?

BYRON. I was about to say that —

MARY. But you did not.

MARY *and* BYRON *laugh.*

POLIDORI. A storm like that, is like God. His hand, from the darkness, fingering his creation.

BYRON. Do not speak so in this company, Polly. With these free-thinkers, they who believe in God go straight to hell.

POLIDORI. I — think the image perfectly fine. The fork of lightning —

He dangles his fingers to demonstrate.

Playing over the water and the mountains, like the Creator's hand.

BYRON. They who live by images shall die by them.

Looks into his glass.

That *is* the brandy talking.

BYSSHE. Shall we go out?

Stands excitedly.

On the lake, tonight?

MARY. Electrical experiments, Bysshe?

CLAIRE (*to* BYRON). Bysshe once flew a kite in an electrical storm, with a cat tied to it.

BYRON. A cat?

BYSSHE. The aim was to galvanise the animal's nervous system.

POLIDORI. I have seen this in madhouses, in France. There was much experiment in the French Revolution, with the mad. The jolt of electricity — to re-align the vital force, through the organs of the body.

BYRON. Ye Gods! You medical men and nature poets! Between you, will you torture us all to death?

CLAIRE. The idea of the cat —

BYRON. The cat aloft!

CLAIRE. Was that the animal be transformed, by natural force —

BYRON. And what was the result of this advanced experiment? Did the dog star bark at the poor pussy?

BYSSHE. The cat fell in the farmyard pond and drowned.

BYRON. A feline Icarus —

BYSSHE. Shall we go?

MARY. If you wish —

BYSSHE. The phosphorescence of waves may well be electrical, what if lightning link with it — and flash across the water —

MARY. Will you come with us, My Lord?

BYRON. I — think that on a vile night, such as this, I prefer the flash of brandy along the waves of thought in the brain.
    MARY, *slyly*.

MARY. The unreal to the real thing?

BYRON. What do you seek to imply?

CLAIRE. The shadow to the substance?

BYRON. Are we talking about Plato's cave, or not gettting wet?

MARY. I, myself, have always been afraid of the story of Plato's cave.

BYRON. Why afraid?

MARY. There is something dark — something sinister about it.

BYRON. But Madam, two thousand years of philosophising rests
upon the parable of Plato's cave. It is meant to be the great
statement of the predicament of mankind.

BYSSHE. Let's do it!

BYRON. Do it?

BYSSHE. This drawing-room — make it the cave.

BYRON. Ah! Now! House party games —

CLAIRE, *clapping*.

CLAIRE. Oh good, good, good, games!

BYSSHE. Where is Plato's *Republic*?

He scrabbles amongst the cushions. He finds The Republic.
BYRON, *an imperious gesture.*

BYRON. Give it to me. I will read Socrates.

MARY. No sir, you will read Glaucon.

BYRON. But he says 'Yes Socrates' all the time —

CLAIRE. A secondary rôle will do you good, George.

POLIDORI. What — what is afoot —

MARY *takes the book from* BYSSHE.

BYRON. You are to be chained, Polidori, hand, head and leg, in
the great cave of philosophical mystery.

POLIDORI. I — protest — I —

BYSSHE. The fire in the cave!

BYRON. Candelabra!

They move the candelabra to the front of the stage. N.B. *the
light from a footlight throws all their shadows onto the wall.*

CLAIRE. Sh! Sh! The voice of the great philosopher, Socrates.

MARY *reads: deep voiced, grave, strange.*

MARY. In a dark cave sit prisoners. Their legs and necks are
chained, so tight they cannot turn their heads.

BYRON. Polidori! At last a rôle in life!

POLIDORI. No, please!

BYRON *whipping off a belt, approaching* POLIDORI.

BYRON. You're going to love this, Polidori! Bysshe, a hand in
this torturing!

BYRON *and* BYSSHE *manhandling* POLIDORI, *sitting him down, facing the back wall, tying his hands behind his back.*

BYSSHE. The human condition, doctor!

BYRON. Have him in rags, whipped and scourged or at least debagged!

POLIDORI. No no!

BYRON *into* POLIDORI's *ear.*

BYRON. Sir deliver yourself into the hands —

He indicates BYSSHE.

Of this advanced experimenter, about to fly you on some metaphysical kite sir, this very stormy night. Sir take the risk, your very being may be electrified into a cinder, you may fall from the sky into some muddy, farmyard pond — but you will be transformed!

POLIDORI. I will argue philosophy — but I do not wish to come to any harm.

BYSSHE *laughs.*

BYRON. What, you think philosophy, you think poetry harmless sir? Sir it can maim, it can mutilate, it can imprison men, women and children, blinded for centuries, it can kill. Sir, I thought you an intellectual — do you not know ideas can kill?

CLAIRE. Sh! Sh! The philosopher.

BYRON *and* BYSSHE *lay back, leaving* POLIDORI *upright, hands tied behind his back. His shadow looms on the wall. He tries to move his head, he cannot.*

MARY. Behind the prisoners, there is a fire. The light of the fire throws the shadows of the prisoners on the wall.

POLIDORI, *little jerks of his head.*

POLIDORI. What? What? What?

MARY. Between the fire and the chained prisoners runs a road. Along the road go men and animals. The prisoners see the shadows on the wall.

CLAIRE. Bysshe!

First CLAIRE *then* BYSSHE *cross the stage, distorting their arms and bodies into shapes that cast shadows on the wall.*

They combine to form animals — birds, cattle, a giraffe.

BYRON. Damme, what animal is that?

CLAIRE. A giraffe, obviously!

MARY. Now tell me, can the prisoners see anything of the men on the road, except for the shadows cast?

BYRON. No, Socrates!

MARY. And so they would believe that the shadows, and the shadows of themselves, were real?

BYRON. Yes, Socrates! Inevitably!

MARY. But now, what would happen to them if they were released from their chains and cured of their delusions?

BYRON. They would go mad, mad, mad!

CLAIRE. Keep to the text, George.

MARY. Suppose one of them were let loose, made to stand up, turn his head. And walk toward the fire. Suppose he was told that what he used to see was mere illusion, do you not think he would be at a loss?

BYRON. Mad! Mad!

A glance from CLAIRE.

Yes, Socrates.

MARY. And if he looked directly at the fire would he not be blinded?

BYRON. Yes, yes Socrates!

MARY. And if he were dragged up out of the cave, and saw the sun, would he not be in terror?

BYRON. Yes yes yes yes! Socrates!

MARY. And now I tell you, our real sun is but the fire in the cave. We are as distant as the prisoners, chained before shadows, as we are from the true sun. Which some call God. Which I call absolute good.

She closes the book.

BYRON. If I were such a prisoner, tell ye what I would do. Bribe a guard. For a gun. Blast my way up out onto the hillside. And make love with the first man, woman, boy, girl or animal in sight! Ye Gods! And *that* dismal parable, is to date the greatest philosophical account of the condition of mankind? The world is bloody — and real — and we know it. Why torment ourselves with ghosts?

CLAIRE. But what would you bribe a guard with?

BYRON. My arse, madam, if need be!

CLAIRE. I see.

BYSSHE *flares up.*

BYSSHE. The fire in the cave is the past, by which we see now. The sun on the hillside, is the future of mankind. It is our future that is the absolute good! Plato himself was a prisoner, religion a flicker in the cave! The mind of man, that is the true sun! We are the instruments of that future light!

BYRON. You are spitting over us, Bysshe. I have noted the more abstract you visionaries become, the more are we all drenched in saliva —

POLIDORI, *suddenly.*

POLIDORI. I!

They look at him.

I — cannot turn my head.

BYRON. Don't be a fool, sir.

POLIDORI. I — am frightened what I shall see!

BYRON. Sir, turn your head. Leave visions to the like of Mr Shelley here. Remain in the realm of the mundane, where you belong.

A pause, then POLIDORI *turns his head without difficulty. Crestfallen he shuffles away on his knees.* BYSSHE's *shadow now dominates the wall.* MARY *looks at it.*

CLAIRE. There there, Polly —

POLIDORI *shrugs her off.*

POLIDORI (*to* BYRON). What — pray what, can you do better than I, when it comes down to it! But for writing verses?

BYRON. Sir, first I can hit with a pistol the keyhole of that door — secondly, I can swim for miles in the open sea — and thirdly, I can give you a damn good thrashing.

POLIDORI. How dare — how dare — how dare —

CLAIRE *releasing* POLIDORI.

CLAIRE. There there, we are only playing, doctor.

MARY. At shadows.

BYSSHE (*to* MARY). What?

MARY. Your shadow.

BYSSHE *turns, looks at the wall.*

CLAIRE. Turn round now, doctor, you'll see a ghost!

POLIDORI *jerks his head and looks at the shadow.* BYSSHE *moves into a monstrous shape.*

MARY. What if —

She pauses.

What if a shadow that we made, upon the wall of our cave —

She pauses.

Stepped down? Walked toward us? Begged — for life?

She pauses.

And we gave it life. What would it be?

A clock begins to chime sedately.

BYRON. Ha! Ha! Midnight! Capital!

He slaps his thigh.

The sun is the other side of the earth, my dear Shelley. Your future's sun? Who knows whether it will give us dawn at all? Let us forget rational, electric experiments and go out — to open graves?

MARY, *to herself.*

MARY. The hideous phantasm of a man stretched out — but not a man, a thing, put together out of graves — by unhallowed arts —

CLAIRE (*to* MARY). Monsters? (*To* BYRON.) Monsters?

She giggles.

BYRON. Of monsters, this is the worst.
Coleridge's witch.

Beneath the lamp the lady bowed,
And slowly rolled her eyes around;

Then drawing in her breath aloud
Like one that shuddered, she unbound
The cincture from beneath her breast;
Her silken robe and inner vest
Dropt to her feet, and in full view,
Behold! her bosom and half her side —
Hideous, deformed, and pale of hue —
Oh shield her! Shield sweet Christabel!

He pauses.

Mm. Well, that is what opium doth for a poet. (*To* POLIDORI.)
In your role as a doctor, you do not have a quantity of that
wondrous substance about you, by any good fortune?

Suddenly BYSSHE *is seized by a fit. Mouth torn open — no
sound — he doubles up tightly and falls on his side.*

BYRON. Sir what philosophical point do you seek now to
demonstrate?

MARY. Don't touch him! Doctor —

CLAIRE. Oh Bysshe —

POLIDORI, *frozen.*

BYRON. Damnation sir, move to him!

POLIDORI. Yes yes, a rule, a rod, a stick, against him biting his
tongue —

CLAIRE *and* MARY *scramble about.*

BYRON. What in Heaven's name is the matter with him?

POLIDORI. A seizure My Lord, with this I *am* of some worth.

CLAIRE *hands* POLIDORI *a pencil.*

But an overloading of the nerves, an excess of agitation in the
fluid of the spinal chord — (*To* BYSSHE.) Sir, this between
your teeth, sir!

BYSSHE *stands suddenly and looks at them. A silence. Then a
thin, high sound from him, staring at* MARY. *He runs off, the
thin sound becoming a screech.*

BYRON, MARY *and* CLAIRE, *frozen.* POLIDORI *turn to
the audience.*

(*Aside.*) Followed him into another room. Calmed him. And
he did confide in me, yes, the 'great' Shelley, he did tell me of

what he had seen! He had looked at Mrs Shelley. And there, standing in her place, was another woman he had known. Naked. With eyes in her nipples, her nipples as eyes, staring at him! Is there no end to their fantasisms? To the indulgence of these revolutionary apostles, with their lives falling apart, their minds in rags? But I did write my account of the evening down and had it printed, in a book! It did bring me a little fame. I left them to their summer. To their diseased imaginations.

He goes off. BYRON, MARY *and* CLAIRE *stay, and —*

Scene Five

BYSSHE *alone. He laughs.*

BYSSHE. I am an atheist, who is haunted by the spirit world! How can this be?

Low.

The — worst ghost I have seen. The most horrid. The most — real — is a phantom that is exactly myself.

He laughs again.

We haunt ourselves. With man-made tyranny.

Even love is sold. Love withers under constraint. Love is the very essence of liberty — we constrain it by the feudal savagery called the institution of marriage. We haunt ourselves, with the ghosts of what we could be, if we were truly free!

Scene Six

BYRON, *coiling a rope.*

Sun and wind. MARY *and* CLAIRE *on a beach,* BYRON *and* BYSSHE, *later, in a sailing boat.*

CLAIRE. I found a letter Byron had written, to his sister, Augusta, it was obscene. It was magnificent.

BYRON *calling, off.*

BYRON. Bysshe! For godsake, are we going on the water? Or are you falling about in another visionary fit?

CLAIRE. The things he wrote to her —

Quoting, by heart.

'Naked — in your arms — no other love for me in the desolation of Europe, desolation of my life — dear Augusta, we have a true marriage, sealed in Heaven witnessed in Hell, forever —'

MARY. You read a copy?

CLAIRE. He had not sent it.

MARY. Ah.

She laughs.

CLAIRE. But it exists, it is in the world.

MARY. He is a writer of fiction, beware.

CLAIRE. Do you mean he really doesn't love her, but cares for me instead?

MARY. Claire, Claire, for the daughter of writers and the mistress of writers, you display great ignorance. Or misguided faith —

CLAIRE. I will overcome his affections. I will use the child. I will — mould him. He will write to me, as he wrote to his sister — 'I wish to have you by my side, to swim with you in the clear water of the lake, naked with you at dawn, when the world is new and young' — that will be me!

MARY. He is a libertine, in love with life — capital letters. They who are in love with life in that way, cause only pain to those around them.

BYRON *throws the rope off,* BYSSHE *comes on and catches it.*

BYRON. I do suppose I am the father — of Claire's coming little 'thing'.

BYSSHE. I do suppose so, George.

BYRON. I mean, to turn the conversation man to man — you have had 'em both, have you not? In your time?

BYSSHE. Rest assured that you are the father of Claire

Clairemont's child.

BYRON. No no, don't go huffy! It's all the same to me, m'dear fella.

He laughs.

Seems that you are intent on populating the world with ghosts, I'm intent on populating it with Byron's bastards. Damme! Why don't I stick to boys? Are we going to sail this bloody boat?

BYSSHE *pulls the rope.*

BYSSHE. Yes, there is hope for a storm!

BYRON *and* BYSSHE *work the rope, as they would a sailing boat, the rope taut between them.*

MARY. Augusta is his distant star. In whosoever's arms he lays, each night, he can look up and say 'There is my true love' — not this woman, man, boy, with dirty feet and night smells. If Augusta were to leave England and come to him, with all the terrible cost to her, the loss of reputation and scandal — he would at once betray her. Probably with you.

BYRON. All very well the carnal act, the act of love, with women, but with a boy you do think — Goddam it, this is the real thing! You ever gone that sweet route?

BYSSHE. Not my nature.

BYRON. What?

BYSSHE. My nature!

CLAIRE. I will tangle him. I will wrench him. Are we not always saying to each other, the world is yet to be made, we are changeable, we will invent a new society and a new human nature?

MARY. A new human nature? Out of George Byron? My darling Claire —

BYSSHE *and* BYRON *raising their voices now, against the sound of a storm.*

BYRON. Tell you the sweetest thing, love of a sister. We talk frankly? Your sister, very fine, ever had her? Come Sir — between the waves and us, our little lusts in a boat!

BYSSHE. We must follow our natures, what more can we do?

BYRON. Y'bloody hypocrite! Where is your legal wife? In England! The two women you are with, Mary y'call your wife, Claire y'friend — concubines, sir! Y'mistresses, sir! All your idealism, revolution in society, revolution in the personal life, all trumpery! The practice of it, sir, the practice doth make us dirty, doth make all naked and bleeding and real!

Angry.

Y'damn theorising! All you want to do is get your end away. And you make bloody sure you do!

The storm.

BYSSHE. I do not care what I do to myself!

I do not, George!

Let's peel open our brains, find the soul itself! Let's blast ourselves with electrical force — cut ourselves open, wreck ourselves, turn ourselves inside out! To find out what we are, what we can be!

That is what poets must do!

I declare I am a public enemy
Of kingly death, false beauty and decay —

BYRON. Bysshe sit down you maniac, there are waves breaking over our gunnel —

MARY. It's no good Claire. You know it. We will go back to England.

CLAIRE. No, we'll stay here, summer will never end, I won't let it — I'll reach out and — hold it, pull it back.

MARY. Summer is over, Byron's new poem is finished and copied — by us. He wants Bysshe to take it, sealed, back to England for its publication. I tell you! When Lord Byron finishes a new poem, summer is truly done for.

CLAIRE. What shall I do? Where shall I —

MARY. Live with us. We will find a small house, with a garden, be quiet, you will have your child.

CLAIRE. I will not have it called Augusta. I will not, will not!

Storm again.

BYRON. Here, you have your adventure, sir! We'll have to swim for it. Come!

He throws the rope at BYSSHE *who clutches it to his chest.*
BYRON, *ripping off his coat.*

The boat is lost. Dive in sir!

BYSSHE. No!

Silence from the storm music and effects. BYSSHE *sits dead
still clutching the rope.*

When will the world marry itself?
When will the true family be
All of human society?

I write poems. But most of the world cannot even read.

So what can I do?

Act as if I were free.

Write, as if I were free.

And at once — the storm.

BYRON. The boat is lost, dive in sir!

Swim!

BYSSHE. Cannot swim! Cannot swim!

BYRON. Ye gods, y'lied to me sir, venturing in a frail boat, in
bad weather?

BYSSHE. Cannot!

Sinking!

Down!

Through the lampless deep!

Of song!

BYRON. Damnation then I will have to stay and hang on with
ye! Ha! God's teeth, will you do anything, my dear Shelley,
to create an heroic episode?

The effects die down. BYRON *and* BYSSHE, *confronting*
MARY *and* CLAIRE *on the beach, the men dishevelled.*
BYSSHE *sullen,* BYRON *in great good humour.*

(*To* MARY.) Thought the boat was awash and done for. Your
husband clings on to it like a leech, announces he cannot
swim, madam! That he'll go down with it. Then damn well
sails it head on into the waves and saves us both.

A silence.

Maybe it was not as bad as that. But! Come my loves, my dears, clean clothes, brandy, refreshments, talk — and then we will retire — to colour up the incident in our diaries! All is well. All is well. All is well.

A silence, then they all relax and move toward each other in a circle.

Blackout.

ACT TWO

Scene One

HARRIET.
I married a poet. Fine poet, was he —
name o' Percy Bysshe Shel-ley!

She giggles then backs away, frightened.

Men in the trees.

She calls out.

Shillin'? Shillin'? Want me for a shillin'?

Low.

Men in the trees, midnight London, Hyde Park, banks of the
Serpentine. I am most refined, *most* refined, yer want me fer
a shillin'? Go down all fours on a grass? Or shall I recite
tastefully, verse he did write for me?

'Whose eyes have I gazed fondly on,
And loved mankind the more?
Harriet! On thine: — thou wert my purer mind;
Thou wert the inspiration of my song' —

Tinkly stuff, in't it dear, rather my arse fer a shillin', dear?
I was but sixteen when I married the poet, sir, where is he
now? 'E is on the continent, sir, on the Con-ti-nont! With
sweet Mary, Mare-ree! Who calls herself his wife, though she
not be, I be, legal-ly. Though she be, intellectually, my
superior.

A hummed scream.

Mmmmmmmmmmmmmmmmmmmmm —

Now I live with a soldier name o' Smith, but he has gone to
India, and I call me Harriet Smith — that none may know I
was had by the poet Shel-ly —

Cruel-ly —

Mmmmmmmmmmmmmmmmmmmmm —

Spitting the lines out.

Who telleth a tale of unending death?
Who lifteth the veil of what is to come?
Who painteth the shadows that are beneath
The wide-winding caves of the peopled tomb?
Or untieth the hopes of what shall be
With the fears and the love for which we see?

Pretty, pretty clever boy, Bysshe!
Ti-tum-ti-tum about death!

All that we know, or feel, or see,
Shall pass like an unreal mystery!

She blows a raspberry.

Yer want t'know 'bout death, mister poet, you go whorin' fer
a shillin' in midnight London!

Dialect change again, quoting her suicide note.

My dear Bysshe, let me conjure you by the remembrance of
our days of happiness — I could never refuse you and if you
had never left me I might have lived — but as it is I freely
forgive you and may you enjoy that happiness that you have
deprived me of — now comes the sad task of saying farewell —

She giggles.

Now I'll go for a swim, go for a swim, like a little girl, by the
sea-shore — wash off the men, swim, I . . .

She drowns.

Scene Two

Winter. MARY *and* BYSSHE *in winter clothes.* BYSSHE *carries
a book in his armpit and logs under his arm. He is reading a letter
that* MARY *has just given to him.*

BYSSHE. A month ago.

A silence.

How can that be?

A silence.

She drowned. And I was not told.

A silence.

Oh the circumstances — Hyde Park, that filthy, filthy lake —
and, and —

MARY. Pregnant. (*To herself.*) Bad news. In England, on a
dull afternoon, in a cold, wet garden.

BYSSHE *flutters the letter.*

BYSSHE. I but wrote a casual enquiry to Hookham, oh, dear
Hookham — how, by the way, is Harriet my wife, and my two
children? And back comes the reply — oh, she drowned
herself, a month ago.

A laugh.

He says it was even reported in *The Times*!

Reads. 'Found drowned'.

Found drowned.

MARY. We must not —

BYSSHE. Not what?

They stare at each other.

Tell you what we must do — take out an order for *The Times*.
I should study the reactionary press more! Then I will learn of
the death of those I love!

MARY. We must be careful, because of this terrible news. Careful
of ourselves.

A silence.

BYSSHE. Do you also see, from the letter, I have received a good
review in *The Examiner*? True, written by Leigh Hunt, a
'good' friend of mine, therefore corrupt, but a good review!
What news! A good review and the death of my wife. Is
not life full, and wild, and a glory, and —

MARY. Stop it! You indulge yourself.

BYSSHE. Indeed?

They stare at each other.

Look, I was going to make a fire. For our little William and
Clara, in the woods, and roast chestnuts and tell them stories
from the flames, of spirits, and — make them laugh and
wonder —

He drops the wood at his feet.

It is Harriet's family behind this! The vile, the abhorred
Westbrooks! They did not tell me, so my silence would appear
horrible. Why? They want the children. The Devil! Why
cannot our children live with Harriet's? Why cannot I have two
families, or three, or four, what in nature forbids it? Ah,
English bourgeois morality, forbids it. What can a poet do,

confronted by the outraged, respectable English — with their bayonets of moral indignation fixed? I can hear Harriet's mother now, that thin, whining, hard done-by tone, all Christianity and naked malice. I am cast as a monster.

MARY. I too.

BYSSHE. It's all in rags, I —

A silence.

I have come to the opinion that there must be a revolution in England, I write for it, every morning, I —

A silence.

And my wife is dead —

He begins to laugh.

And my children stolen and —

Byron's mistress is about to have her child in my house —

House I live in with *my* mistress and *our* children — scandal, scandal, tittle-tattle —

And, in Ireland, English soldiers are murdering Irish liberty —

And, in my garden, neighbours peer over the fence hoping to see me, and Mary, and Claire, all naked, Claire with her big belly, rolling in the cabbage patch —

Quick, quick, inform the *Daily Mail*!

And in the foreign wars of liberation, as we agonise about who sleeps with whom, heroes scream under the torturers, and children pass their mothers and fathers the gun —

Aie, aie! All is hysteria, is it not my love?

MARY. No. It is just The World.

BYSSHE. Just the world.

As I rhyme and rhyme each sunrise, of truth and the sublime —

As each midday comes, with farce, and mud, and the papers, and the post, all the opprobrium —

Opprobrium, good word, doth rhyme with bum —

Well, England! You neighbours, police committees, censors, you 'tut-tutters', you indignant dignitaries, parliamentaries, thin-lipped pedlars of smug moralities, I give you what you want, a shit-smeared bum —

Here, in rags, is the life we Libertarians lead —

Come! Wipe your arseholes! Be satisfied, justified, be *smug*!
I have my dead, but you have yours!

Mine, I will grieve for, s —

A stutter.

S — uffer the wrongs I did them, in p —

A stutter.

Private measure. But you! You great English, bourgeois
public! Your dead are at large. You pass them, everyday,
in the dirty streets of Manchester, of Birmingham, of London!
My ghosts will sing to me, but yours — will bury you!

(*To* MARY). Eh? No, my dear? Hey!

Shamefaced.

What sentiments, from — filthy, private things — to sedition
against my country?

Changes.

Do you think it took her long? It's not that deep, the
Serpentine, took the children boating on it once — S'only two,
three feet deep, the Serpentine —

Deep, in't? I —

MARY, *very angry.*

MARY. I will not have you, and I will not have myself,
condemned to this —

She pauses.

Raving in an English garden.

She scoffs.

The glory of the garden, in which the poet Shelley and the
women and children who love him are —

But weeds? Noisome, troublesome, scratchy, screechy things,
unacceptable —

BYSSHE. Unreviewable?

MARY. You have spoken, let me speak.

She pauses.

I will not have it. That we all be planted in the corner, as ugly
— things, thistles, with poisoned spikes? Tolerated among the
official flowers, all those pale decorated blooms of 'the
nation'? I will not.

We have done nothing wrong.

Harriet was a fool to drown herself. Now that she is dead —

BYSSHE *stares at her.*

We can get married.

A silence.

Then, uproot ourselves? Plant ourselves abroad? Out of this —

A gesture, around them.

English garden, English graveyard? See, Bysshe! How to truly
torture a metaphor, to its bitter end?

She pauses.

If we marry, the courts will give us your children.

BYSSHE. Harriet's children.

MARY. Children belong to no one, but themselves. As you have
often said.

BYSSHE *wanders about, unable to reply. Then —*

BYSSHE. Neither of us believe in marriage!

MARY. You have married once already.

BYSSHE. But —

MARY. But?

BYSSHE. I have no defence.

MARY. You married Harriet Westbrook to give you and her what
strength you could. You were both very young.

BYSSHE. Strength.

MARY. I want you to marry me. It is a practical matter. We must
move through the world, armed as best we can be.

BYSSHE. You are very cold.

MARY. You are very callous.

BYSSHE. Why 'callous'?

MARY. Why 'cold'?

BYSSHE. My darling — well.

Laughs. Flutters the letter.

I receive news of the death of my wife, and you — propose
to me? I mean —

He wipes his eyes, still laughing.

Are we really going to live this?

MARY. There lies your callousness, sir.

She curtseys.

For I live in your household. 'Sir.'

She curtseys again.

BYSSHE. Do not bob up and down like that, do not, I —

MARY. I — I — I — aye, aye, aye, yes 'sir' —

BYSSHE. Stop it! Now you! Stop!

Kicks the logs.

Light the fire, let the — little daemons dance, eh?

MARY. Retreating into poetic imagery again, 'darling'?

They shout.

BYSSHE. Will you marry me!

MARY. Yes! Will you marry me!

BYSSHE. Don't know!

*They stomp around the stage angrily, avoiding each other and
each other's glance. They calm down. BYSSHE kicks the logs
together in a pile. As he does so he smiles to himself —*

Mary, Mary, you are so fantastical, so — daring that I am
ashamed, I —

MARY, *sarcastically.*

MARY. Quote:

My spirit like a burning barque doth swim
    Upon the liquid waves of thy sweet singing,
Blazing into the regions dim

Of rapture — with sails of fire winging
    Its way a-down your many-winding river,
I speed by dark forests o'er the waters swinging —

They glare at each other. A silence.

BYSSHE. Madam, you have been reading my notebook —

MARY. The bloody poem's about Claire! Isn't it!

BYSSHE. You —

He fidgets.

Have somewhat embellished it in the quotation —

MARY. Oh come on, come on! You wrote it, two weeks ago, after Claire sang us Mozart. And three nights ago you told me you wanted to sit up, 'To write'. Don't think you were a-writing, my dear, you were going a-down Claire's many a-winding river. In your boat. No?

Nothing from BYSSHE.

A heavily pregnant lady. But a woman, heavy with child, can with comfort and pleasure, have a man from behind. I should know. 'No'?

BYSSHE, *frozen.*

I do believe men call it 'spraying the baby's head'. Have you been spraying Lord Byron's baby's head?

BYSSHE. Yes.

MARY. Yes.

BYSSHE. Yes.

MARY. 'Course you have.

BYSSHE. Yes.

He pauses.

I —

MARY. The song you wrote Claire is very beautiful. As beautiful as her singing.

She pauses.

Will you marry me?

BYSSHE. Yes.

MARY, *without pause.*

MARY. Are you going to build the fire for William and Clara in the woods?

BYSSHE, *without pause.*

BYSSHE. I must! I've made up a story for the little man and little woman —

MARY. Light the fire, tell it to them, make up daemons, then come into the house — and have tea? Hot cakes?

BYSSHE. Yes!

MARY. Yes.

BYSSHE. Yes.

MARY. After all, somehow we are going to have to domesticate all these grand passions.

BYSSHE. Yes.

MARY. Yes.

They eye each other, beginning to smile.

BYSSHE. I'll go to London. Tonight, if I can book on the Post.

MARY. Yes.

BYSSHE. I'll file a suit for Harriet's children, in the Court of Chancery. Little Charles and Xanthe —

MARY. Yes —

BYSSHE. You and I will bring them up, with our children —

MARY. Yes —

BYSSHE. We will be one great family. And I'll see your father.

MARY. Ah!

BYSSHE. Ah!

They look at each other, laugh, then 'play act'.

I will ask your father, for your hand.

MARY. But my father, kind sir, is a rabid anarchist, much given against marriage.

BYSSHE. Not — !

MARY. Yes, kind sir, my maiden name is Godwin! Oh yes, kind sir, I am the progeny of that monster, he, to my shame, impregnated my mother —

BYSSHE. And art thou, then, horribly infected?

MARY, *a long curtsey.*

MARY. Oh yes, kind sir, see — my white limbs do shine with heresy, — my flesh is the false promise, to they who would be free — Can't keep this up! What's the best rhyme for 'womb'?

BYSSHE, *mock professional.*

BYSSHE. 'Bloom' as in 'flower'? 'Broom', as in 'brush'? 'Boom' as in 'bang'?

MARY. No, gerroff, sir.

In a deep curtsey, head bowed, her dress splayed around her.

Am I not thy tomb? Wherein thou wouldst lie, and gladly die?

She looks up laughing.

My father will be fine. If you give him a loan. Can you?

BYSSHE. I can — from Hookham. I'll exploit his guilt, at not publishing me. Thus, my dear, do we move the money of our friends around, to keep credit.

MARY. And flourish.

Standing, holding hands.

The fire, the children's story —

BYSSHE. Oh. I — yes.

He gathers the logs up clumsily.

MARY.?

They look at each other. BYSSHE *backs away. Stops. Then goes off, bent.*

The words.

A pause.

Oh, you can do the words, can't you, Bysshe. Quote —

Never will peace and human nature meet
Till, free and equal, man and woman greet
Domestic peace; and ere this power can make
In human hearts its calm and holy seat,
This slavery must be broken.

She snorts, very like BYSSHE *does.*

Now how about doing the life, kind —

The mock curtsey again.

Kind sir?

MARY *remains on stage. And —*

Scene Three

The crash of waves. BYSSHE *comes on with bags and rugs, which he piles before them.* POLIDORI *comes on, downstage. He wears a large black cloak which he wraps about himself. At the back, the* GHOST *of* HARRIET WESTBROOK.

POLIDORI. Dover Beach. Waiting for the packet boat to cross to Calais, and I see them! The Shelley menagerie, women, children, bags of seditious material, fleeing the country.

Now good Dame gossip doth say . . . That the Claire Clairemont woman gave birth to a child. Of my Lord Byron's. And the great Lord has taken the child off from the mother. Yes! And all were scandalised by the Mary Godwin woman marrying Shelley and trying to steal away the children of his first marriage. To bring them up atheist. But the Court upheld morality and said 'no'.

These people! Am I condemned to be the nobody at their feast? I will not make myself known. I will dog them. I'll send back tasty bits to the literary magazines. The Shelleys will belong to me.

BYSSHE. A stiff north-easterly! The captain is worried about sailing, there are ten foot waves in the Channel. I've told him 'We go, we go!' Come, bring the children.

CLAIRE. Let's have a ceremony! Scrape off the mud of our country, scrape off all the lies about us — yuck! All the muck of petty little minds. A grand farewell ceremony to England!

BYSSHE. I have already done such a ceremony.

CLAIRE. Oh? What?

BYSSHE. Written to my banker, telling him to pay no more bills. Come! They are ready for us.

MARY *lifts a handful of sand and lets it run from her fingers.*

MARY. Disgrace. Exile. A holiday.

CLAIRE. Summer and hard light. And mountains in the sky again. Life will be a holiday, forever.

A change. A strangeness. BYSSHE *and the* GHOST.

HARRIET. Are you not taking me, Bysshe? I'll be no trouble. I'll slip into the trunk with all the books, I'll be very small, I'll sit on a spoke, on one of the wheels of the carriage, I will hardly be there. Just — a patch, a little stain. Very faint, very light —

BYSSHE. Yes!

A silence.

Yes. Why not?

He snorts.

Hasn't my life become a kind of haunting?

HARRIET. Has it? Oh, poor dear.

She giggles.

And —

Scene Four

Ist May

Blazing light.

From the travelling bags, they take white table cloths, books, bottles of water, parasols. They take off their travelling coats — light, summer clothes. CLAIRE, MARY *and* BYSSHE *sprawl. It's a picnic. The* GHOST *sits at the back, demurely.*

POLIDORI. And now they lie in the sun. In their rented villa, the Casa Bertini, in the Appenine mountains. I mingle with the tourists, look over the wall — whisper in the town 'They are the creatures of Lord Byron, the rake, all of them — even Shelley! He is translating Plato's filthy work, advocating the love of men for boys.' Whisper — scandal — sweet, sweet.

MARY, BYSSHE *and* CLAIRE *with a mess of manuscripts.* BYSSHE *correcting with a quill. They are in mid-flow.*

BYSSHE. You are both utterly, utterly, utterly, totally and absurdly wrong!

CLAIRE. Oh.

MARY. Oh.

CLAIRE *and* MARY *laugh.*

It is always a very bad idea for lovers to start talking about what love is.

BYSSHE. All I am saying is, that we need a theory of the emotions.

CLAIRE. Why? Do we need a theory of breathing? If we did, with all the thinking on it, I believe we would choke —

MARY. Love is — 'The lineaments of gratified desire'.

BYSSHE. What?

CLAIRE. What?

MARY. A line by William Blake.

BYSSHE. That religious madman.

MARY. A *good* line. It means that 'love' can be anything. It shapes itself around the desire of the moment.

BYSSHE. Plato —

CLAIRE. Yes!

Claps her hands.

What does Plato say love is, Bysshe? You're just dying to get him in the argument!

BYSSHE, *rustling his manuscript.*

BYSSHE. The argument between Diotima and Socrates, which proves that 'Love is not a Divine God'. Shall we do it?

CLAIRE. Plato's *Symposium*, in the garden? What of the tourists?

BYSSHE. I will warn them.

Shouts, off.

Love is not a God!

The Greeks did it with boys!

POLIDORI *hisses.*

POLIDORI. Jealous, jealous, I am so —

MARY *and* BYSSHE *read — measured.*

MARY. Observe, then, that you do not consider Love to be a God. What, then, is Love a mortal?

BYSSHE. By no means.

MARY. But what then?

BYSSHE. He is neither mortal nor immortal, but something intermediate.

MARY. What is that, O Diotima?

BYSSHE. A great daemon, Socrates. He communicates between
the divine and the human by science of sacred things,
sacrifices, and expiations, and disenchantments, and prophecy,
and magic. That is his daemonical nature —

He looks up.

Not a god, not a man, nor a woman, not a child, a daemon.

CLAIRE. Daemon —

BYSSHE. A force that flies between us.

CLAIRE. There!

MARY. There!

BYSSHE. There!

HARRIET. Pretty, pretty, how pretty, how pretty —

MARY *kisses* BYSSHE, *they lie in each other's arms.*

CLAIRE. I must go to Venice, Mary, Bysshe. We have not heard
of Allegra, with Byron.

A silence.

I know he means to send for me.

MARY. I am worried about this constant travelling, little Clara is
not strong, Bysshe.

CLAIRE. Then — my darlings, I must be with him. Why can't we
all be together, as we were in Switzerland? That was a golden
age.

MARY. Not really so golden, Claire, remember?

CLAIRE. But — we are all married to each other, is that not true?
Plato's daemon —

She laughs.

Hasn't he run rings round all of us?

HARRIET. Pretty, so very pretty —

CLAIRE. I'll go. Alone.

A silence.

HARRIET. Pretty thoughts, of pretty people, pretty things. On
the grass. Under the trees.

BYSSHE *suddenly stands.*

BYSSHE. I'll go with Claire.

MARY. Oh? Yes?

BYSSHE. We must bring George Byron to heel! He is behaving disgracefully. I'll go with Claire to Venice. I'll see him alone — and tell him what must be.

MARY. *You* will tell *BYRON*?

BYSSHE. We must be practical. What we want to live we must make — it.

MARY. I see!

She stands. Begins to pick up the bags and picnic things.

Well. Very well. You and Claire will go to Venice. And I will stay here and look after the children. Fine.

BYSSHE. We owe it to Claire. To Allegra.

MARY. Oh we do.

BYSSHE. Mary, please.

They look at each other. Then BYSSHE puts his hand to her cheek.

MARY. We were happy here.

BYSSHE. We will come back here. This will take but a few days, a week —

MARY. Fragile.

A silence.

I fear something could break. So easily. So — casually. Without us hardly noticing.

HARRIET's GHOST *hums a little tune, happily.* CLAIRE, MARY *and* BYSSHE, *still.*

POLIDORI. Yes! A little holiday in the Italian sun. Tracking down the literati, keeping track of their little affairs, their little sorrows. What greater delight? What better amusement?

Change.

I wish I was death, I would give them all a disease. They would hate me then, not ignore me. Not spin their 'new love' their 'new world' — they must not win. I could not stand it.

And —

Scene Five

August 23rd

Venice.

Rippling light.

BYSSHE *and* CLAIRE, *hand in hand.* HARRIET's GHOST *at the back.*

CLAIRE. The Grand Canal. My lover's palace.

> *She pauses.*

> Can a man love two women at once?

> *A silence.*

BYSSHE. Can a woman love two men at once?

> *They look at each other, then kiss passionately. At the back* HARRIET's GHOST *laughs. They part.*

BYSSHE. You understand why it is best. That I speak to Byron alone.

> *Pause.*

CLAIRE. If Byron is — cruel about Allegra, will you make love to me tonight?

BYSSHE. Yes.

CLAIRE. Look at the light. It's going hazy.

> *She pauses.*

> We aren't on holiday anymore. I'll go back to the hotel.

BYSSHE. I'll come to the platform with you, for a gondola —

CLAIRE. Oh no. This is Venice. The city where young women go, stepping in and out of boats, between hotels — and palaces. You're so other-worldly sometimes, Bysshe — you haven't noticed the whole of Venice is a brothel.

> *She offers* BYSSHE *her hand. He kisses it, fumbling. She sweeps away and off.*

HARRIET. Naughty naughty, naughty boy.

> BYSSHE *turns round and pretends to throw something at the* GHOST.

> Don't worry! When you touch her, tonight, you can remember touching me, and you will, won't you, husband.

> HARRIET's GHOST *fades — and goes off.*

> BYSSHE *alone on the stage, and —*

Scene Six

August 24th

The Palazzo Mocenigo.

Coloured light across the stage, as from stained glass windows.

BYSSHE alone.

BYSSHE (*to himself*). George Byron. I stand, a petitioner, in your marbled halls!

He laughs. Off, BYRON *is heard rowing, there is a woman's* VOICE *and the sound of breaking glass.*

VOICE (*Italian*). Bastard! Bastard!

A crash.

BYRON. Madam you are unreasonable!

VOICE. I will not have women in my household!

BYRON. Madam *you* are a woman and this is *my* household and you are, horribly, very much in it!

A crash.

VOICE. Bastard English Milord! My husband he will *kill* you! *Kill*!

BYRON saunters onto the stage. He is in an elaborate dressing-gown. Carries a large bottle of red wine, is smoking a long, white clay pipe. His hair is dishevelled, his eyes dark with exhaustion. He is relaxed.

BYRON. My dear Bysshe. Have my footmen not brought you a drink — carrot juice or something? The buggers are all drunk, no doubt. And it's only breakfast time.

BYSSHE. It is four o'clock in the afternoon, George.

BYRON. Yes yes yes. But I have finally gone day into night, night into day.

The woman's VOICE, *off.*

VOICE. My life! My life! It is my life! I will *kill* myself, I will kill you, my husband he will kill us both, bastard!

A crash. BYRON, *cheerfully.*

BYRON. God's teeth! Have y'had a married woman in Venice yet?

BYSSHE. We — I — only arrived this morning.

BYRON. Y'slow sir, slow! They marry young, to old noblemen, and there is a custom. I am the custom. I mean — they take lovers. It is an Italian institution. Her husband always knows, you go to dinner with both of 'em — You even ask his damn permission. The only right he reserves is to suddenly turn nasty and have you knifed and your body dumped in a canal — 'tis all exceedingly wearing on the nerves.

He looks at BYSSHE, *a silence between them.*

You damn revolutionist, carrot juice drinker. I am so glad to see you.

They embrace, BYRON *holding the pipe and the glass over* BYSSHE's *shoulders. They hold, then* BYSSHE *backs away.*

Forgive me, yes I stink of garlic. And my teeth are no better. *And* I had a particularly vicious clap last winter — nearly over that now, thank God. *And* my hair goes grey. Would dye it, but I keep on getting pissed and falling in damn canals! And how are you, my dear?

He eyes him.

In love?

BYSSHE. I — have translated Plato's *Symposium.*

BYRON. Not coming round to boys at last, are ye? Copy? Copy?

BYSSHE. Yes —

BYSSHE, *enthusiastically, takes a rolled manuscript from his shirt, and gives it to him.*

BYRON. A delight, a delight!

He puts it in his dressing-gown pocket and pats it. He pauses.

Nothing else for me? Out of the rotting north, the armed camp, the turgid cesspool — I mean England?

BYSSHE. No.

BYRON. I did think — perhaps you had letters — from Augusta.

Snaps out of it.

No matter! All that is dead. In a dead country. We are in the wide world now. Though —

Pointing the pipe at BYSSHE.

Beware, revolutionary. Venice too, is an armed camp. Austrian soldiers and spies everywhere. The city is not the cradle of civilisation, art and light we dream of. It rots. There is clandestine opposition, I do what I can, I flirt with it — is Italian liberty your cause?

BYSSHE. Liberty everywhere.

BYRON. Ha! Always the abstract. The real thing in Italy is câches of out-dated weapons, forever been turned over by the police, small meetings, infiltrated and betrayed, young men and women being beaten to shit in gaol. You want to get involved, I can introduce you to some people — poor Venice. A prison and a brothel.

BYSSHE. We noticed.

BYRON. Ah! 'We' again! C'mon, do not stand there so damn angelic, who are y'with, who are y'having?

BYSSHE. I came with Claire.

BYRON. Ah.

BYSSHE. She did your fair copy of *The Symposium*.

BYRON. Ah. The bitch was always good when one wanted something copied out. The damn bitch. She was . . .

A silence.

I shock you? Do not let this come between us, Bysshe, I will have none of it —

BYSSHE. I am a go-between.

BYRON. Nothing to go between.

BYSSHE. The child —

BYRON. My daughter, Allegra, is with me. And that is an end to it. I will have her sent to a convent. With a school. I have found the place.

A silence.

BYSSHE. Is that what you wish me to tell Claire?

BYRON. I wish you to tell my daughter's mother, —

An airey gesture.

Everything. Or nothing. What do I care?

BYSSHE. You are harsh.

BYRON. That is how it is.

He shrugs.

You reproach me?

BYSSHE. No.

BYRON. Damnation. Damnation. I know what you did for me, that she had the child in your house, that you give her a roof. But I have no endurance of these things, Bysshe, no endurance at all. It is not my behaviour that gives me pause, it is yours, my dear!

BYSSHE. Why mine?

BYRON. Ha! A little flicker of English puritanism there! You do reproach me, no matter. Your friendship is precious. Come, we will go out. I want to take you somewhere —

He pauses.

And show you something.

Scene Seven

November

Glittering light, haze. At the back, the huge shadowy image of a gondolier, slowly pulling at his pole, it looms towards us and passes.

BYSSHE *and* BYRON *lounge on cushions, as in a gondola.*

BYSSHE (*aside*). And so —

He pauses.

   O'er the lagoon
We glided; and from that funereal barque
I leaned, and saw the city, and could mark
How from their many isles, in the evening's gleam
Its temples and its palaces did seem
Like fabrics of enchantment — piled to Heaven —

BYRON *snorts, raising a glass.*

BYRON. Ha! You poor sod, y'believe in love, y'do, poor bastard. Yet you harm as many as I, you would-be 'moral immoralist'. You shred and tear lives around you as much as I, the cynic, the libertine. Yes, I leave my diseases in married bedrooms, my children in convents — but you! What have you left? A wife drowned in the Serpentine? And who was that other little thing in London, overdosed herself with opium, because of you? Oh yes, the appropriately named Fanny Godwin, your second wife's little sister, all of fifteen wasn't she, when you had her?

BYSSHE. I cannot be —

BYRON. Cannot be what? Responsible? Ha! My darling, darling hypocrite. What a pity it is that you are not —

Wobbles his hand.

Turned the other way too, as I am. We could marry, become two harmless old men, arm in arm on the sea-shore, writing verse in peace, retired from this world — seething, organic world, of flux, and blood, and manic husbands, and jealousy, and babies bursting from wombs and aching cocks, eh?

He laughs.

D'you know where I found myself, one night last week? Halfway up a drainpipe to the balcony of an eighteen-year-old heiress. Dangling in mid-air, d'you know what happened to me?

BYSSHE. The drainpipe gave way?

BYRON. Worse!

BYSSHE. Chest pains?

BYRON. Worse! I looked down into the street and there, dressed for the opera, was the Venetian correspondent for the London *Daily Mail*. Spotted! And then, ah then —

A silence.

BYSSHE. Well, what? Did you go up to love the heiress, or down, to thrash the journalist?

BYRON. For a moment both delights had an equal attraction. No. I despaired.

BYSSHE. Come, come —

BYRON. No no — despair. Perhaps it takes a high-blown, high-flown personality, such as I have engineered, to be caught in a scene of outright farce, to feel —

An airey wave.

That profound emotion. Up a drainpipe?

BYSSHE. A good story —

BYRON. Is it not, is it not. Actually, I went down and bribed the spy to silence. Now is *that* within my received character, yes or no?

BYSSHE. No.

He pauses.

No —

BYRON, *angrily.*

BYRON. Then believe what I say, you tight-arsed, 'Libertarian', 'free-lover', 'free-liver'!

BYRON *looks away, dangling his free hand in the water.*
A silence.

BYSSHE. What are you telling me? You went home, reformed?

BYRON, *good humour back at once.*

BYRON. Not at all — waited 'til the spy was well away — then went to the servants' door — another bribe — and up to her. Sweet thing. Fair hair. Down on her thighs, unshaved skin — soft, like feathers. I am not telling you that I have reformed, I am telling you that I have despaired.

BYSSHE. What right do you have to do that? You do not have the right. Despair? Easy, George! Cheap merchandise for a writer. You will end up silent or making a pretty lyric out of the phrase 'I have nothing to say'.

The people of England — they may well have the right to despair. So would you — if you were a mill-hand in Manchester, or a child down a mine, or a mother to a labourer's children in a filthy hovel —

BYRON. Perish the thought —

BYSSHE. But for a poet to despair? Obscene! We claim to be the poets of the people of England. How dare we — luxuriate in denouncing the human cause as lost?

The great instrument of moral good is the imagination. We must not let it become diseased! We must be optimists for human nature!

  We might be all
We dream of, happy, high, majestical.
Where is the love, beauty and truth we seek
But in our mind?

Poets are the unacknowledged legislators of mankind!

BYRON. You talk Utopia. We are where I want to take you. Come on dreamer —

He stands.

BYSSHE. What is this island?

BYRON. A madhouse Bysshe!

He laughs.

Come on! We are the wide world's tourists, no?

The stage darkens.

Come on, I want you to meet a true 'citizen of the world'.

BYSSHE (*aside*). The oozy stairs.

Into an old courtyard. Black bars.
A face, looking down. Hair of weeds.

The intendent took us into that terrible place.

The madman sat by a window. He said —
'I met pale pain, my shadow'.

A silence. Then BYRON, *in the shadows, with the madman's voice.*

BYRON.

I met pale pain, my shadow.
How vain
Are words.
Oh — from my pen the words flow as I write
Dazzling my eyes with scalding tears . . .
What I write
Burns the brain
And eats into it.

BYRON *again as the madman*, BYSSHE *flinching away, as if approached.*

Sir, sir, kind sir — you have a childish face — sir, sir, a rhyme — of the fate of poets . . .

Most wretched creatures, they
Are cradled into poetry by wrong
They learn in suffering what they teach in song.

BYRON (*in his own voice. He laughs*). See, my dear? A poet in an asylum. Is he not a lesson to us all? A sweet irony, no, Bysshe? You write to change the world. And the world has its revenge — it overwhelms you with its cruelty.

The madman laughs, BYRON *laughs.*

Scene Eight

Light. BYRON *gone.* HARRIET's GHOST *at the back.*

Hotel room, CLAIRE *and* BYSSHE, *kissing. She backs away.*

CLAIRE. So Byron will not see me. So no matter!

She spins, false good spirits.

BYSSHE. Why did he take me there? A joke? A warning? A —

CLAIRE. What of Allegra?

Nothing from BYSSHE.

What haven't you told me?

BYSSHE. Byron is putting Allegra in a convent, with a school.

CLAIRE. Oh no.

BYSSHE. He can, he's her father —

CLAIRE. Oh no.

BYSSHE. He has the right.

CLAIRE. Oh no.

A silence.

I'll — go to him. I'll dance naked for him, I'll paint myself,
I'll let him put me in chains, any filthy thing he wants — I'll —

She freezes, fists clenched.

Not! No, I will not be — diminished by this. By the cruelty of
a Lord. From now, I will look to myself.

BYSSHE. Yes.

A pause.

We — will conquer our fears.

The GHOST *giggles. The light shifts. And —*

BYSSHE. I will have nothing of madmen. Poetic indulgence. I
will see the real world.

Scene Nine

November 1817

BYSSHE, *aside.* HARRIET's GHOST *at the back.*

BYSSHE. I can see it. St Peter's Field — the outskirts of
Manchester. A great crowd, some 60,000 working men and
women. Armed only with banners.

And then, from nowhere — the militia. The brutal attack. In
ten minutes, a massacre. Eleven dead, four hundred and
twenty-one cases of serious injury, one hundred and sixty-two,
men women and children with sabre wounds.

And where was I, the poet? Impotent in Italy, in the sun.

He turns. Hotel room. MARY *and* CLAIRE. *They are
awkward in their movements, distressed.*

The world is catching fire, the oppressors have bloodied their
hands! But what excites the educated classes? The behaviour
of the rich and famous in bed.

CLAIRE. Bysshe, it would be better if you did not talk. Not now.

BYSSHE. Why?

He looks at CLAIRE, *then* MARY.

What's the matter?

MARY. Ha!

A silence.

BYSSHE. What? Is little Clara worse?

It's nothing, a stomach upset, a cold on her chest. She's a
child of the new age, the dear little ones, they will have to be
tough as steel, soldiers, for what is coming —

CLAIRE. Be quiet, be quiet, can't you tell what has happened?
Are you so insensitive, isn't it screaming off us? Your daughter
died, an hour ago, while you were out in the street.

A silence.

BYSSHE. No, a little cold, and we are in Venice! A city of the
rich! Of hypochondriacs! Of art! And science! And light!
There are legions of doctors in this rotting hell, I'll go out,
get medicine, for a little child with a bad tummy —

MARY. Let me hit him in the face, let me pull out his hair,
scratch out his eyes —

CLAIRE. No Mary, stop it, stop it, stop it!

She restrains MARY, *who subsides.*

BYSSHE. I'll go and see her — kiss her, breathe life back —

MARY, *low.*

MARY. You will stay where you are. You will keep away, you will be still.

Utterly still.

A silence.

It was you who made me bring her to Venice. The cruellest thing you have done to me. Impossible, impossible journey, with a sick child —

BYSSHE. There was nothing impossible about it! I drew up a time-table! For the family, the servants, you had only to keep to it, it was all absolutely clear! There was no reason for anything to go wrong!

MARY. You accuse me? Do you come into this hotel room, dreary, dreary hotel room, find your daughter dead and accuse me —

BYSSHE. Yes!

You dessicated, withered bitch — yes!

He looks down.

I —

Low.

No, of course I do not accuse you.

MARY. I am glad to hear it, for I do accuse *you*.

CLAIRE. It's the grief, only the grief, the grief talking, please my loves, do not —

MARY. Accuse you. For the cruelty, pointless cruelty of all your schemes. The endless, mad-cap journeys, in the heat, in dirty coaches.

The endless —

hopeless —

schemes, and dreams, and —

She calms herself, then continues.

What have you achieved, Bysshe?

BYSSHE. I have written — of the Peterloo massacre. I have written 'The Mask Of Anarchy'. Let it be — a poem — for our daughter.

MARY. Oh! Can't you hear yourself? Do you know what you're saying?

Is the price of a poem — the death of our child?

'The Mask Of Anarchy'! No one will publish it. Will Hunt, in *The Examiner*? No, he knows he will go to gaol for seditious libel.

She scoffs.

The great revolutionary, English poem — unpublishable! Bury it in your daughter's coffin, poet.

BYSSHE. We do what we can! I write what I can, I —

He covers his eyes with his hands.

At the massacre — they carried the word 'love' on a banner.

MARY, *looking away.*

MARY. Oh yes, put the word 'love' on a banner, put the word 'life' on a banner.

CLAIRE. But we are still in love. We all are, with each other. The sorrow of this — will bind us together.

A silence.

MARY. Yes.

All still.

Yes.

CLAIRE *steps forward, hoping they will form a circle, as in earlier scenes — they do not.*

Scene Ten

July 1818

Beach. The Gulf of Spezia. Crash of waves. The stage empty.
BYRON *and* BYSSHE *walk on.*

BYRON. A newspaper.

BYSSHE. Yes.

BYRON. Run — and written by us?

BYSSHE. A voice in England — radical, fierce, uncompromising —

BYRON. With wonderful reviews of our own work, no doubt —

BYSSHE. It will be a banner! A beacon! That is why I have asked Leigh Hunt to come out and join us.

BYRON. The worthy, boring, Leigh Hunt. I see you are as — hot as ever, my dear.

His eyes wander over the landscape.

BYRON. Our two boats moored up together! D'you think 'The Bolivar' is ostentatious?

BYSSHE. Highly, George.

BYRON. Good! You admire the brass cannons?

BYSSHE. Do they work?

BYRON. Work? What does that matter?

He laughs.

Do you like the moulding on the prow? Does it not make the boat look more fearsome?

BYSSHE. It is all excellent, George.

BYRON. As for your boat —

He sniffs.

Is she not shallow in the water?

BYSSHE. How could a boat named the 'Don Juan' be shallow?

BYRON. Cutting, cutting sir — was damn flattered you named her after my poem. I do not object to plagiarism — when it flatters.

BYSSHE. I am thinking of renaming her 'The Ariel'.

BYRON. Yes, more airy-fairy, more like you.

He looks away.

Your women, walking the beach, I see. Still the same menagerie. How is she?

BYSSHE. Claire?

BYRON. You know whom I mean.

BYSSHE. Changed. Well. Different.

BYRON. Much —

He pauses.

BYSSHE. What?

BYRON. After —

BYSSHE. Come, George! They have both had children by us, who died in this country, it is not like you to flinch from raising the subject.

BYRON. Allegra. That damn convent, I felt like breaking in, shooting nuns left, right and centre! Ha! And your wife?

BYSSHE. You know she miscarried a child? Two months ago?

BYRON. Ye Gods. Two men together, two women together, on a beach. But, but, but!

Slaps his thigh.

We have not met enough, Bysshe. What have we done for three years? Barged about this bloody country, you with your holy family, I with my whores. A prison of open air, hard light. I'm thinking of going to Mexico — there is a revolutionary war there. Or Greece. Though the Greek clap be just about the worst in the world — as I well remember. But all this writing about tyranny, eh? In the end you get itchy fingers. Violent verses pale. You want to actually put a bullet in a fat neck.

MARY and CLAIRE walk on. They stop when they see BYRON. CLAIRE goes to turn away, MARY stops her.

(*To* MARY.) Madam. (*To* CLAIRE.) Madam.

MARY. My Lord.

She curtsies. CLAIRE does not.

BYRON. Well! Shall we all dance upon the beach again, my loves? Shall we send up Shelleyan balloons, loaded with lightning experiments? Steal some fire? Shall we, eh?

MARY. Forgive me. I am not too well, today, My Lord.

The two women walk by them, and go off.

BYRON. A war. If only there were a war in England, not that endless — slow, sullen defeat. Why don't the bastards take up arms against such a government? Then we poets would be of some use, we'd do the songs, the banners, the shouts, but no. Sullen silence.

He pauses.

Is Williams down there re-rigging your boat?

BYSSHE. I want it to sail faster.

BYRON. Huh!

BYSSHE. I will race 'The Bolivar' to Livorno, when we go to pick up the Hunts.

BYRON. Oh the Hunts, those bloody children, why do these well-meaning literati have so many of 'em? All so healthy, and so — eh? I am so damn restless.

They look at each other.

Well, well! Let's go play with our boats, like good little boys.

He stomps off. BYSSHE *stays on the beach. Then* MARY *and* CLAIRE *come on.*

CLAIRE. Do you know, that is the first time I've seen him — since our daughter died? Is that not terrible — or farcical? He looks crabbed. Much older.

MARY. What of the plans with the Hunts?

BYSSHE. We will sail both vessels to Livorno. You stay here. We will bring the Hunts — if things can be made quiet, between them and George —

MARY. Why cannot they come over land?

BYSSHE. We — will sail. Jane Williams would very much like to sail, perhaps —

MARY, *bitterly.*

MARY. Yes. Jane Williams.

BYSSHE. What is the matter?

MARY. What can be the matter?

A silence.

BYSSHE. Williams is re-rigging for me. I must go and help.

A silence.

We are well! It will be fun!

He goes off.

CLAIRE. Jane Williams, his boatman's wife?

She laughs.

MARY. Have you not listened to the pretty little love lyrics, being read each night, after supper, as if out of thin air?

She laughs.

And — I found the manuscript of the new, long poem he is writing. At the bottom of the page, in tiny, tiny writing, were the words — 'Alas, I kiss you Jane'.

CLAIRE *looks away.*

CLAIRE. Not to be diminished. I will join —

She pauses.

The subterranean. The subterranean community of women. I'll travel. I'll see Islands. And the snows of Russia. I will never marry, for I was married once.

She looks at MARY.

To you and to him.

MARY. Do you know what the new poem is called?

CLAIRE. No.

MARY. Guess.

CLAIRE. How can I?

MARY. Guess! Guess! Guess!

CLAIRE. Mary, stop it —

MARY. It is called 'The Triumph Of Life'.

She doubles up, shaking with laughter. CLAIRE *does not laugh.*

'The Triumph Of Life'! 'The Triumph Of Life'! 'The Triumph Of Life'! 'The Triumph Of —'

And —

Scene Eleven

The stage darkens.

POLIDORI *walks about the auditorium, a glass of wine in his hand, wearing a smoking jacket.*

POLIDORI. Oh yes, I knew Shelley in Venice well, oh yes, many
an evening, went to brothels together, talking literature the
while, oh yes, Shelley's mistress, had her myself, oh yes yes,
'course I was the model for the diabolical, in Mary's novel, oh
yes, had her, many-a-time, gave her the plot for the damn
book — yes, no, well not quite, but to all intents and purposes,
I saw Bysshe Shelley jump into his boat, in Livorno Harbour,
with the storm coming, my opinion? Suicide, yes, no doubt,
an utterly unstable little prick, y'get m'innuendo — yes, I'll
have more wine, kind of ye —

Wandering out of the auditorium.

Yes, m'literary reminiscences, course y'know about the body
when it washed up? The fish had had the eyes out, and eaten
the testicles, what dinner? Kind of ye, most —

He has gone. And —

Scene Twelve

BYSSHE. *A sail. Dark stage, his face. NB. No 'storm effects'.*

BYSSHE.
As I lay asleep in Italy
There came a voice from over the Sea
And with great power it forth led me
To walk in the visions of poetry

I met murder on the way —
He had a mask like Castlereagh —
Very smooth he looked, yet grim;
Seven blood hounds followed him:

All were fat; and well they might
Be in admirable plight,
For one by one, and two by two
He tossed them human hearts to chew
Which from his wide cloak he drew

And with pomp to meet him came
Clothed in arms like blood and flame
The hired murderers, who did sing
Did sing! Did sing! Did sing!

He pauses.

And Anarchy, the ghastly birth
Lay dead earth upon the earth,
The Horse of Death tameless as wind
Fled, and with his hoofs did grind
To dust the murderers thronged behind

A rushing light of clouds and splendour,
A sense awakening yet tender
Was heard and felt — and at its close
Words of joy and fear arose

Men of England, heirs of Glory,
Heroes of unwritten story,
Nurslings of one mighty Mother
Hopes of her, and one another;

Rise like Lions after slumber
In unvanquishable number —
Shake your chains to earth like dew
Which in sleep had fallen on you —
Ye are many — they are few.

He pauses. A change.

The waters are flashing,
The white hail is dashing,
The lightnings are glancing
The hoarspray is dancing —

The Earth is like Ocean
Wreck-strewn and in motion:
Bird, beast, man and worm
Have crept out of the storm —

A silence. A change.

When the lamp is shattered
The light in the dust lies dead —
When the cloud is scattered
The rainbow's glory is shed —

Change, at once.

And 'fear'st thou?' and 'Fear'st thou?'
And 'Seest thou?' and Hear'st thou?'
And 'Drive we not free
Over the terrible sea,
I and thou?'

He pauses, and to a broken, odd rhythm.

Mother of many acts and hours — free
The serpent —

These are the spells —
    by which to reassume
An empire o'er the disentangled doom.
To suffer —

    woes which hope thinks infinite
To forgive wrongs darker than death or night
To defy power which seems omnipotent —

To love, and bear —

    to hope till Hope creates
From its own wreck the thing it contemplates

This is —
    to be
Good, great, and joyous, beautiful and free.

Sh! Sh! 'voluptuous flight' — 'volup — tu — ous flight!'

He laughs.

Ha! An easy rhyme there — with 'night'.

A blackout.

And —

Scene Thirteen

A blast of storm effects — briefly — they die down, the lights come up. At the back, HARRIET's GHOST. BYSSHE's *body is furled in the sail upon the stage.* BYRON *stands behind it, looking at it. He keeps his distance. The* GHOST *stands at the back.*

BYRON. We'll burn the body on the beach.

I loved him.

Thus is another man gone, about whom the world was brutally mistaken.

And in the name of all the mercies, look what the sea did to his flesh.

He shouts.

Burn him! Burn him! Burn him!
Burn us all! A great big, bloody, beautiful fire!

A blackout.

GREENLAND

To Wolfgang Lippke

'We're here to build cathedrals'
Joseph Beuys

Notes

To be performed by a company of four men and four women.

The action of the play takes place on 11 June 1987, and 700 years from then.

Greenland was first performed at the Royal Court Theatre on May 26 1988 with the following cast:

Act One
— US —

JOAN	Jane Lapotaire
BILL	Ben Onwukwe
POLICEMAN	Larry Lamb
BETTY BLAZE	Sheila Hancock
SISTER ANNE ⎫ Evangelists	Janet McTeer
BROTHER GEORGE ⎭	David Haig
ROGER, A Reporter	Ron Cook
MARY	Jane Lapotaire
CENTURION	Ben Onwukwe
JUDY, Betty's Daughter	Lesley Sharp
BRIAN	Larry Lamb
DOT, Brian's Sister	Sheila Hancock
PAUL, LORD LUDLOW	David Haig
MILLY, Paul's Wife	Janet McTeer
VAL	Lesley Sharp
JACKO ⎫	Ron Cook
ANDREW ⎬ Paul's Friends	Ben Onwukwe
HUGH ⎭	Larry Lamb
DON	Ron Cook
JEFF	David Haig
BUSKER	Carol Sloman

Act Two
— THEM —

DRAW ⎫ Beachcombers	Ron Cook
A'BET ⎭	Lesley Sharp
JACE, A Jeweller	Ben Onwukwe
SIU	Janet McTeer
ANNETTE, An Archaeologist	Lesley Sharp
SASHA, Her Assistant	Ron Cook
OH' ⎫	Ben Onwukwe
LAI FUNG ⎬ Lovers	Lesley Sharp
SALLY ⎭	Janet McTeer
SEVERAN-SEVERAN, An Historian	Ron Cook
PALACE, A Nurse	Janet McTeer
GREENLANDER	Carol Sloman

Director Simon Curtis
Designer Paul Brown
Lighting by Andy Phillips
Music by Stephen Warbeck

ACT ONE

Scene One

Lights up.

7 a.m. Thursday, 11 June, 1987.

JOAN *there. She is dressed in a well cut coat. 'Good' shoes. She wears a large Labour Party rosette.*

JOAN. Mum? Dad?

Today your daughter will be elected to the House of Commons.

Yup! Your Joan, your Joanie, is going to change the world.

A laugh to herself. A pause.

You'd have been proud. Even you Dad, you old Stalinist. If only you were here.

Straightens.

Right! The only time today you think like that, my girl!

BILL *comes on, fast. He carries three clipboards, loaded with papers, a bulging briefcase, and three large electric megaphones. He too wears a large Labour Party rosette.*

BILL. The turn out at the committee rooms is great. A lot of helpers.

JOAN. I saw Punk Eddie hanging around the Park Grove committee room. Bill! Now keep him and his lot off the street.

BILL. Punk Eddie is dead keen . . .

JOAN. Bill! I am not going to have a mad Glaswegian with red eyes and a green, three foot high Mohican haircut, knocking on doors telling people to vote Labour.

Not today. Today we get it right. Today we are going to win.

BILL. OK.

They look at each other. They grin. Then BILL looks at his watch.

The polls opened. Just then.

JOAN. Let's go.

Walking off together. JOAN talking fast.

I'll go out with the megaphone van at ten. I'll do Safeway's Shopping Mall at lunchtime. And we'll have the first check of the turnout at twelve, then every two hours. What about drivers and cars for the old folks?

BILL. Tremendous . . .

They are off.

Scene Two

*Noon. South London. Outside a school. A cardboard sign –
'Polling Station'.*

A young POLICE CONSTABLE *stands, hands behind his back.
He claps his hands. He blows into each glove at the wrist. Then
he looks one way, then the other. Feeling unseen, he quickly gives
his balls a scratch. Then he puts his hands behind his back again.*

BETTY BLAZE *comes on. She is in her early sixties. She wears a
sensible plastic mackintosh and a flamboyant hat with feathers
and fruit. She carries a copy of the 'Daily Telegraph'.*

She opens the 'Daily Telegraph'. She kneels on it in prayer.

BETTY. Oh Lord Jesus. I kneel down in a dirty street of London.
For I would see thy Angel with burning sword, oh Lord. A
sword of light.

The CONSTABLE *starts, is about to move forward. Then he
recognises* BETTY.

CONSTABLE (*aside*). My God. It is. It's her.

BETTY. Let darkness not fall in England, on this thy sweet land.

For I would that all were praise, over all the roofs, all the
gardens, the houses, yea high in the tower blocks and on the
motorways, praise, yea in the churches, in the dens of iniquity,
in the discos, the strip clubs, all praise, yea even in the studios
of the BBC, hallelujah.

For my heart is heavy, sweet Jesus.

Suddenly cross. She looks at her watch.

Well, where are they? I do hate things not happening when
people say. Oh, whoops, sorry Lord!

Finishing the prayer off.

For my heart is heavy and thine is the kingdom, the power and
the glory, amen.

*She snaps out of the prayer. Stands. Picks up the 'Daily
Telegraph'. Puts it in her copious handbag and turns to the*
CONSTABLE *with a beaming smile.*

Good morning Officer!

He nods.

BETTY. I hope the voters are flocking!

CONSTABLE. Bit quiet so far, but . . .

BETTY *interrupting.*

BETTY. And voting the right way!

CONSTABLE. Well as I see it . . .

BETTY. The Devil does his work, even on Polling Day.

Both of them looking one way, then the other. Nothing happens.

BETTY *looks at her watch.*

BETTY. Really! I know they are the South London anti-pornography committee and good souls, but why can't God's people . . . keep to a timetable?

Two local Christians come on, 'SISTER' ANNE and 'BROTHER' GEORGE.

SISTER ANNE. There she is, bless her.

BROTHER GEORGE. Mrs Blaze!

BETTY *glances at them.*

SISTER ANNE (*aside*). She's famous for her hats. Amongst the crowds, the TV cameras, photographers from the newspapers, demonstrators – the hat. She said once: 'When I do battle for the Lord, I like a harvest festival on my head.' (*To* BETTY.) What a wonderful hat, Mrs Blaze.

BETTY. Oh thank you dear. When I do battle for the Lord, I like a harvest festival on my head.

SISTER ANNE. But you've said that before . . .

BETTY. Any gentlemen of the press?

BROTHER GEORGE. I telephoned the Methodist Recorder.

BETTY. Yes. Well. That will strike fear into Satan's hordes.

BROTHER GEORGE *is nonplussed.*

BETTY *beams at him.*

Well! When does this blasphemy start?

BROTHER GEORGE. I think they are a bit late.

BETTY. We are in the right place?

SISTER ANNE. The Anglican Vicar was going to let them do it on the steps of the church!

BETTY. We must all pray for the Church of England. Oh!

ROGER, *a top tabloid reporter, wanders on. He has a camera.*

SISTER ANNE. It's that strange man. Who was hanging around the Baptist hall . . .

BETTY. It's a big boy. From Wapping. No one say anything.

SISTER ANNE. You mean . . . (*Panicking.*) A real reporter? . . .

BETTY. Not a word! I'll do the interviews. He loves me. (*Aside.*) Why has one of the heavies come down to this little do? On Election Day? (*To the* REPORTER.) Hello Roger! Here I am!

BROTHER GEORGE *looks along the street and goes off.*

ROGER. Hello Betty! Getting your knickers in a twist for the Lord again?

BETTY. Now Roger! I don't want any of that from you!

ROGER. Devil's party myself, Betty.

BETTY. You do the Lord's work without knowing.

BROTHER GEORGE *comes back on, quickly.*

BROTHER GEORGE. They're coming! And it's worse than we thought!

SISTER ANNE. Oh! My tummy's turning.

BETTY (*to the* CONSTABLE). Constable! Do nothing until I make a complaint!

CONSTABLE. Oh, right . . .

BROTHER GEORGE. Let us pray!

SISTER ANNE. Sing!

BROTHER GEORGE. Praise the Lord!

BETTY. We'll go over the street. Hide in the chemist's doorway. Come on!

BROTHER GEORGE. Oh. Isn't that rather . . .

BETTY. What?

BROTHER GEORGE. Sneaky?

ROGER. You've got a seasoned moral campaigner here, old man. Don't teach Saint Betty how to suck eggs.

BETTY. Quite right dear.

As if about to cross a street, through the traffic.

I'm rushing straight to Broadcasting House after this one. On call for *News At One*.

ROGER. Messing about in politics, Betty?

BETTY. Naughty, naughty! God is politics. Go on everyone! Dodge the traffic . . .

They 'cross the street' and hide for a moment, the CONSTABLE is alone on the stage, nervous. He takes his radio from his lapel, at the ready.

Off, loud tinny music. A 'Dies Irae'.

Enter a street theatre troupe. A ROMAN CENTURION with a whip. MARY, Christ's Mother. They plant a banner, between sticks, the stick implanted in orange boxes. The banner reads 'PASSION OF A WOMAN VOTER'. They set a tea-chest. On the tea-chest a placard, which reads 'NOBODY CARES. VOTE FOR NOBODY'.

NB: The actors in the passion play have half-face masks. Incongruously, hanging around their necks over their Biblical costumes, they have electric megaphones.

The CENTURION cracks his whip on the pavement.

CONSTABLE (*to himself*): Oi oi!

He begins to mumble into his radio. The taped music goes into a ska beat. The CENTURION and MARY chant, blasting through their megaphones.

MARY. The housewife voter crucified . . .

CENTURION. Jesus Christ, who was she . . .

MARY. Daughter of woman, not of man . . .

CENTURION. She would not vote for man! Man's world! Man's taxes, man's holy Parliament! So crucify the bitch!

The CENTURION cracks the whip on the pavement.

Enter a female CHRIST, dragging a cross. She is wearing a half-mask and is naked but for a traditional Christ loincloth, a housewife's turban and pink fluffy slippers. The pipe of a vacuum cleaner is draped around the cross. Instead of the 'INRI' sign at the top of the cross there is a board, on it the words 'DON'T VOTE'.

MARY (*megaphone*). She shall rent the temple of Parliament! The great seal of men and power shall be cracked! Westminster, She shall throw you down, stone by stone!

As MARY *rants,* CHRIST *and the* CENTURION *insert the cross in a slot in the top of the tea-chest.* CHRIST *ascends the cross in the traditional position. The* CENTURION *cracks the whip on the pavement.*

The heads of BROTHER GEORGE *and* SISTER ANNE *poke around the corner of the stage.*

SISTER ANNE. Ooh I say!

BROTHER GEORGE. Disgraceful!

CHRIST. Sisters. We will not vote for the man and his works. And today thou shalt be with my Mother in Paradise.

The CENTURION *spreads his arms wide. 'John Wayne acting'.*

CENTURION (*megaphone*). Truly this was the daughter of God.

ROGER, *camera at the ready,* BETTY *and* SISTER ANNE *and* BROTHER GEORGE *tumble toward the scene. The* CONSTABLE's *radio crackling.*

All speak at once:

SISTER ANNE. Stop this outrage!

BROTHER GEORGE. Stop that actress's breasts!

ROGER. I gotta get the pix! Betty, I want you with the bint on the cross!

SISTER ANNE. Filth! Cover yourself, cover it up!

ROGER. Jesus! Jesus! Look at me! Poke 'em out Jesus, Jesus!

Then:

BETTY. Oh you sinners, silly-billy people! With your filthy minds, misguided, mocking the faith of decent folk . . .

She is suddenly still. And, at the moment, everyone is still. CHRIST *and* BETTY *are staring at each other.*

The CHRIST *removes her half-mask.*

Judy!

CHRIST/JUDY. Oh Mum, what the fuck are you doing here?

BETTY. Judy!

CENTURION. Fuck. Her Mum has turned up.

MARY. Great, this is great for the play . . .

CENTURION. Oh Gawd! I'll never work again.

SISTER ANNE (*to* BROTHER GEORGE).
Her daughter?

ROGER, *photographing at speed.*

ROGER. That was the tip off and this is the story folks!

BETTY. Judy! Get down off that cross at once!

JUDY. St Paul said 'I am crossed out in Christ!'.

BETTY. He said no such thing you stupid girl.

JUDY. Mum! I'm thirty-three years old! As old as he was!

ROGER. Great, oh great!

BETTY. Wicked! I'll get you down off there myself . . .

BROTHER GEORGE. Constable . . .

CONSTABLE. Right, all of you . . .

A scrummage. The actors and the two Christians in the mêlée with BETTY *and* JUDY. *The* CONSTABLE *wades in.* ROGER *circles the scene, photographing.*

ROGER. Betty! Betty! What d'ya think of your daughter doing this? Betty!

All speak at once:

CENTURION. Get back, just get back . . .

BETTY. You wicked, wicked . . . God if your father . . . Oh you girl . . .

MARY. Freedom o' speech! What about freedom o' speech!

ROGER. So fucking speak, darling . . .

SISTER ANNE. Sing! Someone, sing a hymn!

Then:

ROGER. Deposition from the cross! 1980's style. Raphael you should'a been living at this hour.

The cross keels over, with all of them falling, in slow motion, into a heap.

Disentangling themselves.

CENTURION. Run!

MARY. Judy come on!

CENTURION. Come on!

MARY. Judy!

CONSTABLE. Not you!

MARY *and* CENTURION *run off. They are heard offstage, shouting 'Judy' . . . 'Judy' . . . But the* CONSTABLE *keeps his hold on* JUDY's *arms.*

SISTER ANNE. Give her something to cover her up.

BROTHER GEORGE. Er, here Miss . . .

He takes off his coat and puts it around JUDY.

SISTER ANNE *stands, helping* BETTY *up. The* CONSTABLE, *one hand on an unresisting* JUDY's *arm, the other at his radio, is sending for help.*

CONSTABLE. Incident at 2 Dog Lane School Polling Station, assistance required, two suspects, going towards West Peckham Estate . . .

The radio crackles.

SISTER ANNE. Oh Mrs Blaze, I am so sorry, we had no idea your daughter . . .

A pause. Embarrassment.

JUDY (*at* BETTY). You make everything dirty. Everything.

BETTY. I? I make dirty?

ROGER. Come on Betty! Interview time.

BETTY. Give me this one Roger. After all the stories I've slipped you. You'll bury this one . . .

JUDY. Listen to her! Listen to her!

The CONSTABLE *pulling* JUDY *away.*

CONSTABLE. Now now.

BETTY. Be fair to me, Roger.

A pause, all looking at ROGER. *Then he backs away.*

ROGER. All right. Don't worry Betty girl. I'll see you all right in the story.

BETTY. Oh! Bless you dear. I'll say a little prayer.

ROGER. That will come in handy.

He is going. He turns.

(*Aside.*) Fifteen years we've printed her muck. She's got it coming to her. If Labour get back in, it'll be no holds barred. But if it's Thatcher again, the paper'll kill the story. The days of right-wing gurus will go on for ever.

He sniffs.

Think I'll go down the Walworth Road. See if I can get a shot o' Kinnock picking his nose. You never know y' luck . . .

He's gone. The sound of a police car's siren. The CONSTABLE *pulling* JUDY *off.*

CONSTABLE. We will want statements from you all.

BETTY. I'll come with you . . .

> JUDY *spits on the ground before* BETTY. *Who is frozen.*
> *The* CONSTABLE *and* JUDY *go off.*

SISTER ANNE. The Porn Committee . . . have laid on a tea. At the Baptist Hall. There are cakes, there are buns . . .

BETTY. What I need . . . Need now . . . Is a stiff scotch.

SISTER ANNE. Oh?

BETTY. You go on. I'll have a little prayer.

SISTER ANNE. The Baptist . . .

> BETTY, *a flash of violent temper.*

BETTY. I'll find the wretched hall!

SISTER ANNE. But the Police . . .

BETTY. I'll talk to the Police. Just go!

> SISTER ANNE *and* BROTHER GEORGE *pause, then turn away, walking off.*

BROTHER GEORGE. Whited sepulchre.

SISTER ANNE. No, surely . . .

BROTHER GEORGE. Feet of clay, there.

SISTER ANNE. I don't think . . .

BROTHER GEORGE. I do.

> *They are gone.* BETTY *alone.*

BETTY. To be a brand . . . Put to the burning. Oh, to catch fire!

> *She covers her face with her hands. The sound again of a police siren.*
> *She goes off.*

Scene Three

5 p.m. South London. Amongst flats.

BRIAN *before us. He has a Harrods plastic bag, much abused. It is full of cans of lager.*

BRIAN. The . . .
> fuurst . . .
> la la larger . . . !!

And he holds up a can from the bag, like a magician producing a rabbit from a hat.

First since lunch-time, that is.

A woman's VOICE, shouting down at him.

VOICE. Brian! You han't made your bed!

Looking up.

BRIAN. Oh! Dot! Right! (*Aside.*) My sister, Dot. Live with her. Got a wank pit in her spare room.

VOICE. You lazy bugger!

BRIAN. Oh, right! (*Aside.*) Just 'til somthin' turns up. Y'know, while I steady myself.

VOICE. These sheets are disgustin'! You said you'd take 'em down the laundrette.

BRIAN. Give over, Dot! Not in public . . .

VOICE. They're grey! They got beer all over 'em!

BRIAN (*aside*). I mean it's only a poxy council flat. Poxy South London. You'd think it were the fucking Ritz with her. Hoover, hoover . . . (*Shouts up.*) Can't you take 'em down? I got to see a man in a pub . . .

DOT. You're a lazy, dirty, lazy bugger!

BRIAN. Give us a break, Dot! They open in half an hour. (*Aside.*) I dunno. Days are so short. They just go.

A bundle of two dirty, single sheets is thrown down onto the stage.

DOT. Do your own fuckin' washing. And don't come back 'fore you do!

BRIAN. What do you want to do? Humiliate your own flesh and blood?

DOT. You heard!

Above, a door slammed.

BRIAN. Dunno at all. Survival o' the fittest in't it.

Picking up the sheets, putting them under his arm. He walks off, sheepishly. As . . .

Scene Four

LORD LUDLOW (PAUL) *comes on. He is dressed in evening dress. He is well built, straight-backed. His dress is immaculate. He carries a portable telephone, of the latest design. He is dialling. He stands, legs slightly apart, 'manly', 'suave' in his manner. Harrovian accent.*

PAUL. Meanwhile in another neck of the woods, as they say, a great deal of money is being lost.

Into the telephone.

Jacko, you fucker. Are we or are we not having dinner tonight?

Listens.

'Course I'm not going to the fucking Garrick, last time I dined there I had to sit next to some fucking little High Court Judge. The little cunt threw his custard pudding all over me. No I've booked a table for four at Swanson's.

Listens.

What the fuck do you mean, 'Mustn't gamble' tonight? It's General Election night. The whole fucking country's at the gaming tables. Could lose all, come the dawn find it's a Moscow shade of red. Where would you and I be then? . . . Right. In the hills, Jacko . . .

He pauses. Lowers his voice. MILLY *his wife comes on. She is in her early thirties, drawn, withdrawn. She carries a perfect white carnation.*

Just a little chemmy. Something light. After a light supper. The Club will stand you half of anything, if you're with me. They like an Earl and his friends at the tables. It encourages the Arabs. Do this for me?

Listens.

Thank you Jacko.

Palms the aerial of the telephone down. Husband and wife look at each other.

A silence.

Then she holds out the carnation. He takes it. He gives her the telephone.

A silence.

Then he begins to try to put the carnation in his button hole.

Children . . . ?

MILLY. Little John rang.

PAUL. Enjoying themselves?

MILLY. His sister was sick.

PAUL. That fool of a husband of your friend Florence. Taking kids on a helicopter trip. I'm not sure I approve.

MILLY. Why do you not approve?

PAUL. It gives them ideas.

MILLY. And what ideas are those?

PAUL. You know. That everything comes easily.

MILLY scoffs.

MILLY. Well you should know all about that.

A pause.

PAUL. Milly, I don't want to bitch.

MILLY. Am I coming to Swanson's tonight?

PAUL sighs.

PAUL. Well are you?

MILLY. I don't want to sit any more, amongst your cronies.

PAUL. No.

Fumbling with the carnation.

Fucking flower . . .

She closes her eyes. A slight sway. Then she opens her eyes. She takes the carnation brushing his hands away. She begins to fix it.

PAUL. Things narrow. You know? Narrow down and I . . . It could all come to pieces, you know. And I've done my best.

He floods with rage. Clenches a fist. Hits it against his side. Then rubs his hand. She stands her ground. They are close together. Then, clumsily, he tries to take her face in his hands to kiss her, but now she flinches away.

He looks at the carnation.

PAUL. Carnation. Death flower. What will you do? Watch the box?

Nothing from MILLY. He turns and goes.

MILLY *alone, not moving.*

Then she puts the telephone down. Lifts her arms and undoes her hair. She shakes her head, her hair falls.

The telephone rings. She does not answer it.

From the pocket of her skirt, she takes out a large joint of marijuana. She puts it slowly in her mouth, wetting the skin. She takes out a small gold cigarette lighter. She lights the joint. She inhales deeply. She blows the smoke out.

The telephone stops ringing.

MILLY (*aside*). I want to be back in the early seventies, in a secret Chelsea garden. Flowers, by the river, in the sunshine. Drinking wine. Giggling. Feeling naked in a short skirt, my legs long and golden. And a handsome young aristocrat, leaning over me, helplessly in love.

PAUL comes back on, a strange distortion on his face.

She instantly steps away.

MILLY. No don't Paul! Oh my God!

He hits her in the stomach.

PAUL. I am in hell . . .

MILLY. Bastard!

PAUL. Don't you see that!

He punches her in a kidney. She doubles and falls. (Aside.) I have forty suits in my dressing room. They are of silk or wool. Identical. They all have the same pattern and cut. Blue, a light stripe.

Clenches his fists.

Life should be so . . . good!

He steps on her head. She yells and rolls.

Looky. It's all right. Don't lie there crying.
Looky here.

He takes a fistful of jewels, diamonds, from his pocket.

I went to Cartiers. All the cash I could put together. Thousands worth. Pure, simply cut. So we are all right Milly. If the country goes to the dogs. If the reds take over. If the bastards come for us . . .

He sags, half kneels.

I'll stay in tonight. We'll watch the box. Crack a bottle of the burgundy, we . . .

He pauses, a hand covering his face. Then suddenly he stands.

He holds up a diamond bracelet.

Here. With love.

He throws the bracelet on the floor before her. He goes off, raging, fists clenched.

A silence. MILLY *dead still.*

Then she moves painfully. She picks up the joint. It is trodden. She picks up the bracelet and dangles it before her face.

In a very faint, high clear voice she sings a few lines from the Eagles' song, 'Desperado'.

MILLY.
'Why don't you come to your senses
You've been out riding fences
        For so long now . . .
These things that are pleasing you
Can hurt you somehow . . .
Oh it's hard to tell
        The night from the day . . .'

She stays on the stage. She hides her head in her arms, bundled up, the telephone before her.

Scene Five

BRIAN *comes on. He carries his Harrods bag and the bundle of dirty sheets. He has an unopened can of lager in his hand.*

BRIAN (*aside*) Where was I? Yeah, that first bite of the first can of a long, long night.

The drinker approaches.

Now some wankers make nothing of this moment. Your scum of the earth, your average boozer, your Millwall supporter, just go rip-bang-wallop.

Whereas your 'artiste', your Leonardo of the lager
can . . .
He holds up his left hand, then just its third finger.

God, I'm dying. That taste o' orange peel, with the fizz. No! I got to get some self-discipline. The whole night ahead to get out a' control . . .

He puts the Harrods bag down carefully. He pulls the sheets around his shoulders. He adopts the drinker's stance, legs apart. Holds out the can in his right hand. Finger to the ring.

Here she blows.

Up where the air is fresh 'n' clean.

He pulls the ring. Lager squirts. He sups, wandering off.

Two Labour Party workers come on, BILL, working class, and VAL, middle class. Rosettes, armfuls of pamphlets. Shoulder bags.

VAL. I wanted to come out earlier.

BILL. Oh yeah?

VAL. But the children. And Hippolyta's in Portugal.

BILL. Hip what?

VAL. Our au pair.

BILL. Gotcha. (*Frowns*). Hippolyta, isn't that Greek?

VAL. But her boyfriend's Portuguese.

BILL. Ah. Well. That'll be why.

VAL. Why what?

BILL. Why she's in Portugal. (*Aside.*) Help!

VAL. She has her own room. And we give her English lessons. She's free to eat with us . . . And she's got her . . . (*Weakening.*) own key.

BILL. Look, eh, Valerie in't it?

VAL. Val.

BILL. You done this before?

VAL looks puzzled.

Canvassing for Labour.

VAL. No, actually. Actually, I'm a bit nervous.

BILL. Don't worry, it's a doddle. When did you join the party, Val?

VAL. Last week, in fact. I thought I had to do something.

BILL. Good for you. (*Aside.*) Save me, save me Trotsky!

VAL. What about you?

BILL. Oh . . . I'm Union section. NUT.

VAL. You . . . are a teacher? (*She is scared.*) Not Militant . . .

BILL. Heavy duty workerist tendencies more like, comrade.

VAL. Workerist?

BILL. Roll the Union on etcetera. Look love, shall we get on tryin' to drag Neil Kinnock by his remaining hair, screaming into Number Ten?

VAL. Let's. They say the Labour Party is a broad church.

BILL. Very like a church. Smell a' mothballs and the lead nicked off the roof – right, these call backs. In the flats. These are promises, but the sods haven't turned up at the polls yet. We know from the cards. You clock the system.

VAL. Er . . .

BILL. It's a straightforward knock-up. I'll do numbers one to a hundred, you do a hundred and up . . .

VAL. We're going to split up?

BILL. I'll do a couple o' doors with you. Just say have you voted yet? If they want a babysitter, sit with the baby, while they pop round.

VAL. Oh.

BILL. Just get the buggers to vote.

VAL. All right . . .

BILL. Don't worry. These are our people.

BRIAN *crosses before them. Carefree, contemplating his third lager can.*

BRIAN. (*aside*). Can number three. Your first five cans are the lower slopes of Mount Piss-up.

Rips the ring off the can.

VAl. Shall we do him?

BILL. Scraping the barrel a bit.

VAL. Surely he, too, is the great electorate.

She frowns.

But why has he got dirty bedsheets round his neck?

Grins.

Takes all sorts.

BILL. He won't even be on the electoral register . . .

But she is confronting BRIAN.

VAL. 'Scuse me, do you vote?

    BRIAN *is stunned. He stares at her.*

BRIAN. Do I what?

VAL. Will you, tonight?

    BRIAN *looks puzzled.*

VAL. It's only just gone five. You've got until ten. So vote. For the Labour Party.

BRIAN. I got a secret life, you know.

VAL. We've all got our lives, but what about the country? What has Margaret Thatcher ever done for you?

BRIAN. What are you? The Government?

VAL. No, no, we're Labour.

BRIAN. Stuff the Government.

VAL. Labour Party, not the Government. Though we want to be!

BRIAN. Why do you want . . . (*A sweep of an arm.*) To run my life?

VAL. I don't want to run your life . . .

BRIAN. Coming up in the fucking street, trying to run my life . . .

    BILL *intervenes.*

BILL. That's enough, friend.

BRIAN. And who are you, Hitler?

BILL. On your way, friend.

    He and BRIAN, *eyeball to eyeball.*

Have a pamphlet.

    He pushes a pamphlet against BRIAN's *chest. It flutters to the ground.* BRIAN *backs away. He lurches up-stage then turns, abusive from a distance..*

BRIAN. Gov'ment . . . Police . . . Labour . . . Man on the fucking telly . . . All you, keep off! You don't know me! You don't know my secret life!

    BRIAN *goes off.*

BILL. Don't let it worry you.

    She smiles.

VAL. Was that what they call the lumpen proletariat?

BILL. Not the real thing, not at all.

VAL. Oh Lord.

BILL. Tell you what, I'll do the flats. You do Craven Grove. More your thing. I'll still do a couple of doors with you to get you going.

She is angry.

VAL. No. I can handle Craven Grove. Every house costs over a hundred and fifty thousand. Much more my 'kind of thing'.

He looks at her, unsmiling.

BILL. The point of doing this, is to get a Labour Government elected.

VAL. 'Yes, comrade'.

A pause.

BILL. See you back at the committee rooms, then. Oh. No canvassing while EastEnders is on the box. Knock 'em up while Dirty Den is doing his stuff, sure vote loser.

VAL. Right. (*They part. Aside.*) Pig.

BILL (*aside*). God Almighty. We're going to lose.

They go off.

Scene Six

MILLY *still on the stage, huddled before her telephone. She does not look up.*

MILLY. I don't want anything. I'm not ambitious. I just don't want to be who I am.

The telephone rings five times. She does not look at it. It stops ringing.

Not much to want.

At the back, PAUL, 'JACKO' *and two other male friends,* ANDREW *and* HUGH, *come on. 'Street lighting' – blueish, light from polished glass, passing cars.*

JACKO. ⎱ London Nights. Out there . . .

PAUL. ⎰ What did I drive here? The fucking BMW or the fucking Volvo . . .

JACKO. The discos whirr, the roulette tables whirr, the brains of drunks, the wheels of the traffic, whirr whirr, films in the cinema projectors, hamburgers slapped on ten thousand plates, fifteen-year-old girls on high heels, the punters the punted, the muggers and the mugged, the pigeons in Trafalgar Square, whirrrrr!

ANDREW. Pissed again . . .

JACKO. London Nights . . .

PAUL. Fucking keys.

Fumbles in his pockets. Diamonds spill.

HUGH. My God, Paul, what's all this? Burglary?

PAUL. S'mine . . .

ANDREW. Loot?

HUGH, *slurred.*

HUGH. Second Earl a'Ludlow, se's a fucking cat burglar!

PAUL.	You buggers . . .
HUGH.	Pink Panther! S' a fucking Panther!
JACKO.	London nights! Diamonds in the gutters, 'long with theatre tickets, spewed up Chinese takeaways, old johnnies . . .

ANDREW. Paul what the fuck are you doing?

PAUL. Reds.

ANDREW. What?

They are picking the diamonds up. A WOMAN TRAMP wanders past.

PAUL. Stash. Go to the Welsh hills. Small arms.

ANDREW. Pursued by whom?

The TRAMP has picked up a diamond necklace. She stands, swaying, looking at it.

TRAMP. You'sha, whatsh a?

ANDREW *relieves the TRAMP of it.*

ANDREW. Thank you, Jeeves.

The TRAMP, lurching off.

TRAMP. You'sha, whatsh a?

HUGH. Come on you drunken farts, let's all go on to Mary Anne's.

PAUL *pocketing the jewels.*

JACKO. What is it Paul? Is it Milly?

  PAUL *holding up a car key*.

PAUL. S'all right I'm in the Volvo.

ANDREW. Mary Anne's, one and all . . .

  ANDREW *and* HUGH, *peeling away*.

JACKO. Paul!

  PAUL *holding* JACKO's *lapels*.

PAUL. Look Jacko, will you do this for me? Go on to where . . .
  there you're going. I'll be with you. Say I'm with you.

JACKO. Brigade spirit?

PAUL. I'm fucking with you all the time right?

JACKO. My dear fellow, don't . . .

PAUL. With you. With you.

  He runs off.

JACKO. Paul!

ANDREW. Where is the drunken Earl?

JACKO. A piss up a dark alley. He's with us. On we go.

HUGH. What's the time?

ANDREW. Twelve o'twelve-thirty.

HUGH. Fuck and damnation!

ANDREW. What?

HUGH. I forgot to vote.

  They are going off.

ANDREW. What do you want to fucking vote for?

HUGH. Well I'm the only one of you who can. You buggers are
  all in the House of Lords.

JACKO. Never pissed on those portals myself.

  Point of principle . . .

  They are gone.

MILLY. If I were not me, what would I . . .

  . . . wear?

  What would I know? What would I think?

  What would be the colour of my hair?

  How would I . . .

Move? Smile? Turn . . .

Where would I live?

Who . . .

would I love?

At the back of the dark stage, a spotlight, very bright, switches on then at once dies. In it a figure of a WOMAN, *in a strange, long dress, barefoot, with* MILLY's *long blonde hair. The figure is turning on the ball of a bare foot, a shrugging gesture, which may mean 'hello', or may be dismissive – 'hard luck'.*

The figure gone. MILLY *starts and glances over her shoulder. She shivers. She remains on the stage.*

Scene Seven

MILLY, *on the stage huddled before the telephone.*

JUDY *comes on. She carries a pair of garden shears. Her arms are full of cut and mutilated flowers. She strews the flowers about the floor, lethargic gestures. She stands, looking out, the shears dangling from her hand.*

BETTY *comes on. She stops.*

BETTY. Judy. Thank God you got back home, dear.

Nothing from JUDY. BETTY *gushes.*

Oh I'm dead on my feet. First the BBC wanted me on *Newsnight Special*, then they didn't. Was I furious! I made a scene they won't forget. And thank the good Lord, it looks like Mrs Thatcher is back in.

It's wonderful to think that God is working his purpose out, through an English Prime Minister.

She realises. She lifts her glasses and looks around the floor.

JUDY *lets the shears fall from her hand. They clatter on the stage.*

What have you done? The garden.

She pauses. Then she rushes off. She comes back onto the back of the stage, as if out to a garden. She has a flashlight. She flits it about her in bewilderment.

JUDY *(aside)*. Why do I hate her so? Because everything I do, is what she does. She is a fundamentalist, I am a fundamentalist. She to one extreme, I to another. I can only be what she is, the other way round. I know the way she thinks, I feel it in my own thoughts. I hear the edge of her voice in my voice. When I am her age, I know my body will be just like hers.

BETTY *at the back, rushing about, 'in the garden'.*

BETTY. How could you . . . how could you!

She stops. The flashlight on a particular spot.

Oh look. My lilies too. Little madam! Give her a good thwack on the backside! Her father . . .

But her father is in America. With a harlot from Chicago . . .

Oh please!

Flitting the flashlight 'around the garden'.

Don't tell the media that! So many humiliations. I know I am, to many, a laughing-stock. But that about Hugh, I could not bear . . .

Someone there? *Express, Sun, Star?* They don't throw Christians to the lions now, they throw them to mockery. Which is worse?

No!

Closes her eyes.

Is a wrecked garden in Wimbledon to be my Gethsemane?

She trembles, mouth open. Wet lower lip.

When I was a little girl, nine years old, I read John Bunyan's *Pilgrim's Progress.* Under the bedclothes, at night, with a torch. There were fearsome pictures. The Slough of Despond. The Castle of Giant Despair. I wanted to scream.

Oh Lord, this world is a terrible place.

She composes herself. She goes back 'into the kitchen'.

Well you ungrateful little madam . . .

JUDY. Don't start Mum . . .

BETTY. Arrested, naked in the street for all to see? And what are the police going to do?

JUDY. No charges. You know there'll be no charges! You rang the station! And got me out, because of who you are!

BETTY. For which I get no thanks?

They glare at each other.

A pause.

Look at the state of your life . . .

JUDY. I was chucked out of my flat, that's all . . .

BETTY. No money, thirty-three, having to come begging to me for a roof over your head . . .

JUDY. You said you'd love me at home . . .

BETTY. But you've been here six months! Sleeping 'til midday, out to heaven knows when. You would think, with all I do for people, the Lord would give me a daughter . . . but no.

JUDY. Mother, has it never struck you that we both want the same thing?

BETTY. Never!

JUDY. You and your Christian lunatics, your anti-porners, your clean-up TV campaigners, in your gospel halls? I and my friends, street-theatre clowns, squatters, in our resource centres in shabby shops? We all want a new world. That has . . . Light. That's human, and decent, and . . . Clean?

We both want . . . A new Jerusalem?

BETTY. Clean? You say the word 'clean'? Wash your mouth out, girl. What was that thing I found in your room?

JUDY. Thing?

BETTY. On top of the wardrobe?

JUDY. You've searched my room?

BETTY. That wicked, filthy thing!

JUDY. You mean my vibrator?

She smirks.

Try it Mum. Next time you feel a prayer coming on.

From BETTY *a deep sound.*

BETTY. Ooooh, ooooh.

JUDY. We must . . . Oh I hate talking like this . . . Mum, we must find our real selves.

BETTY. We must find God.

JUDY. Have you seen how people are living out there? On the estates? Their only chance is to save themselves.

BETTY. Salvation is Heaven's gift. It is certainly not the gift of a Lesbian theatre company performing in the nude. 'Find your real self?' Will you do that with some battery operated, plastic carrot, that you stick up your private parts?

JUDY. Sometimes I think it's you that's got the dirty mind.

BETTY. Nothing shocks me, girl. When you campaign against immorality, you learn the worst.

None of it shocks me.

A pause.

It just makes me fall to my knees and pray.

JUDY. I'm not going to kneel down and close my eyes with you Mum. I've done that so often, just not to have this argument . . .

BETTY. Just a little one.

JUDY. No.

BETTY. A quick word with Him . . .

JUDY. No!

BETTY. 'Jerusalem' . . . Ooooh . . . I can see your 'holy city' my girl. The city of perpetual indulgence. Your only church a VD clinic. Abuse of the body, slavery to all that's base.

JUDY. I can see your 'Jerusalem'. A police state. All human desires, censored. 'Hallelujahs' broadcast on megaphones at each street corner. And lovers torn apart by cops at night.

A pause. They look at each other, appalled.

BETTY. Don't have anything more to do with those people, Judy. Those . . . 'women'. Please.

JUDY. Do you want to meet my lover? She is very sweet. You'd like her.

BETTY. Ooooh. I . . .

JUDY. Mum.

BETTY. Don't touch me!

They are looking at each other, BETTY, *mouth open, wet lower lip. Then she rushes off.*

JUDY (*aside*). Just one crack. In the lines of a famous face. Just one glimpse that you may be wrong, Mum.

JUDY *looks about her. She picks up the garden shears. She opens and shuts them a couple of times, despondently.*

Well come on, you stupid cow. Come back and tell me Jesus forgives. We'll have a cup of cocoa, then I'll kneel down with you in tears. For a bit of peace and quiet. I . . .

The sound of a car starting.

Mum? Mum?

Car lights pass across the back wall of the stage.

Mum!

JUDY *rushes off and back on at the back of the stage.*

Where's she gone? (*Aside.*) How strong is she? Not that much, after all?

A look of horror, very like BETTY's *wet lip look.*

I should know. I do know. Oh God, what have I done?

She rushes off.

The stage remains strewn with flowers until the end of the act.

Scene Eight

MILLY *alone. The stage now littered with flowers.*

PAUL *lurches on. She looks up at him sharply.*

PAUL. Shorry.

MILLY. What did you say, what did you say to me?

A silence.

PAUL. Sorry, slipped up.

MILLY (*aside*). You look at the eyes for the tell-tale sign. The muscles in his cheeks, gone slack. The sign that he is over the edge.

PAUL. Fair's fair.

MILLY (*aside*). I married an Earl. 'My elevation' said my friends, bitchily. My ascension into the clouds.

PAUL. The bracelet. It was thirty thousand. Give it back to me.

MILLY. Oh. (*Laughs.*) Do you mean this?

She dangles the bracelet before him.

PAUL. Rush of blood to the head. (*Both still.*) I'll leave you alone. I'll go. Loosh myself!

(*He hiccups.*) In the hills.

MILLY. Ha!

She swallows the bracelet. They look at each other, shocked.

MILLY, *oddly matter-of-fact.*

I swallowed it.

She begins to giggle.

PAUL. That's my life! Milly, Milly . . . Godsake, get to the bathroom . . . spoon, tongue . . . Get it out. God! What? Mustard, hot water . . .

Her giggles are uncontrollable.

Here!

He grabs her. She pummels him with her fists and squirms away, laughing.

MILLY. What you going to do? Wait down the loo pan? Hey? Where is my Lord? My Lord is down my loo . . .

PAUL (*aside*). I always eat the same thing. First course, Scotch smoked salmon. Second, lamb cutlets, hot in winter, in summer, jellied. Then strawberry ice-cream.

The best meal in the world. Again and again . . .

Fist clenched, into a rage.

Again! And again! And again!

He grabs MILLY *by the hair. She grabs his legs.*

Again! Again! Again! Again!

He stops. Lovingly.

Oh Milly, Milly, let me pat you on the back. Give you a rub? Let's go and make love . . . You must cough it up. You . . .

She is hit by a pain.

MILLY. Oh! You'll . . . have . . . to split me open. Split me, you bastard.

Bad pain.

Oh!

She looks up startled. She cannot speak. She has a spasm. They look at each other. She puts a hand out to him.

PAUL. Worth it. Ha! Thirty grand!

She tries to speak.

Cheap at the price! My freedom!

She tries to move towards him. He takes a step away, then runs off, weeping.

MILLY, *her hands to her mouth, has a convulsion. Then she is still. She takes her hands away from her mouth. She has got the bracelet up. She stares at it. She begins to laugh.*

The telephone rings. She lifts it at once.

MILLY. Oh Geoffrey my darling, the bastard . . .

She begins to laugh.

No I'm fine, fine. I'm coming round to you, now. Now.

She holds the bracelet up, looking at it. Then goes off quickly.

Scene Nine

Elsewhere, South London. Outside a town hall.

Off, raucous singing of 'For he's a jolly good fellow'.

BILL *comes on.*

BILL *(aside).* Defeat. Rage. Strategy. I am knackered.

VAL *comes on.*

VAL. All those Tory hooray Henrys, celebrating. The flesh crawls.

She bumps into BILL.

Oh hello.

He does not recognise her.

Remember me? We canvassed. Seems light years ago . . .

BILL. Oh yeah. Valerie in't it?

VAL. Val . . .

BILL. Come for the town hall wake?

VAL. They said there was a recount. On Election Special. I mean, the people I'm with were getting maudlin. And most of them are Alliance anyway. So I thought I'd come down here . . .

BILL. Right.

VAl. Is there any hope?

BIll. We've lost.

VAL. How do you know?

BILL. The inside word is a hundred and fifty-two votes.

VAL. Why bother with a recount then?

BILL *shrugs.*

BILL. Be bloody minded. Keep the bastards up all night.

VAL. But round here was Labour for years. I mean – the state of the flats . . . Why did we lose? The candidate?

BILL, *blank.*

BILL. How do you mean?

VAL. L . . . Loony left? I mean, she was on the Liberal Party hit list . . .

BILL *scoffs.*

Two other party workers come on, DON and JEFF. They carry a sagging banner. DON has a big bunch of red roses, which are the worse for wear.

VAL, *voice trailing out . . .*

VAL. And didn't she go to see the Sinn Feiners, with Ken Livingstone . . .

DON. Roses! Roses! I am sick of roses!

Throws them down and kicks them about.

JEFF. A hundred and fifty-two votes, a hundred and fifty-two stinking, stupid lazy bums, who couldn't get off the settee away from the box, down to vote.

DON. I don't want to wave a rose like a wally. I want a red flag.

VAL *is determined to join in.*

VAL. Yes, but I think people quite liked the Kinnock rose. President Mitterrand's got one . . .

JEFF. And what have they got? A pig Tory, thirty-eight, chin of pink sausage over 'is collar, all after-shave and pissed in the Turf Club . . . You fucking idiots, that what you want?

VAL. I don't think we should blame the electors.

They all stare at her.

I mean this is a democracy.

JEFF. Yeah. A democracy of fools.

A pause.

DON. Coming on to rain. Better roll the banner up. Don't want it to shrink . . .

Begins to do so.

JEFF. Right!

Claps hands.

Who's for the All Night Victory Barbecue?

DON. What Victory?

JEFF. All right, the All Night Defeat Barbecue. We better get over there. The Party bought fifty double litres of Rioja, not to mention fifteen sacks o' chicken drumsticks.

DON. Have to have it under umbrellas. With this rain.

JEFF. Joan over there already?

BILL. Dunno.

DON. Well, where is she?

JEFF. Yeah, where is our comrade Candidate? At this our darkest hour . . .

DON. That speech was bloody odd. With a recount going on.

JEFF. Should be here with the walking wounded.

They are looking at BILL.

Bill?

BILL. I know where to find her.

DON. Then do so, Comrade.

BILL. Go to the barbecue. I'll bring her.

He walks off, one hand in a pocket, the other closing his lapels to his throat.

DON. Oi, oi!

JEFF. Really?

DON. Very much so.

VAL. 'Scuse me . . .

They ignore VAL.

JEFF. Since when?

DON. Last party conference but one. When Neil purged the Militants.

JEFF. And our local Robespierre purged our Candidate's knickers?

DON. Now, now . . .

VAL. 'Scuse me but can I join in?

They look at her.

Can I come to the barbecue?

JEFF. You in the Party?

VAL. Yes, I joined to do some canvassing.

DON. And how was it?

VAL. It . . .

A pause.

Was one of the most horrible experiences of my life.

JEFF. Comrade!

DON. One for all and all for a plastic cup o' Spanish plonk!

JEFF. Or ten.

DON. One for all . . .

They enclose arms around either side of VAL.

JEFF. For one.

DON. Close the ranks. We're all terrorists now.

Heavy rain. They flinch.

Fucking rain. We can't move the barbecue indoors. We'd burn the scout hall down . . .

They scuttle off.

Scene Ten

On Southwark Bridge. Night.

JOAN. *She is well dressed, an elegant raincoat. She wears a large Labour Party rosette. Her hair is wet. She looks 'down into the water'.*

BILL *runs on. He sees her at a distance and stops.*

BILL. Bridge over the Thames. Before the City of London, the fortress, the banks.

A forgotten bridge at night.

He approaches JOAN.

JOAN. Ah yes, Bill.

BILL. Does the candidate weep?

JOAN. Not at all. We nearly won.

BILL. Why did you disappear?

JOAN. Work on my speech. For the Victory Party. Is the barbecue . . . ?

BILL. Well underway. It's horribly late, Joanie . . .

JOAN. It'll go on for hours. Sausages and red wine for breakfast.

BILL. Looks like it.

JOAN. Neil sent a message. He said he was very pleased, very proud.

BILL. What would he have said if we'd won? That he was sick as a parrot?

JOAN. Deeee . . .

BILL. ⎫
JOAN. ⎭ Featism.

BILL. OK. OK.

She grins, standing confidently before him.

Are you all right?

JOAN. What did the *Daily Express* call me? Tough cookie?

BILL. Labour Left's Boadicea?

JOAN. Left loony harpy . . .

BILL. That was *The Sun*.

She laughs. They look at each other.

JOAN. You go and keep them sweet, love. Keep the barby going under umbrellas, if needs must. Cooking in bad weather, that's what we're in for, the next five years. Socialists lighting their fires, in the hard rain?

BILL. That the speech?

JOAN. Something like.

She shrugs.

I know, I know, but they'll all be pissed.

BILL. Sure you don't want me to hang about?

JOAN. No. My car's at the end of the bridge.

BILL. Fine.

A pause. He goes to her, they embrace and kiss. He steps back.

Half an hour. No more.

He hesitates, then turns away.

JOAN: Bill?

He turns back.

Do you have a crystal clear idea of what a just democratic, socialist England would be like? A communist England?

BILL. Hey now . . .

JOAN. No! Really like. To breathe in. Go through a door in. Get on a bus in, if buses there will be. Do you have any idea?

BILL. No. 'Course I don't.

JOAN. Nor do I.

BILL. Babbling of Utopia?

JOAN. Yes. I am.

BILL. A communist society would be made by its citizens. It would be up to them if they had buses. Or doors, come to that.

JOAN. So by definition Utopia cannot be described?

BILL. Did Marx?

JOAN. William Morris tried.

BILL. Oh yeah. Endless country dancing, with the sun out all the time.

JOAN. People want to know what we want, Bill. On the doorstep. And we can't describe it. Only flat, lead phrases . . . Dignity of working people . . . Right to work . . . Healthcare, pensions, decent life . . . blah, blah. I mean what, what life?

BILL. I don't know why you're talking like this. You know all the answers.

JOAN. Yes. I do. It is pointless talking of Utopia. What matters is the here and now. Concrete struggle. On the concrete.

BILL. Strategy. The gains, the losses.

JOAN. Gains, losses.

BILL. The real world.

JOAN. Oh yes. The dear, cracked concrete . . . the real world. Which we love so much. I am just so angry!

BILL. 'Better a long, cold anger . . .

JOAN. . . . Than a brief fire.'

BILL. Well. (*He shrugs*). There you go.

JOAN. Yes.

BILL. Ide . . . ol . . . ogy.

JOAN. Ideology. Don't worry, the candidate has the line. Hard and secure. Go down to Brighton tomorrow, shall we?

BILL. Oh yeah! Let us do that.

JOAN. Look at the sea.

BILL. Fish supper?

JOAN. Book into the Ship Hotel? A night, double-room, shower?

BILL. You bet your arse, mate.

JOAN. I will, I do.

A pause.

Twenty minutes, Bill.

He nods. He turns away.

BILL (*aside*). We made love, the first time, on this bridge. Night like this too, rain. Under the walls of the City of London. The castles of money. Leant against the parapet, standing up! She didn't give it a moment's thought, though I was scared sick. Eyes over her shoulder, the while. A panda car coming along? 'Primary school teacher bonks Labour Candidate on a London Bridge?' Who says there's no romance on the Left?

He goes off.

JOAN (*aside*). Upon the candidate let all the sins . . .

She scoffs. A pause.

They're all at it back there. Heating their arguments in bad wine in polystyrene cups. The post-mortem, the old rows. The left shouting 'not enough socialism', the right shouting 'too much'. The centre – Cheshire cats, grinning, relieved the party lost, 'cos now they can really sort out people . . . like . . . me.

And a wind will come . . . Whirl us all up, into the trees. Committees in their birds nests. Tree sways. Wind and rain. Red rags, twigs.

She stamps her foot. Stamps again and whirls, once.

All blown away. God I need a fag. No you don't. You gave up for the campaign.

She waits a second.

Yes, you do.

She takes out cigarettes and matches, lights up and sucks blissfully.

An empty beer can flies onto the stage.

And BRIAN comes on. He still has his Harrods bag and bedsheets. He is very drunk. He is having a football fantasy.

BRIAN. N' a long cross, deep from deep midfield! And the striker! Runs thirty fuckin' yards! Into the box! And with his noddle, bang!

BRIAN makes a lurching attempt at a few yards run, a jump, a header. He falls over. He is crying. He wipes his eye with a corner of the bed sheets.

Split second. So fuckin' beautiful. What I'd give for that.

He staggers to his feet and goes off sadly, head bowed. He and JOAN have not seen each other.

JOAN blows more smoke.

JOAN. The angels . . . (*She looks into the smoke.*) cannot tell the living from the dead. (*She shivers.*)

No, not religion! I can't go that way! The fate of burnt-out comrades . . . Old communist poets, kneeling before the Pope . . . Angels?

If there are angels, they are . . . (*She pauses.*) Us?

BRIAN strides back onto the stage making a cricket batsman's forward drive, a mighty six. His Harrods bag swings from his wrist and pulls him round.

A bloom of light. A batsman in full whites, white helmet, executing the stroke expertly. The light dies.

BRIAN. Out o' the ground!

JOAN turns. They stare at each other.

(*To himself.*) Oooh. Legs.

He wipes his nose on his sleeve. Staggers a side step.

Hello shweeheart!

JOAN (*to herself*). Mm. Now is *that* angelic? Sometimes it's a fucking drag, to believe we are all born good . . .

BRIAN. Tight little bum under there, I can tell. La mumba bumba!

He makes a grotesque wiggle of his backside. As, for a few seconds, a shaft of red light blooms. In it a young woman in a WHORE's outfit – black corset, black stockings, suspenders, high heels, red carnation in her hair. She moves her hips and knees, as if mocking BRIAN's movement. The light dies.

BRIAN, approaching JOAN.

Come fly with me?

JOAN. Where do you want to be kicked? Front teeth or balls?

BRIAN. Hunh? Don't y' fink I can fly?

JOAN, to herself. Looking away.

JOAN. Oh London. All your sons.

BRIAN hefts himself, with difficulty, up 'on the parapet'. That is, he squirms on then stands gingerly and walks along the very edge of the stage.

JOAN. What are you doing?

BRIAN. Here I do, I can!

JOAN (*aside*). Oh no. Another waif and stray. (*At* BRIAN.) Get down! You'll fall in the river.

BRIAN, *terrible singing of a line from 10cc.*

BRIAN. 'Too many broken hearts have fallen in the river.'

JOAN, *fast, a line in her head from the same song.*

JOAN. 'Communication is the problem to the answer.' (*At* BRIAN.) You'll fall! You know, 'Drown?' 'Glug glug?'

BRIAN. I'm gonna fly! Ferra second! It'll . . . Be boo . . . tiful.

He looks at her in horror.

I can't move.

JOAN. Tough shit.

BRIAN. Help me.

JOAN. Join the Labour Party?

BRIAN. Yeah! Anythin'! Get me down!

JOAN (*aside*). Ah well! Organisation. That's what the people need.

She hitches up her raincoat and skirt and climbs up 'on the parparet', nimbly. She faces BRIAN. She holds out her hands.

JOAN. Just take my hands and we'll jump. That way.

Lightly.

Not that way.

A silence.

BRIAN. No.

JOAN. Take my hands. Jump down.

BRIAN. I got a secret life . . .

JOAN. Here.

She takes his hands. He pulls back. They lose balance. They fall from the bridge into the river. That is: they teeter on the edge of the stage, fighting for balance. A rushing sound, air and blood in the ears. They snap rigid, both arms up. Light, deep blue and green.

BRIAN. Glug.

JOAN. Glug.

*A blinding flash of white light illuminating the entire stage.
BRIAN and JOAN, their heads right back, mouths wide.*

Blackout. And . . .

Scene Eleven

PAUL *is there, in a patch of 'street lighting'. He is hunched
holding his belly.*

PAUL (*aside*). Born noble. To be put to the test.

But the times are mean.

Oh to live in apocalyptic times. A war. So a man can put up a
good show!

But not bloody likely, in the England of the eighties. The dog
days of little shopkeepers. No red revolution, no chaps from the
old regiment in North Wales.

What test then, in these times, for the high born desperado?
Build up mighty gambling debts. Choke a wife . . . Life out of
her . . .

Hides his face.

Elsewhere on the stage, JUDY.

JUDY (*aside*). Someone you love runs out of the front door in
London. What do you do, where do you go?

The Mall? She loved royal occasions. Tower Hill? She used to
preach there, with the loonies, before the media took her up . . .

Come back Mummy, you bitch. I don't want you to go away. I
want to hate and scream at you!

A pause.

I'm afraid.

The light around JUDY *dies.* PAUL *again, to the edge of the
stage.*

PAUL. To throw oneself into a test. A swim.

The Hellespont.

Chuck yourself away, to fate.

PAUL *looks down. Light elsewhere on* BETTY, *who is on her
knees. Near her a broken, rusted child's pushchair. Light off the
water. She is under Vauxhall Bridge at low tide.*

BETTY. Down. Under the bridge. River of faith. Dear God this is a dreadful place, at the heart of the world.

A pause, mouth open, listening.

Yes Lord, my life Lord.

She crawls forward.

A walk on the filthy water.

The brilliant flash of white light that illuminates the entire stage. At the back JUDY and MILLY, the telephone to her face, are revealed.

BETTY *kneeling, hands snapped up above her head.* PAUL, *standing on the edge of the stage. The blue and green 'drowning light'.*

ACT TWO

1. SUMMER

A green and red stage.

Scene One

Seven hundred years from then. A dawn.

BRIAN *lies unconscious, soaked. Marshland. He is face up. It rains.*

A man and a woman, DRAW *and* A'BET, *watch him. They are swathed in oilskin cloaks.* DRAW *holds a large, asymmetrical umbrella above them.*

DRAW. Do y' get anything?

A'BET. Oh he's in luck. And alive.

  A pause

DRAW. He doesn't? No.

A'BET. No.

DRAW. All night, y'reckon? In this weather? Out in the marshes?

  They wait, listening.

A'BET. That's what he says.

DRAW. A man in trouble. Tasty.

A'BET. Hunh hunh.

  They move towards BRIAN. A'BET *starts.*

A'BET. Oh.

DRAW. What?

A'BET. He's a boozer.

DRAW. How d'you know that?

A'BET. I know. I was.

DRAW. To see what it was like?

A'BET ⎱ And what was it . . .
DRAW ⎰

A'BET. Flashes o' yellow. Orange. Black. Y' head a red pimple.

DRAW. Like that!

  He laughs. They approach. A'BET *bends and, as if with an osteopath's hold, lifts* BRIAN. *A hand on his side.*

A'BET. Bad lungs.

DRAW *stifles a cry. He and* A'BET *stare at each other, at a loss.*

A moment.

DRAW. He's dying.

A'BET. No one dies like that.

DRAW. He must be.

They look at each other, at a loss.

Leave him?

A'BET. His heart's strong, though. Liver's swollen though, but nothing good food, good nights won't right.

DRAW. But what was that out of him, just then?

A'BET. He's violent.

DRAW. Good reason to leave him alone. He'll be flying, through something personal . . .

A'BET. I don't think this one knows how t'do that.

A pause.

We'll get him into the boat, and back to the house. And advice.

DRAW, *in sudden agreement.*

DRAW. Yes, we're right.

DRAW *swirls his cloak and gathers* BRIAN *up, over his shoulder. Their apprehensive mood is quite gone.*

So! When were you a boozer?

A'BET. Oh, in my teens.

DRAW. Beer, wine?

A'BET. Wine, wine. I wanted to be an artist. On walls.

They are walking away.

DRAW. Graffiti? Figures?

A'BET. Sort a' . . .

A gesture.

swirls. Wine made the swirls more . . .

DRAW. Swirly?

A'BET. Swirly.

DRAW. Why did you stop?

A'BET ⎫
         ⎬ Ran out of walls.
DRAW ⎭

They stop and look at each other.

A'BET ⎫
         ⎬ Ran out of wine.
DRAW ⎭

They laugh and go off.

Scene Two

JOAN *shivering. Bedraggled. She looks at her hands. She holds her head. She peers forward from between her fingers.*

JOAN. Water? Little . . .

She frowns.

Islands?

Covers her eyes.

Shaking! Stop!

She controls herself. She looks again.

There is water. There are islands. Paths. Footbridges. Are there buildings there or not?

She controls a wave of panic and tries again.

Smoke. What, chimneys? Beyond the trees. Nothing's near, no, everything's near.

She holds out her hands, looks at them, turns them over, then stuffs them in her mouth with panic. She speaks through her fingers.

It is not fair. For a paid-up atheist to fall into the river. And wake up to find there is life after death!

No. I'm ill. Get to casualty. St. Thomas's.

She looks about, waves.

Taxi!

Off a whirring sound that rises and falls like a child's whizzer toy. She scuttles away.

JACE, *a jeweller, comes on. He carries a small lathe. It is shining, metallic, inexplicable. It is on a tray around his neck, the strap is multi-coloured, glittering with stones that catch the light. He has a large, irregularly shaped bag slung across his shoulder, it is elaborate, straps, many small pockets. He has a cape, its hem is studded with coloured stones.*

He squats. He sets up his lathe. The tray has little legs which unfold, to make a low table.

JACE (*to himself*), Damp, when you get the damp air. Condensation. Mol-ec-u-lar. That be. That.

As if someone has said something.

What?

Ai! Talk to m'sel. I do, I do, not a thinker. All in things. Who do need thought?

Nowt but in things.

He touches the lathe. It whirrs – the 'whizzer' sound. He takes a small cylinder of heavy metal from a pocket of his bag. He puts the metal cylinder into the lathe. He concentrates.

Tricky, tricky.

He shifts on his haunches and puts his hand on the lathe.

Shining. Perfect in zeal.

The noise of the lathe rises to a high pitch. JOAN *dashes from her hiding place.*

JACE *loses concentration and cuts his hand. He yells. The lathe dies down. He holds his wrist. Blood.*

Oh no, hand! What you doin'? Hand, oh!

JACE *and* JOAN *stare at each other.*

Y' help me here.

JOAN. What?

JACE *holds out his hand.*

JACE. Bandanna.

JOAN. I don't . . .

JACE. Inna bag!

JOAN. Oh, yes.

She goes to his bag.

What am I looking for?

JACE. Blue! Blue bandanna!

She takes a blue, square cloth from his bag.

She looks at it. Sniffs it. He is holding out his injured hand, trustingly.

JOAN. How do I do this?

JACE *in pain, bewildered.*

JACE. Whatever way you do.

JOAN. Er . . .

She folds the square into a triangle. She wraps it around his injured hand. He looks at her quizzically.

JACE. Y' from the Americas, then?

JOAN. America? No.

JACE. Are y' sick? You are, y're shrammed cold. Little bottom pocket of the bag, go on, take one.

She does so and takes out what looks like an old-fashioned sweet, in a twist of paper.

JOAN. Sweets?

JACE. Y' what?

JOAN. What are these, Fisherman's Friends?

JACE. Y' what?

She puts 'the sweet' into her mouth.

That'll warm y'.

She retches and spits it out.

That don't warm y'?

JOAN. Water . . .

JACE *takes out a jug from his bag, takes a cork out and hands the jug to her. She drinks.*

JOAN. Have you got the whole world in there?

JACE. Right. All my world. M'sel, in that bag.

JOAN. Why did you think I'm from the States?

JACE. All from states, in't we? Health, mind . . .

JOAN. No . . . Why did you think I'm from America?

JACE. No offence. Y' smell strange that's all. Y' stink.

Very interested.

What that come from, what you eat?

JOAN. Look, I'm from London. Here.

JACE. The Thames Valley?

JOAN. London.

JACE. Yup, there's so many names. For places. N' people. Names like weeds, cropping up all over. One of my kids, so many love the blighter he's got about thirty names on him. To me he's Hoppy, though. Always will be. That was my name, when he was born. His Mum took it from me for him. You're still shrammed, here.

He lifts his cloak. She hesitates, then snuggles beneath it. He puts his arm around her.

If you're lost, don't think I can find you for you. Sorry. Your bad luck hitting me. I not got much up top.

JOAN (*aside*). Arrive in Heaven? To be picked up by a thick angel?

JACE. And I can't work now, by the look of it.

He holds out his hand.

JOAN. What . . . work do you do?

JACE. Jeweller, in't I.

He takes out a stone and shows it to her.

JOAN. That's so beautiful.

JACE. Here you are then.

He gives it to her.

JOAN. How much?

JACE. How much? Well I haven't got many of 'em, that's half a year's work there. But I got another five stashed away.

JACE. No, what do you want for it? I mean, you want me to buy this?

JACE looks puzzled.

JOAN. You want me to have this? A gift?

JACE. You don't *have* it do you? A jewel. A jewel belongs to itself. All you can do is carry it around. Lose it. Pass it on. Chuck it away.

JACE. But . . . What's it worth?

JACE. To me? My life of course. What's it worth to you?

JOAN stares at the palm of her hand.

JOAN. I don't know, I don't know.

JACE. Seeing I've bust m'hand, d'you want to take over?

JOAN *is lost.*

The jewellery. I'll teach you.

JOAN (*aside*). An entrepreneur, in Paradise?

JACE. Come on, there's a house I use. There'll be people having breakfast.

They stand, their arms around each other under the cape.

JOAN. Where is this house?

JACE. By Southwark Bridge.

JOAN. Southwark Bridge?

A pause.

(*Aside*). The future. It's . . . crowded.

Scene Three

PAUL *sneaks onto the stage. He carries a thick stick, as a club.*

PAUL (*aside*). Why do other people . . . always have to be there? With their boring, stupid little lives?

Packed into a room when you open a door. Breathing on you in their thousands when you walk down a street.

Give me . . . Desert Island Discs. One book of my choice? Good hard Swedish porn. One object of my choice? A grand piano at concert pitch. A Steinway in the jungle. I'd teach myself to play, plink plonk, year after year. J. S. Bach, 'The Well Tempered Clavier', dawn to dusk, on a coral beach, against the sound of the sea in an empty world.

I'd be happy.

A 'Greenlander' comes on at the back, looking about, cautiously. Her name is SIU. *She wears a large brown leather cape, head and face hidden by a hood. The cape swirls with a hiss over the stage as she turns this way then that.*

That weirdo again. It's been following me for hours whatever it is. Some kind of bloody hippy.

(*To* SIU) All right you.

NB: SIU *is played by the actress who played* MILLY *in Act One, but at first a man's voice comes from the figure – a trick, an actor in the wings speaking the lines.*

SIU *turns towards* PAUL *and is still.* PAUL *brandishes the club.*

I warn you, you freak! I have a fucking mean golf swing. So bugger off.

SIU (*voice-off*). Sorry, love. I not been well . . .

SIU (*on-stage*). . . . Very down. Very sick, actually . . .

SIU (*off-stage*). . . . Still am.

A pause. PAUL looks off-stage. Then back at SIU on-stage when she speaks.

SIU (*on-stage*). . . . Some days are better than others. I think it's lifted. Then it comes back. Usually round this time a' day . . .

SIU (*off-stage*). . . . It grips me . . .

SIU (*on-stage*). . . . It gets me very bad.

PAUL. Sick?

SIU (*on-stage*). I don't want to put to any trouble . . .

SIU takes a step toward PAUL.

PAUL. Stay there!

SIU (*on-stage*). I don't want to bother you at all, really, I don't. Now with what I've got . . .

PAUL (*aside*). Fucking Ada. (*To SIU.*) Just stay there!

A pause. Both still.

SIU (*on-stage*). Oh! (*Laughs.*) No, you can't catch it . . . (SIU *off-stage, laughing.*)

SIU (*off-stage*). What a queer idea you got about disease!

PAUL about to speak.

SIU (*on-stage*). You're safe, really!

SIU (*off-stage*). Funny. Each age has got its own diseases. Hundreds of years on, you've got a whole new choice o' what to die from.

SIU (*on-stage*). Though die you do, don't you.

The masked SIU on-stage, a graceful shrug, hands out, palms exposed.

PAUL stares. Then he spins. He looks off-stage again, then at SIU on-stage.

The danger is I'll catch something from you.

Falters.

It's a mental illness. You, I think . . . have got it too.

A wheel with numbers, it's spinning in your head. Green tables.

Low lights. You go deep . . . You're drowning, in a little glass in your hand.

You . . . 'gamble'?

Your name's Paul.

PAUL. What are you? Some kind of mind reader? Some two-bit ventriloquist? Some cheapo kind of fucking Variety act?

SIU (*off-stage*). Vent?

SIU (*on-stage*). . . . Trilowhat?

SIU (*off-stage*). Oh no . . .

SIU *on-stage, shaking her head.*

SIU (*on-stage*), Variety? What's that?

Paul about to speak, but she has got it.

No! No! I couldn't do nothing like that! What, stand up, sing 'n' dance? Speak? Front of a crowd? All of 'em, turned on me?

SIU (*off-stage*). I'd be sucked into the crowd . . .

SIU (*on-stage*). Torn to rags . . .

SIU (*off-stage*). Ripped to bits . . .

SIU (*on-stage*). I've got the same trouble as you. Crowds. I disappear into . . . other people.

What we have between us, the natural thing . . . the flow between each other, the way we wing . . .

Falters.

What we are to each other . . .

PAUL, *a sudden thought, he looks down and she catches it.*

Yes Paul, that's it! As you thought then . . . 'Like being in love'. She has your face you have hers.

PAUL. Hunh!

She points at him, angrily.

SIU (*on-stage*). Don't sneer at it! Don't sneer at being in love! It's something I can't ever have.

Distressed.

For me, it's too strong. I can't control it. He becoming her, she him . . .

SIU (*off-stage*). She him . . .

SIU (*on-stage*). Him her . . .

SIU (*off-stage*). I you . . .

SIU (*on-stage*). You I . . .

SIU (*off-stage*). Throw my voice to divert you, turn you away, turn me away . . .

PAUL, *raising the club.*

PAUL. You should be in the bin, with the key thrown away. Broadmoor. High security hospital.

SIU (*off-stage*). No. All the world is my hospital.

SIU (*on-stage*). You are my hospital.

And the on-stage SIU *takes off her face mask. It is the* MILLY *actress. With* MILLY's *characteristic gesture, she loosens her hair and shakes it free.*

SIU, *with* MILLY's *voice.*

Do you want the diamonds, Paul?

PAUL. Whatever you are . . .

SIU (*on-stage*). Don't you want the diamonds, Paul?

PAUL. Pervert, kink of nature, whatever . . .

SIU (*on-stage*). You want the diamonds. I know . . .

She throws her head right back, her throat exposed. Her hand snakes up, then fingers down, as if to plunge her hand into her gaping throat. An image of horror.

PAUL. Whatever you are! You won't get me!

He runs at her, swinging the club, two-handed. He swings it sideways, not near her. But it may as well have been — without a cry she is thrown aside by the blow, clutching the side of her head.

PAUL *stumbles onto all fours, letting go of the club. He is breathless. He catches his breath and looks at the silent figure. He crawls to her. He touches her head. He stands, looking at his hands, as if they are covered in blood.*

He is still. Then he whirls around, to where SIU *off-stage spoke.*

What? What have you to say to me?

A silence.

I'll show you! How a man can live like an animal. Free, of the lot of you!

He picks up the club. He scans the landscape. Then he runs off, bent double.

Scene Four

Blankets of bright colours. Tapestries. BRIAN *huddled up.*
SASHA, *the* 'CRICKETER', *and* ANNETTE, *the* 'WHORE',
watching him. SASHA *taps his pads, one then the other, then
bends the tops of the pads.*

SASHA. What do you think these things are for?

ANNETTE. What . . .

She stretches one of the suspenders out.

. . . do you think these things are for?

The suspender snaps back, stinging her.

Ow!

She licks a finger and rubs her thigh.

SASHA. When I said I'd come and work with you . . . and I'm
glad to work with you, don't get me wrong . . . it's just that I
never thought I'd be in for dressin' up. I mean, we're
archaeologists.

ANNETTE. Archaeology's a human science . . .

SASHA. . . . Human science, yeah you keep on sayin'. But
shouldn't we . . . y'know, dig the odd thing up? Bit o' spade
work?

ANNETTE. We dug these clothes up. From his head.

SASHA. You think he really . . . got this clobber on his mind?

ANNETTE. The visionary said so. And my workshop had no
difficulty in making them. The visionary must be right.

SASHA. The visionary.

A disapproving sniff.

I have had most unfortunate experiences with visionaries. I
spent a year in a sleeping bag in the Sahara because of one of
'em.

ANNETTE. Why?

SASHA. I got very deep into psycho-drama theory. Too
complicated t'go into.

ANNETTE. Try.

SASHA *sighs.*

SASHA. There's a two-thousand-year-old Arabic story. It goes . . .
ready?

She nods.

'Destitute. Friendless. In a foreign land, Maruf at first mentally conceived, then described, an unbelievable caravan of riches was on its way to him. But this fantasy did not lead to his exposure, or disgrace. The imagined caravan of dreams took shape. Became, for a time, real. And arrived.'

A pause.

ANNETTE. And that's what you were doing in a sleeping bag in the Sahara Desert for a year . . .

SASHA. On a visionary's advice, yup.

A pause.

ANNETTE. Well?

SASHA. Well what?

ANNETTE. Did your caravan become real, and arrive?

SASHA. Oh yeah, it arrived all right.

A pause.

Came out of the haze. Like a sailing ship. Over the sand. I nearly died.

A silence, SASHA looking away.

Well out of all that, now. Or am I? Archaeology, I thought. A little heavy diggin', I thought. Cataloguing old beer mugs 'n' doorknobs. But seeing your workin' methods, I'm not so sure.

ANNETTE, *pulling at straps on the corset.*

ANNETTE. Maybe these costumes are religious.

She means the cricket bat.

SASHA. You mean – a wand?

He waves the bat.

Yeah. Does have a holy feel. And white, for innocence? But what about you, black and red, with your arse hanging out?

ANNETTE. I could be a nun.

SASHA. A what?

ANNETTE. A bride of Christ? You are Christ, dressed in heavenly white.

SASHA. Yeah but if it's a fertility ritual, me the God you the bride, why . . . have I got my cock shut up in a cage under m' pants?

ANNETTE. Maybe it's potency. God's cock can break through anything.

SASHA. I . . . I don't think we're gettin' this quite right.

BRIAN *stirs and groans.*

Hey.

ANNETTE. Here we go. Now remember what I said. He'll recognise us, if we're dressed right . . .

SASHA. If . . .

ANNETTE. Archaeologists dream of this. After years of staring at bones, bits of metal and plastic, dug out of the dirt. A conversation with someone from the past. Nervous?

SASHA. Deeply.

SASHA *and* ANNETTE *hold hands apprehensively.*

BRIAN *sits upright. He stares at them. A silence.*

ANNETTE. 'Ello, love.

BRIAN. Gor.

ANNETTE. Whatever y'want, feel free.

BRIAN. What are you?

ANNETTE. What d'you think?

BRIAN *shakes his head. He realises he is naked beneath the blankets.*

BRIAN. 'Ere! I'm starkers! What you doing to me?

ANNETTE. Anythin' you want, jus' say . . .

BRIAN. My boat come in, has it?

SASHA *and* ANNETTE *look at each other.*

SASHA. Boat?

ANNETTE. Could be a reference to Christ meetin' Peter by the shore of Lake Galilee. (*To* BRIAN.) Are you a fisher of men, dear?

She makes a move towards BRIAN, *who panics.*

BRIAN. No. Get off! Get off from me!

In a panic BRIAN *gathers the bedding about him and lurches off.*

ANNETTE. I think . . . we got it wrong.

SASHA. I think . . . human science leaves much to be desired.

ANNETTE. We did somethin' to him. But what?

SASHA. Let him go for a day or so. We'll catch up with him. Look . . . let's have a night.

They look at each other.

So, why don't you go 'n' put something sexy on?

ANNETTE. I don't fancy you.

SASHA. No? Not even dressed as a god?

He waves the bat.

ANNETTE. No.

They smile and go off hand in hand, talking.

So in the desert, how did you navigate?

SASHA. Stars. But I had the idea o' making a song-line of the journey . . .

ANNETTE. Difficult, no? Shiftin' sands?

SASHA. But not impossible, if your song-line's sung with a star map . . .

ANNETTE. I've heard of this, the Bedouin . . .

And they are gone.

Scene Five

For a few moments, the stage empty. The light shifts.
JOAN comes on. She carries JACE's lathe around her neck. She puts it down and squats before it. She opens her hands, frowns, bites her lip and takes a deep beath. She puts her hands on the lathe. It does not work.

JOAN. Damn, damn, damn!

Don't panic Joan. It is a machine. You switch it on, you switch it off.

She tries again and fails.

I do not understand. How does anything work here? I mean . . . where is the nearest Post Office? The nearest police station? Where is the town hall? Who do I complain to?

JACE comes on behind her. He stands on one foot, pivoting on a heel, curling his toes.

She turns and glares at him. He shrugs and goes off.

She stands.

There has got to be someone in charge here. There has got to be a committee. With sub-committees. And by-laws and policy statements and people arguing and fixing agendas, and knifing each other in the town hall, I mean, real life!

She picks the machine up.

Jace! Jace come back here. Wandering about . . . What does he do all day? Jace!

She goes off after him.

Again, for a few moments, the stage empty, the light shifting.

Then three lovers – OH', LAI FUNG and SALLY come on, giggling. They carry huge, fluffy woollen capes, rugs, pillows and scarves of many colours.

They wear half-face masks.

OH'. Catch our death a' cold . . .

LAI FUNG. Cold feet?

OH'. Out a' doors? After all that rain . . .

SALLY. Yes come on . . .

LAI FUNG. Here! Go!

And they throw the capes, rugs, pillows, scarves into the air, billowing them up.

Get 'im, Sally!

SALLY. Yeah c'mon man!

LAI FUNG. Man!

SALLY. Man!

OH'. Fuckin' in the open air, this far North a' the equator? It's not healthy . . . Ow!

SALLY, *a rugby tackle on his midriff, they disappear under the pile of improvised bedding . . .*

LAI FUNG. Time to sort our married lives out!

OH'. Yeah but can't we just talk about it!

SALLY. Love in action's what we need!

OH'. Oh.

A moment. The pile of bedding still.

Right!

Yelps. The bedding bulges about. Items of clothing are thrown out.

LAI FUNG. Quiet!

SALLY. What?

The bedding pulled about, then LAI FUNG's *head appears. She looks about.*

OH'. What?

LAI FUNG, *retreating.*

LAI FUNG. People we don't want. Lie still!

The bedding is still. A moment, then PAUL *comes on. He is very muddy. He has the club. He carries a mangled, dead rabbit.*

PAUL. Three days.

And I did it.

I actually did.

Killed a fucking bunny rabbit. Shit.

He laughs, exhausted, head and shoulders sagged.

How the hell am I going to eat this thing? No! Wild man of the woods, me, I am officer material. True Stock! Born to eat raw rabbit, yup! In the back of beyond. God help me I killed her. No! No!

He straightens. His face set.

Look after the body and the mind. Get a grip.

He starts. He is alert. He looks about.

There must be a place, cave, true, deep wood, wild. For the wild man. Living hidden.

Whirls round. Eyes flitting. He scuttles off.

A moment, the bedding still. Then LAI FUNG's *head appears, slowly.*

LAI FUNG. All clear.

Scene Six

OH', LAI FUNG *and* SALLY *making love underneath the bedding, which humps, wriggles and moves about an area of the stage, like a huge ladybird. Grunts, laughs and whistles are heard from beneath.*

BETTY (*aside*). What clean air. I wish I had my walking shoes.

She narrows her eyes, looking into the distance.

The glory of thy world, for the simple soul, oh Lord. How beautiful it can be.

How . . . it can hover . . . before your very eyes.

Creation in its wondrous garments.

She sings quietly to herself hymn no 50 from 'Hymns And Psalms', the Methodist hymn book.

Behold the mountain of the Lord
  In latter day shall rise
On mountain tops along the hills
  And draw the wondering eyes.

A screech from the lovers. BETTY *sees them. She jolts with shock.*

SALLY. Don't do that!

OH'. Na go on!

LAI FUNG. Let me!

OH'. Ow!

SALLY. Don't!

OH'. Who is fuckin' who here!

BETTY. Oh I say, how dreadful!

She watches, transfixed.

(*Aside.*) That a body could stand so near!
And they not blush!

OH'. Na, c'mon, fair do's! I am here y'know!

BETTY (*aside*). It's not true I'm against sex.

SALLY. Hold her then. For me.

BETTY (*aside*). I'm just against how sex is used.

At once, LAI FUNG's *head pops out from the tangle of bedding.*

LAI FUNG. 'Scuse me?

BETTY. Ooh! You hussy . . . (*Aside.*)
When you look at them they have that awful look. On their skin. All this sex, it's an illness. And they always are, y'know. Sick. Dirty. Why I've got a book at home, pictures of terrible diseases . . .

LAI FUNG. How is sex used then?

BETTY (*aside*). And they have that sneer, on their lips. All the so-called libertarians have nasty lips.

LAI FUNG. 'Scuse me, you're against sex?

BETTY (*aside*.) The lip, the skin. And she so young!

LAI FUNG (*to* SALLY). 'Ere Sally, what do you make of this woman out 'ere?

SALLY'*s head pops out.*

(*To* BETTY.) What do ya think sex should be done for, then?

BETTY. Love.

They stare at each other.

Between one man and one woman. For life.

They stare at her.

Only when married.

SALLY. What a disgustin' idea.

BETTY. Only in marriage. Within the temple. The Sanctuary.

BETTY *is greatly distressed and near tears.*

SALLY. She must be one of those weirdo perverts, from New Amsterdam.

BETTY. The garden of fidelity. Private. The red rose and the white rose, the lawn, behind the hedge, safe for the children's sandpit. You've got a man under there, haven't you! I know it! Oh you young people, get married, before you ruin yourselves, get married before it's too late.

A silence.

SALLY. Really weird.

LAI FUNG. But I am married.

BETTY. What?

LAI FUNG. I'm married to this man.

She hits OH'*s head, on top of the bedding.* OH', *from beneath.*

OH'. Don't do that!

SALLY. And I'm married to her.

BETTY. What?

LAI FUNG. She was married to him, under here, two years ago. And so was I.

BETTY. What?

LAI FUNG. But they had a row and broke up.. Then she married me.

BETTY. What?

LAI FUNG. Yeah. I was still married to him, and now I was married to her. An' seeing as I was with both of 'em . . .

SALLY. It just seemed a good idea f' the three of us, to give it another go.

LAI FUNG. Which we're doin'.

SALLY. Or trying to. We respect each other.

LAI FUNG. Yeah, we're very respectable.

OH', *from beneath the bedding.*

OH'. I've got a problem here! Massive interruptus! For cryin' out loud, someone do somethin' for me . . .

SALLY. Hang on can't you? There's a woman out here. In trouble.

She shakes herself, a little wriggle to settle her clothing. A characteristic gesture.

SALLY. Come under here, with us.

LAI FUNG. Yeah come on love.

OH', *his head appearing.*

OH'. What is goin' on out here . . .

LAI FUNG *pushes his head back down out of sight.*

SALLY (*low, to* LAI FUNG). Can you get her name?

LAI FUNG. Think so. (*To* BETTY.)
Beatrice? Be-at . . . Betty? Come on love. S'warm under here.

BETTY. I. Oh!

LAI FUNG. Like . . . when you were a little girl? Under the bed clothes? With a light? Betty?

BETTY. Get!

BETTY *struggling, wringing her hands.*

Thee behind me!

LAI FUNG *and* SALLY *glance at each other and shrug.*

SALLY. Anythin' you want, love, we're easy.

BETTY (*aside*). The light, it's going hazy. My skin, it's going shiny. Like theirs.

And I do get bitter! I do! Because of my campaign against all the filth they think that I am ugly. And have no thoughts myself. No stirrings.

Desires. Oh I . . .

LAI FUNG, *over her speech.*

LAI FUNG. . . . You're beautiful, Betty . . .

BETTY. . . . At home in my summer house where I work, at the bottom of the garden, behind the rambling roses, I have a collection of pornography. Under lock and key . . . I tell you, the Marquis de Sade would blush at my library.

LAI FUNG. . . . Don't think of yourself as ugly, Betty, why do that . . .

BETTY. . . . All for my work of course. To defeat the Devil, first know the Devil's ways. But late at night, my husband away, I will take out the terrible books, the vile magazines, and look at them. And not as a Christian. Not at all.

As a . . . creature of nature.

SALLY. Nature? Dodgy, very dodgy. It's true the world of nature's a mirror. But it swims about in front of you. It's not fixed. It folds up, inside itself. Distances an' shapes, change. If you're going to learn from nature, it's always 'now you see it, now you don't'. We're part of the mirror, part of what we're looking into. We distort it. Nature changes with the weather, in your mind.

LAI FUNG. Sally believes in psychic weather. Isn't she sweet? C'mon.

She extends an arm to BETTY. *Then* SALLY *does.*

SALLY. Yeah, c'mon love.

OH', *from underneath.*

OH'. I hope you two know what you're doin'. Even I have a limited capacity y'know.

They ignore him.

A pause.

The two young women, each with an arm raised in invitation.

BETTY *moves towards them. Stops. Wrings her hands. Then moves another few steps.*

Then, turning away as if talking to someone there.

BETTY. Please don't look. Please don't. Just for a minute.

LAI FUNG *and* SALLY *have not moved.* BETTY *takes the final few steps, and takes* SALLY's *hand. She kisses it.*

And suddenly, with a shriek of laughter, the two young women pull BETTY *down under the bedding, flipping it over her head.*

Voices from underneath.

OH'. What's all this?

SALLY. Just another one!

BETTY. You wicked, wicked little thing! You wicked, wicked little thing!

SALLY. Ouch!

OH'. Dear, oh dear, oh dear!

Lights down on the heaped hump of clothes and bedding, which moves about the stage energetically.

Scene Seven

BRIAN *comes on. In a Greenlander's cloak. He carries the bedding under an arm.*

BRIAN. (*aside*). Night with some . . . fuckin' weirdos. Some fucking kind of house. Took me in. Great beer 'n' all. Bit real ale-y.

He sniffs. He suddenly thinks.

Why do I tend to avoid people? 'Cos they're all after somethin'. Other people are mean sods who want you by the balls, 'n' that is that! Pass along the other side o' the street, with a can o' lager in your hand, that's my philosophy. That way you don't get hurt.

He frowns.

So, what are these weirdos after? Free bed, free meal, free beer? They got to want somethin'.

He frowns.

What do I want? I want to bowl Ian Botham for nought at the Oval. Then flatten him in the bar afterwards.

Then I want to go home to a tart with legs that are so long they go up to her armpits. Yeah. That's what Brian wants.

He shrugs.

Wantin' what you know you'll never get. It's kind o' peaceful.

He frowns.

What I really want . . . I've not ever . . . really said. Have I?
I need a drink.

That fuckin' twit in cricket gear. And his bird. I think I'll sort
'em out. And if it's free beer all round here, I am away!

He goes off.

Scene Eight

BETTY, OH', SALLY *and* LAI FUNG *have been on stage
meanwhile, still beneath the pile of bedding.*

BETTY *pokes her head out.*

BETTY. Oh dear God what have I done!

OH'. I am utterly shagged dead by this woman. She just exploded.
Exploded! All over me.

BETTY. Where are my clothes, give me my clothes this instant!

BETTY, *as if pulling her clothes on under the blankets.*

LAI FUNG. S'all right Betty . . .

BETTY. Take your hands off me!

BETTY *scrambles from beneath the bedding, her clothing in
disarray, pulling it to rights about her. She stumbles forward on
to her knees and prays.*

Jesus don't forsake me. Don't abandon me, into their filthy
hands.

Right!

She stands.

All of you! Out of there!

OH'. What now? I can't do any more, I'm utterly spent . . .

LAI FUNG. C'mon. Let's see what she's got in mind.

BETTY. Get dressed and get out of there!

SALLY. We're comin'.

*The three lovers, exhausted and dishevelled, crawl out from
under the bedding, pulling their clothing on, wrapping their
cloaks about them.*

BETTY. On your knees.

They hesitate, then kneel in a row.

Hands together!

BETTY *demonstrates. They copy her.*

OH'. Not goin' to tie our hands up now, is she?

BETTY. Eyes closed!

OH'. Dear, oh dear . . .

LAI FUNG. Sh!

BETTY. Now! Pray!

A silence. Then the three lovers shift and peek at each other. Giggles.

SALLY. What is this?

LAI FUNG. Dunno.

BETTY. No talking! Right, repeat after me! 'Lord look down upon we sinners'.

The lovers, raggedly.

LOVERS. 'Lord look down upon we sinners.'

BETTY. 'Wash us clean in Jordan's waters, cleanse our dark and sinful hearts, let us walk in light.'

The lovers pause, bewildered. Then, raggedly.

LOVERS. 'Wash us clean in Jordan's waters, cleanse our dark and sinful hearts, let us walk in light.'

BETTY. 'Amen.'

LOVERS. 'Amen.'

BETTY. Oooh!

Shakes herself.

That's better. Right! I know what Jesus wants. He has called me to found a church in this dreadful place. You are the first of millions that I will convert for Him. We will build a Church and we will start today. Come on dears!

She strides off.

SALLY. What do we do?

LAI FUNG *shrugs.*

OH'. Why do I feel that woman hasn't begun to fuck us over yet?

LAI FUNG. We'll see it as a task.

SALLY. Task?

LAI FUNG. An experiment. Can we really love this woman?

BETTY *comes back on.*

BETTY. Come on! Best foot forward, for the Lord!

She goes off.

OH'. Oh well. Let's be suckers for experience.

The lovers go off.

Scene Nine

PAUL *comes on. He is gnawing a cooked leg of the rabbit. Fur hangs from it.*

PAUL. I cooked this rabbit! And it's raw!

He throws it off-stage and backs away at once. A figure in a cloak walks on, head shaded by a large, wide brimmed hat.

You dogged me for days.

A pause.

Wales I thought. Snowdonia.

A pause.

If I do nothing else, I'll find the wilderness.

He turns. Another cloaked figure, bareheaded, comes on. PAUL stands between them.

What are you? Police?

FIRST. We were looking after Siu.

PAUL. After who?

SECOND. The woman you killed.

A pause.

PAUL. Nothing to say to you.

The SECOND figure produces a blowpipe from beneath the cloak, takes her time loading it, then uses it. PAUL clutches at his arm and swivels to face her.

FIRST. It's to slow you down, you'll be all right m'dear . . .

SECOND. But you're an ugly sod, if we're gonna get near y' . . .

FIRST. With what you done.

PAUL, *pulling at the dart in his arm.*

PAUL. Hide. Mountains. Or some . . . island.

FIRST. Not a square inch of the planet . . .

PAUL. Desert, forest . . .

SECOND. Not touched by human heel.

PAUL. Snowdonia.

The FIRST *laughs.*

FIRST. Snowdonia? S' a housing co-op. Pleasant. Bit chilly in winter.

SECOND. Siu.

FIRST. The woman you killed. She was sick.

PAUL. Nothing to say.

FIRST. We didn't know you'd do that to her. We'd have stopped y', had we known, for your sake. We apologise.

PAUL'*s knees go. He topples.*

SECOND. He's a drowning man.

PAUL. You . . . apologise . . . to me?

SECOND. That's justice.

PAUL, *on all fours, slurred.*

PAUL. What are you, the hanging judges, come for me?

FIRST. Judge?

PAUL. Judging me.

SECOND. Judge y'. How 'd we do that?

PAUL. Condemned.

SECOND. Well you are, in't you. Condemned. Nothing we can do about that.

PAUL. To what?

They stare at him.

To what . . .

Tries to drag himself . . .

What sentence?

SECOND. He thinks he's going to be shut up. Prisoned.

FIRST. Barbaric.

PAUL. What's going to be done to me?

FIRST. That's up to you. But it'll be a terrible thing, I tell y'.

SECOND. Just remember the old story, 'bout what justice is. In an old-fashioned court. A man was found guilty o' murder.

FIRST. Yeah the judge put on a black hat, to condemn him to death.

SECOND. But the judge said 'For this murder, I condemn you to life'.

FIRST. And the man . . .

SECOND. Walked from the Court, free. Into the road outside.

FIRST. 'N killed himself.

The two 'Greenlanders' pause, then turn and sweep off the stage, quickly.

PAUL. No. Help me. Someone.

He shakes his head.

No.

He crawls away.

Scene Ten

SASHA *still dressed as the* CRICKETER *comes on, uncertainly.* BRIAN, *off.*

BRIAN. Guard! Take guard. Like I showed ya!

SASHA. Er . . . Yes.

BRIAN (*off*). This ball's soft!

SASHA. It's red though . . .

BRIAN. But it's got to be hard! If it's gonna be a cricket ball!

SASHA. Sorry, Brian. The workshop got it wrong.

BRIAN *wanders on at the side. He is dressed in cricket whites. He has a red ball in his hand.*

BRIAN (*aside*). Afternoon in Utopia. With a soft cricket ball. I begin to find that is bloody typical.

He looks at SASHA, who is adopting a ludicrous batsman's position. BRIAN sighs.

No, no, no, no!

He manhandles SASHA into position. A reasonable stance achieved.

I mean, what games do you play?

SASHA. Ball games? Football.

BRIAN. Really?

SASHA. Zen football.

BRIAN. Right. Football? Two goals.

  SASHA, *puzzled.*

SASHA. No, one goal.

BRIAN. What, like a kick about? All right! One goal. Two teams.

  SASHA *looks puzzled.*

BRIAN. What's the matter? Eleven-a-side. The team. The lads.
  Y'know, never walk alone. One f'all 'n' the rest are wankers. A
  fuckin' football team!

SASHA. You mean groups, playing? How can that be?

  A pause. BRIAN *frowning.*

BRIAN. No hang about. You got one goal . . .

SASHA. Right.

BRIAN. Two players.

SASHA. Huh, huh.

BRIAN. Kickin' a ball into the goal . . . With a goalkeeper?

SASHA. No, they are their own goalkeepers.

BRIAN. Don't get it.

SASHA. It is a hard game to play.

BRIAN. Sounds it.

SASHA. Just a moment!

  And he makes an immaculate practice stroke.

BRIAN. Yeah! Yeah, you caught on.

  SASHA, *an elegant slow motion sweep.*

  Yeah y' got it . . .

  SASHA, *very excited.*

SASHA. And the ball down the other side . . .

BRIAN. Off, the off . . .

  SASHA *executes a reverse sweep, in elegant slow motion.*

  'Ere we go! (*Aside.*) I'll show this crapola Charlie.

  BRIAN *strides off purposefully, rolling up a sleeve.*

  SASHA, *to himself, under his breath.*

SASHA. Line of the ball. Concentrate. Move feet. Pitch of the
  ball. Follow through. Instinct. The cat.

BRIAN (*off*). This one's got your name on it mate!

A silence. SASHA poised. He makes to lift the bat. But the ball bounces on the stage and hits him in the face.

BRIAN, 'following on' from the wings wildly, leaps on to the stage with a shouted appeal.

Haaaaa izee?

SASHA goes down covering his face with his hands.

ANNETTE, her clothes torn, crawls round the edge of the proscenium, huddled, hugging herself. Scratches on her skin bleed.

On yer bike, on yer bike! Played on! Off! Off!

SASHA gasps for air.

Nah c'mon. It was a soft ball.

SASHA. I . . . played it hard.

BRIAN. What?

SASHA. Like it was a hard ball.

Magician's trick here –

BRIAN *picks the ball up. He looks at it, bewildered. He drops it. It is a hard cricket ball.*

BRIAN. You people.

You take me up d'yer? I tell you! No one takes me up!

To ANNETTE.

Hey, cunt?

SASHA (*to* ANNETTE). What . . . ?

ANNETTE shakes her head, a single jerk. BRIAN, panicking.

BRIAN. Inna long grass!

Back o' the jolly old cricket pavilion, what ho? Gave 'er one! 'Ey?

You asked for it, cunt! Don't tell me you did not. Stuck your fanny right up to me. Look at yer, tart!

Sorry. I'm sorry.

Looks from one to the other.

Why don't you do somethin'? I mean to me. Call the Old Bill. Kick me in the goolies. Scream 'n' shout! Go on! Go on!

A silence. They are dead still.

I gotta get a drink somewhere!

He lumbers off, near tears.

A silence.

Then SASHA *pulls a glove off with his teeth. He looks at his hand. Then extends it to her. 'A question.'*

ANNETTE (*low*). No, I'm all right.

She shakes her head back.

Just because a man put his thing in me, why should I weep? A rodent. Falls in your lap.

A gesture.

Knock it away. I just . . . want a bath. Then I will make love with you. Restore.

Touching his bruised face.

SASHA. Conversation with a man from the past.

He stands, goes to her, a hand extended. She does not move.

ANNETTE. Why . . . am I dangerous to him? Why . . . is he dangerous to me?

SASHA. Dunno. What we take f'granted . . . threatens him. Things like kindness?

ANNETTE. I didn't realise.

SASHA. What?

ANNETTE. How in the past they suffered. And how it made them so ugly.

A pause.

SASHA. Come on, love.

She stands. They are walking off hand-in-hand, relaxed, easy together.

ANNETTE. Summer almost done.

SASHA. Yeah, after all the rain, 'be a fine autumn. What do we do about him?

ANNETTE. He is his own problem. There's nothin' kinder to say.

They are off.

2. AUTUMN

A vermilion and ochre stage.

Scene Eleven

The light shifts, a rainy day, an evening, a sunrise and then a fine clear sunny Autumn day. The colour of the stage changes to Autumn.

JOAN comes on. Her clothes are now nearly entirely changed to Greenlander styles. She has the jeweller's lathe around her neck. She sets it before her and squats.

She opens her hands. Frowns, bites her lip and takes a deep breath. She puts her hands on the lathe.

It does not work.

JOAN. Each day. Week after week.

JACE comes on behind her. He stands with his characteristic manner, on one leg, looking at her.

I can feel myself becoming like them. Slowing. Dreaming. I mustn't! I won't let go! I . . . (*To* JACE.) Oh, bugger off!

JACE smiles and hops a complete turn. She sits back, closing her eyes to control her temper. Then, aside.

I am in a world where everything I have ever dreamed of, has happened.

In here, all value is the value of labour. No one works, but everyone is busy. There are those who even love the sewers. I met some women, fanatical sewer builders. They told me they had tunnelled under the streets of what was once Los Angeles. Bendy sewers, of a plasticy stuff, earthquake proof.

How do they maintain essential services, chemical factories for basic materials? By traditions. 'Guilds' I thought, but no. You may spend two years growing tea. Just . . . get into tea growing. If you get fed up, you drift away. Build a boat, drown sailing in the Indian Ocean. But there's always tea to be had. I go mad! 'How is it organised? Production and supply?' They shrug and say 'There are enough people in the world'.

'But what,' I say, 'if everyone wants to grow tea in India?'

Again, a shrug. 'There'd be a lot of tea' they say.

It can't work! There are no politics! No one decides anything!

No one's in charge! I just die for . . . some authority! A little
touch of leadership, a bit of bracing tyranny! God what am I
saying?

JACE. You still gettin' wrong are you? 'Tween you 'n' the
machine?

JOAN. I try every day. Like you said. The bloody thing must be
bust!

JACE. That it?

JOAN *pauses, angry.*

JOAN. No, no, all right. That is not it. The machine is fine. It is
me that is wrong.

JACE. Oh.

JOAN. As you know. But will not get angry about. You just make
it work and say 'that's how'. And shrug and piss off. And stand
on one leg.

JACE *scratches his crotch.*

Scratching yourself.

JACE. Right.

He continues to scratch.

JOAN. Look could you, do you think you could please stop doing
that?

JACE. Oh, right.

He stops scratching. He still stands on one leg.

JOAN (*aside*). They are always there. Looking at me. Waiting for
something. Blank. See through. Like ghosts. Passing through
you. Some of them are really beautiful, but they shift. Yes,
future ghosts, future selves . . . No personality fixed. One
moment, like mental defectives, picking their noses. The next
talking mathematics, or philosophy beyond anything I can
fathom.

Like him. He can't even read. But he spent all the late summer,
when his hand had healed, making a stone that . . .

She shakes her head, closing, her eyes.

He said it was cut in seven dimensions, I looked at it. And God
or the Devil or something help me, it was. And, worse for me,
just for a second I saw how it was done . . . I was terrified. I
found tears streaming down my face.

She opens her eyes.

Then we went down to the South Coast to throw the stone into the sea. Why? I don't know. Perhaps because he's just thick as pigshit.

JACE, still balanced on one leg, is now picking his nose.

Jace!

JACE studies the bogie on his little finger. He reinserts the finger into his nostril.

JACE. Yeah, love?

She stands and strides up to him. He is abstracted, removing the finger again and staring at it.

JOAN. Jace, now tell me. Just tell me what has happened in the last seven hundred years.

He stares at her.

JACE. What? History?

JOAN. Yes, yes.

She nods. A pause.

JACE. Well.

He laughs.

I picked m'nose.

JOAN. F' . . .

She turns away.

JACE. An' you asking me the question. That's history now.

That's why it can't work. 'Cos a history of the world would . . . itself . . . be . . . history.

JOAN. All right, sorry I asked.

JACE. Tho' . . .

He begins to scratch his crotch again.

You could have a history of the world, if it went backwards.

JOAN. All right!

But he is lost, following his train of thought.

JACE. If you could get past the first second. 'Cos you have t'prove the world didn't come into existence a second ago.

He claps his hands.

Then!

JOAN. Well it didn't did it!

JACE. Didn't it?

> *He smiles.*

> Sexy thoughts, eh?

> You 'n' I. Just appeared.

> *He claps his hands, with a shout.*

> Now!

> *The smile.*

> Complete and beautiful.

JOAN. And you with one leg.

> *He looks down.*

JACE. Oh dear.

> JOAN, *working herself up into a rage.*

JOAN. You're like a child, or a happy dog. Infuriating, happy, stupid dog, woofing about, tongue out, you make me want to . . . Oh!

> *She thumps his chest with her fists, she boxes his ears. He laughs, weaving like shadow boxing, then dances away. Then he starts to box her ears in return.*

> Don't Don't!

> *He stops, looking at her. Gravely.*

JACE. Told you I weren't that bright.

> *A pause. Then they hold hands.*

> There's a man I'll take y' t' see. A fusty sod. Calls himself the last reactionary, even.

JOAN. The last reactionary?

JACE. Last on Earth, he reckons.

JOAN. Take me to him, now!

JACE. It'll be a journey, that. We'll have to kit ourselves up.

JOAN. Why, where's he live? (*Aside.*) The North Pole? With Frankenstein's monster?

JACE. In the hills. Outside Moscow.

JOAN. The Lenin Hills?

JACE. Yeah! You been there?

JOAN. Once. I went with an organisation called the Labour Party.

JACE. Oh really? What's that for, childbirth?

JOAN. Not exactly.

JACE. Severan-Severan is the man. I'll wake him up on radio. Let him know we're coming. Should be there in two months.

JOAN. Can't we drive?

JACE *looks puzzled.*

(*Aside.*) The engineering of drugs beyond anti-biotics, no cancer, no meningitis, no rheumatism, arthritis, no cholera, no schizophrenia, no AIDS, the ability to slip into six, seven, God knows what dimensions. But to build a simple combustion engine . . . That does not even occur to them. Why are the complex things easy, the simple beyond their reach?

They are going off.

JACE. We'll go through old Poland. Those Polish jewellers are crazy. They're makin' jewels out o' river silt.

JOAN. Silt?

JACE. Mud.

JOAN. Jewels out of mud. That does sound reassuringly Polish.

They are off.

Scene Twelve

BETTY *comes on. She is exhausted. Her clothing, as with* JOAN, *is beginning to change. She has huge boots on, with rags tied around them, and carries, half-folded, one of the asymmetrical umbrellas.*

BETTY. Heat! What have they done to Autumn? Oh, shade.

She puts the umbrella up and half collapses, half sits down.

Then she looks about, nervously.

Where are they? Oh I hope they've gone. Just for half-an-hour. Week in week out, dogging me.

But they're good, or they're very, very good. They say their prayers. I have converted three sinners!

So why do I feel . . . So fucking irritable?

A short scream.

She slaps a hand to her mouth.

And on to the stage come OH', SALLY *and* LAI FUNG, *still wearing face masks.*

SALLY. Praise the Lord!

LAI FUNG. Praised be He!

SALLY. Yea in the morning . . .

LAI FUNG. And in the evening . . .

OH'. The going down of the sun . . .

SALLY. Praise we Him.

BETTY (*sotto, aside*). Oh here they are again, oh no.

LAI FUNG. Praised be He!

OH'. For He giveth!

SALLY. He taketh away!

BETTY. Oh shut up! Shut up can't you!

A silence.

SALLY. Have we sinned, Sister Betty? If we have, tell us in what way.

BETTY. You're . . . too bloody perfect!

LAI FUNG. And the Lord looked upon Noah and he was perfect.

SALLY. Sinless.

OH'. And the Lord looked upon Noah's wife.

SALLY. And she was perfect.

LAI FUNG. As we want to be.

SALLY. Though we know we are not.

LAI FUNG. We are sinners.

BETTY *lets the umbrella fall. She goes on all fours. She points at them.*

BETTY. I know what you are. You are my gaolers. I am in hell. And you are my keepers.

Weeping, a tiny voice. Her face to the floor.

Oh Jesus, Jesus, gentle Jesus, help me.

SALLY *makes to move towards* BETTY. LAI FUNG *restrains her – a touch on the arm.*

OH'. Why do they think they are in hell, or in gaol? When they are at liberty?

SALLY. Maybe they like to suffer.

OH'. He don't.

He turns aside. A blitz-drunk BRIAN staggers on. He carries a wine skin. He falls over.

BRIAN. S'a man inna woods?

OH'. Sorry, mate?

BRIAN. All y' got's fuckin' sweet wine. S'piss! Inna woods 'ey said. Still!

LAI FUNG. Sufferin' in liberty. Seems to be the fashion this Autumn.

OH' (*to BRIAN*): You want the alcohol still? In the woods? The path's along by those houses.

BRIAN. Got ya'. Right. See ya.

OH'. Right.

BRIAN. I didn't wanna hurt her.

S'nature. S'what made me do it to her.

Too much fer a man t' bear!

He looks at them. Swaying. He looks at BETTY, her face down on the ground.

Thas' right, love. Eat the dirt. Thas what it's about. All about.

He staggers off.

BETTY. Oh!

She suddenly sits bolt upright.

Temptation on the brink again! So sorely, Lord.

She begins to pray fervently, lips moving.

OH'. I'm gonna give it to her.

SALLY. I don't know whether we should . . .

OH'. We got it . . .

SALLY. It'll hurt her.

OH'. She's cryin' out for it. She's been cryin' out for it f'months, while we've been taggin' along. Singing her stupid hymns.

I say give it her! Once 'n' for all. Bang.

SALLY. Violence, we don't have the right.

OH'. Well?

A pause.

SALLY. Let's do it.

They advance on BETTY, standing around her. She opens her eyes. She flinches.

BETTY. What are you . . . What is it?

She is frightened.

What are you going to do to me?

OH' *swings his bag from his shoulder, opens it. Puts his hand in.*

Violence! I knew what you were all along. You people. Godless. Warped.

She grabs LAI FUNG's *wrist.*

You're such a . . . pretty young thing. So lovely. Why ruin yourself, sully yourself, filthy stuff running down your sk . . . skin?

LAI FUNG *looks at her in horror and pulls her wrist away.*

OH'. We just got you this.

He takes a Bible out of his bag.

Friends scouted for it.

SALLY. Found one.

OH'. A library in Peking.

SALLY. It's been on its way to us, all Autumn. Here. Seein' you told us so many stories out of it.

OH'. Could be.

BETTY. What?

SALLY. You thought – 'The last Bible in the world'.

BETTY. The last Bible in the world?

BETTY *takes the Bible, gingerly. She holds it in her lap.*

SALLY. A present.

A silence.

Then BETTY *opens the Bible. She stares at it.*

LAI FUNG. We gotta leave you now, Betty. 'Gotta see how the children are.

BETTY. You've got children?

LAI FUNG. Two girls.

SALLY. They're with our other husband, in Northumberland. He wants to go off, so we're taking 'em back.

LAI FUNG. Go off fishing.

BETTY. Oh.

LAI FUNG. The children understand. They know we've been with you.

A pause.

SALLY. We tried to love you, Betty. But we don't.

OH'. No hard feelings.

BETTY *turns a page of the Bible, shakes her head, unable to speak.*

Hallelujah!

SALLY. Hallelujah!

They turn and walk away.

OH' (*to* LAI FUNG). So much for the new Christian Church.

SALLY. Gonna take some time. Wash all that out of us.

SALLY *and* LAI FUNG *kiss on the mouth.* SALLY *turns and watches* BETTY *turn another page.*

Then slowly, she tears it out, throws it away. It floats over the stage.

A 'routine'. BETTY *both losing and destroying her faith, tearing 'the last Bible in the world' to pieces, laughing and crying.*

When she has done, the stage is littered with torn pages, the ripped covers.

A silence.

BETTY. What have they done to me?

De-converted me. Me!

How did they do that to me? They never said a word. They . . . gave me their love. Then took it away. And I just knew that Jesus . . . never died. And all my life, *Pilgrim's Progress*, all the prayers . . . it's fallen away.

What shall I do, without the cross to lead? What's going to become of you Betty girl, without salvation?

LAI FUNG *comes back on. She removes her mask. She played* JUDY.

BETTY *not looking at her.*

BETTY. Judy?

3. WINTER

A white stage.

Scene Thirteen

SEVERAN-SEVERAN *is wheeled on to the stage, fast. He is small. He has a withered arm. He is bundled up and swathed in cloaks and scarfs. Huge mittens. An elaborate 'Russian' hat. His wheelchair hangs with bags, books, boxes. Two high aerials rise from the back of the chair and whip about in the air. Flags are upon them.*

His chair is pushed by a young woman, PALACE. JOAN and JACE follow. JACE wanders about during the scene.

Everyone wears heavy winter clothing.

SEVERAN is talking, torrentially. He has a Germanic accent. He sways and writhes in the chair as he argues, waving his arms.

SEVERAN. We continue this confrontation in the open air. Temperature! Reading!

PALACE *consults a thermometer, that hangs from the chair.*

JOAN (*aside*). Through Poland. The plains. Rivers. Slowly, for months. The endless villages. The people on the road. As if we were not travelling at all. Everywhere a city, everywhere parkland, fields. A world that's . . . enfolded in the mind, as much as there. Really they are dirt poor. And I began to understand. If we are to have a future, it will be on a planet we have wearied and worn, near to death. To live there, the future will have to be ascetic.

PALACE. Minus eleven degrees.

SEVERAN (*to* JOAN). You are disturbed by the cold?

JOAN. It's . . .

SEVERAN. Good! Pain! To concentrate the analysis. What analysis? In a state of happiness? With the death of contradiction, the death of mind. As a declared reactionary, it is my function to make as much trouble as possible, in their insipid ideal. If it kills me my aim is to be the last tragedian on earth. Indeed . . .

He thumps the arm-rest of the chair.

I hope it does kill me! To achieve a tragic, as opposed to an heroic death, in a society of free communistic value, that would be a victory!

PALACE (*to* JOAN). He has tried for years to shock. You mustn't let him get y' down. We love him very much.

SEVERAN *turning, waving his fists at* PALACE, *who, practised at this, dodges out of his reach, skilfully.*

SEVERAN. Damn passivity! Is the dialectic at rest forever? What is at war with what? Peace is senility, worst in the young! Is human nature now a mere mirror to itself? There are people abroad who believe that human nature is changed, for the good, forever. Bunk! There is a worm in man . . .

PALACE. Worm in woman too? . . .

SEVERAN. In the end we are all selfish, self-obsessed, with a dark heart. Human nature? It is evil and it will out.

PALACE, *angrily.*

PALACE. Ah Severan, but what human nature? The human nature of victims and slaves? Or the human nature of free men and women? Which? Tell me that, you silly old fart!

SEVERAN *roars and takes a swipe at her. She ducks.*

SEVERAN (*to* JOAN). So! On your journey did you ask your question? The last seven hundred years? What happened?

JOAN. I did, Mr Severan.

SEVERAN. And never got an answer?

JOAN. Never.

SEVERAN. Like this?

Pointing, with a jerk, over his head at PALACE.

You! Palace! Darling Simplicissima! Enlighten our guest. What has happened in the last seven centuries?

PALACE *shrugs.*

PALACE. Well. This morning . . . I painted my nails.

SEVERAN. Display this major historical event!

PALACE *takes off a glove and holds out her hand for* JOAN *to inspect. Each nail is painted a different colour and glitters.*

There! She's right! That is what history has become! Painted nails!

JOAN. Amazing . .

SEVERAN. Hologram nail varnish. Bah!
Millennia of struggle! For decoration on a young woman's hand.

JOAN. Yes, but . . .

PALACE *looks directly at* JOAN. *She smiles.*

SEVERAN. Oh there is a beauty in it, yes. For that lovely little hand to glitter so, Robespierre rolled the tumbrils and ended, crouched beneath the table in the Hotel de Ville with his jaw half shot away. That, hundreds of years on, a girl may paint her nails. Is this a human wonder and a glory, or is it an historical disgrace?

JOAN (*to* PALACE). Don't get cold.

PALACE. S'all right.

She puts the glove back on.

SEVERAN. And that is the answer. For a world at peace, the only authentic history is an endless 'now'. All about me see that as liberation, freed of the past. Freed of the ravages of the old Adam! 'Liberation'! To me it is a living death. So! Was your journey pointless?

JOAN. Can y'ask that?

SEVERAN. Hunh!

A pause.

Hunh! I see you are halfway to being one of them.

He thumps the wheels of his chair with his hands.

Take me back inside! I want to sweat in the sauna! A good birching! A good scream! (*To* JOAN.) Stay in the guest house as long as you wish. (*To* PALACE.) Crack my spine! Break my neck! (*To* JOAN.) Goodbye, citizen of the past. May misery and suffering never entirely desert you, so that you remain human. Go!

JOAN (*to* PALACE). Oh God, did he . . . ?

PALACE. Yes. He mutilated himself, to live like this.

JOAN. But . . .

SEVERAN. Go! Go!

He is wheeled off, fast.

JACE. Did the great man help out, then?

JOAN. No.

JACE. What a joker, eh?

JOAN. Not really.

JACE. One o' the world's comedians, love. He's known half round the world for it.

JOAN. He wants to be tragic, he said.

JACE. Same thing for him, isn't it?

PALACE *walks back on. She stands calmly, dead still.*

PALACE. Severan is embarrassed. He has to ask me to say what he cannot.

A pause.

JOAN. Thank you.

PALACE. Of the late twentieth-century, almost nothing remains. We have more from the eleventh, the twelfth century, than we do of the twentieth.

JOAN. But . . . Libraries.

PALACE. Acid paper. We dug up two books, from sand deposits. As faint as a neolithic posthole. We think we made out one of the titles of the books.

JOAN. What was it?

PALACE. 'No Orchids For Biggles'.

JOAN. Oh no.

PALACE. Severan would like to know if it means anything to you.

JOAN. No. No. But film, Eisenstein, Fellini, Bergman . . .

PALACE. Combustible, says Severan.

JOAN. The millions of hours of TV . . .

PALACE. Electronics. Will-o'-the-wisp. Not a trace. There are bits of plastic in the archaeological record. For example, this was dug up in the Thames Valley. Could you look at it for us? We believe it is a dildo, an aid for masturbation.

PALACE *rummages in her 'Greenlander' bag. She takes out a bottle of Fairy Liquid.* JOAN *stares at it.*

A pause.

JOAN. It's a bottle of Fairy Liquid.

PALACE. Pardon?

JOAN. Put it away.

PALACE. It is not a sexual aid?

JOAN. Put it away!

JOAN *covers her face with her hands.* PALACE *puts the bottle back into her bag.*

A pause.

PALACE. Forgive me if I distress you, but that is the major artefact we have from the early lost enlightenment.

JOAN, *hands away from her face.*

JOAN (*aside*). Which is what they call our time . . . The early lost enlightenment.

As I talked to her, to Severan-Severan through her, I fell into mourning for my life. (*To* PALACE.) A nuclear war?

PALACE. Never was one.

JOAN. Names. (*Aside.*) I went through the US Presidents, Wilson to Reagan.

PALACE. Nixon. Yes.

JOAN. What . . .

She hesitates.

What language did Nixon speak?

PALACE *shrugs.*

PALACE. Spanish, of course.

JOAN (*aside*). There remained the knowledge of the destruction of the Jews by the Nazis, but no knowledge of the First World War. No novels, no poems, three paintings by Picasso, done in his old age. Fragments of one play. I think it was *Just Between Ourselves* by Alan Ayckbourn. Severan seemed to think it was a crude, satirical reworking of Penelope, by Euripides. (*To* PALACE.) Sorry? *What* by Euripedes?

PALACE. Penelope.

SEVERAN-SEVERAN *shoots on to the stage in his wheelchair, and slews to a halt. He is agitated.*

SEVERAN. From the Library of Alexandria. We have reconstructed it.

JOAN. You mean dug it up?

SEVERAN. We got the books out again.

JOAN. Dug them up . . .

SEVERAN. Dug out, in a way. 153 plays by Euripedes, 87 by Sophocles. Most of them pretty rough.

JOAN. You have the library of Alexandria . . .

SEVERAN. The mathematics of Ajax Parocoles. Also much trivia. The autobiography of Pontius Pilate. By the way, if a paragraph in it is to be believed, Christ was never crucified, Barrabas was. Understand!

He hits the wheels of the chair.

Enlightenment lost. Dark ages. The collapse of the West, the 'stripping' of America in the twenty-first century, interminable decades, a medievalism, out of the Soviet Union . . . These writers you speak of? James Joyce? William Faulkner? Rilke, Brecht, Solzhe . . . ?

JOAN. Solzhenitsyn.

SEVERAN. Struck from the record forever. In those interminable decades, brutish, censored, authoritarian. For 250 years what you call 'State Capitalism' was the iron model for Government in 'the mainland' Northern Hemisphere. North America? A garbage heap of the Third World. Do you feel the weight of it? The wasted years? The dread?

JOAN. But how, then . . .

PALACE. Tyranny got tired.

SEVERAN. Hunh! History died.

PALACE. Two generations. Ninety years. Out of a second Medieval age, a new Renaissance.

SEVERAN. Bah! A way of putting it.

PALACE. There was confusion. We still study that time. To understand the forces within the movement for the beloved community. How, after the centuries, we began to talk to each other.

SEVERAN. After all the struggles, the revolutions, the human cost, the mulch, the bodies, the great ideas, mulching down . . . There never was a final revolution to give birth to this revolutionised world of theirs . . . their 'beloved community'. Bah!

PALACE. Just life after life, lived through, as best they could be lived. Ordinary life triumphed and made an extraordinary world.

SEVERAN. A mass defection! Humanity defected! Just . . . walked away! To piss in the hedges, walk in the woods, mooning about. Bah. I hate it so. Give me something to fight against, give me anguish, give me struggle! I think I'll break my arm! Someone, break my arm for me!

He huddles down in his winter clothing.

JOAN (*to* PALACE). The beloved community?

PALACE. Yes.

She shrugs.

Us.

4. SPRING

A yellow and green stage.

Scene Fourteen

There is a circle visible on the stage, as if grass has been scuffed away to make it.

BRIAN *comes on. He carries two improvised 'goal posts' — sticks with wooden bases, and a soft football made of cloth.*

BRIAN *puts the posts down. He raises his arms above his head. He is cheerful.*

BRIAN. Sixty-seven days without a drink. What 'n utterly horrible experience.

He bends and touches the ground. Up.

(*Aside.*) What's borin' about being dried out is that you 'ave no alternative . . . 'cept to be a really good man. Spare a thought for the poor sodding alki. No grey areas! You're a fuckin' saint or a fuckin' sinner. Sixty-seven days a saint . . .

Hup!

Bends, touches the ground. Up. PAUL *comes on. He is entirely dressed as a 'Greenlander'. He has a wooden bowl. He sits down, the bowl before him.*

BRIAN *looks up from his exercises and is startled to see him.*

(*To* PAUL.) I did that, f'a bit. 'Cos of something I did.

PAUL. Don't let me . . . Embarrass you, mate.

BRIAN. You don't get me, I was a criminal. Somethin' I did.

PAUL. Ah.

BRIAN. Workin' on the roads now. Fuckin' terrible the roads round here. Still. Least y'got the right to go 'n' dig up roads, if that's what you're into.

PAUL. I . . .

He looks away.

Have to be like this for the rest of my life.

BRIAN. What did y'do?

PAUL *shakes his head. But* BRIAN *has got the thought.*

You killed her?

PAUL *startled.*

PAUL. You can do that?

BRIAN. Yeah. Dunno how. Two weeks in to gettin' off the booze
. . . And just like learnin' to ride a bike. First time you swim, it
. . . She didn't choke, y'know.

A silence.

Mill . . . Milly? But er . . . I 'ave to tell you. She went off with
another bloke . . . Graham, no . . . A Geoff.

PAUL, *suddenly his old self.*

PAUL. Geoffrey Hamish-Simpson? That little fucker? That fucking
little wimp ran off with my wife?

BRIAN. Sorry.

PAUL *buries his head in his hands.*

PAUL. I've been on the road. Months. Looking for . . . the
gallows.

BRIAN. Don't happen like that, does it. You've been hung. The
moment you did what you did.

PAUL. Yes.

He shakes his head.

Yes.

BRIAN. Er . . .

Looks one way, then the other.

Fancy a game of footy?

PAUL *looks up.*

Or what passes for it round here. Actually, it looks impossible.
But it knackers you. Right! A circle.

He scuffs round the circle on the stage.

A goal line, cuttin' the circle in half. One goal.

He puts the posts down.

On y' feet!

PAUL *stands. He shuffles into the circle.*

Stand back to back.

They do so.

That half circle in front of you, that's your area. This is mine. I can't go in yours, you can't go in mine. An' we score inta the same goal. Right?

PAUL. Ah . . .

BRIAN. You can kick off.

He plumps the ball down at PAUL's *feet. He crouches, back to* PAUL.

Go!

PAUL *looks down at the ball, bewildered.*

Let's be 'aving y'!

PAUL *toys with the ball. Then he suddenly moves one way.* BRIAN *anticipates him.* PAUL, *suddenly lively, switches the other way. Turns round the circle. Shoots.* BRIAN *stops it. They stand panting. Then* BRIAN *feints.* PAUL *finds himself wrong-footed.* BRIAN *swivels out of his area and scores into* PAUL's *side of the goal.*

Right! Again!

BRIAN *kicks off. Again* BRIAN *feints* PAUL *the wrong way and scores.*

JOAN *and* JACE *come on, upstage. He sets up the jeweller's lathe and works at it. After a few moments* JOAN *takes over. The lathe works for her.* JACE *stands on one leg.*

PAUL. Sod! The minds that conceived this game are fucking perverse.

BRIAN. Y'can say that again . . .

They play on.

BETTY *comes on, hand in hand with* LAI FUNG, *the actress who played* JUDY. *They are dressed in white and yellow cloaks. They are holding hands and in mid-conversation.*

BETTY. Kew Gardens . . .

LAI FUNG. A collection, like a library of plants . . .

BETTY. No, no, no, not . . . But living.

LAI FUNG. The land will be difficult, 'specially by the river. But if you get a neighbourhood to join in, they'll move the houses.

BETTY. Or we could build a big glass house. Oh! What an idea. A big hot house. A tropical climate! For folk who dream of living in the heat . . . You do meet 'em. It'll be the old Crystal Palace. A cathedral . . .

LAI FUNG. Now Betty.

BETTY. I'm still religious dear! I just don't believe in the mucky bits anymore.

They look at each other. They embrace, kissing fully on the mouth.

The stage darkens. A rumbling sound. Like a heavy cloud passing.

It clears.

JOAN looks up, alarmed.

JOAN: Jace? What is it?

He does not respond. The two other 'Greenlanders' come on. They are drinking from wineskins, and merry with the drink. The 'HE/SHE' figure is one of them.

JOAN stands, looking about her.

FIRST GREENLANDER. Brian. Have a drink.

BRIAN. Nah, I can't not ever. I'm a cripple, f'life.

FIRST GREENLANDER. Nah you're stronger than that. You're just a normal bloke, Brian 'n' that's all.

BRIAN. Oh. Well.

He takes the wineskin. He drinks.

Fruits a' the earth eh?

JOAN walking downstage. Again the darkening effect, with a rumble. More pronounced.

BRIAN *hands the wineskin back. The 'Greenlanders' turn away.*

PAUL *is staring at the 'Greenlander' who was 'SIU onstage', who makes a sign of greeting to him.*

Any of you want a game?

They do not hear him.

I said any of you want a game . . .

They cannot see him. They walk through the circle, brushing past him as if he were not there. SIU *walks towards* PAUL *who holds out a hand. But she walks past* PAUL *as if he were not there.*

The stage finally darkens. A roaring sound. JOAN *at the end of the stage,* BRIAN *comes to edge.*

BRIAN. Where are y'?

And they are in a repetition of the 'drowning sequence' at the end of Act One . . .

Blackout and –

Scene Fifteen

Early morning, 12 June, 1987.

Dark stage, but for the London lights.

JOAN *can just be made out, moving on her hands and knees. She is soaked.*

BILL *calling, off.*

BILL. Joan! Joan! Are you down there! Joan! Please, oh please! Joan!

JOAN, *shivering. Can hardly speak.*

JOAN. Bill?

BILL *comes on.*

BILL. Joan, oh God . . .

JOAN. There was a guy, he . . . Where is he . . .

BILL. What guy?

JOAN. Off the bridge . . .

BILL. We'll get you to St Thomas's . . .

JOAN. We've got to find him!

BILL. We'll ring the coppers. Please Joan.

JOAN, *a sudden change.*

JOAN. No, it's all right. They won't let him go.

BILL. Yeah the river police . . .

JOAN. Look.

BILL. No Joan, I'll carry you . . .

JOAN. I said – look.

From her clothing she takes something, with difficulty. She holds out her fist. It is closed. She opens it. A jewel from the lathe.

BILL. What is it?

He stares.

That's . . . beautiful. Where did you get that? From the river?

JOAN *holds up the jewel above her head. A beam of light from the side of the stage hits it. Light splinters across the stage and out over the auditorium.*

Blackout.